A Daily Dose of
Mindful
Moments

A Daily Dose *of*
Mindful
Moments

Applying the Science of
Mindfulness and Happiness

Barbara Larrivee

Shoreline Publications

Library of Congress Cataloging-in-Publication Data
Names: Larrivee, Barbara, author.
Title: A daily dose of mindful moments: applying the science of mindfulness and happiness / Barbara Larrivee.
Description: Includes bibliographical references and index. | Santa Barbara, CA: Shoreline Publications, 2018.
Identifiers: LCCN 2017961997 | ISBN 978-0-9651780-0-6 (pbk.) | 978-0-9651780-1-3 (ebook)
Subjects: LCSH: Mindfulness (Psychology). | Positive psychology. | Happiness. | Meditation. | Attention. | Awareness. | BISAC: BODY, MIND & SPIRIT / Mindfulness & Meditation |
Classification: LCC BF637.M4 L37 2018 | DDC 158.1/2—dc23

Cover and Interior Design by Constellation Book Services

ISBN: 978-0-9651780-0-6

First edition: 2018
18 19 20 21 22 23 24   10 9 8 7 6 5 4 3 2 1

Printed in the United States of America

To my parents

Table of Contents

PART 2

Applying Mindful Moments to Live a More Mindful, Less Stressed and Happier Life

Introduction

The search for greater mindfulness is afoot with everyone jumping on the mindfulness meditation bandwagon as the promised path. There's no doubt that mindfulness meditation is good for you. The simple act of allocating time for yourself, doing nothing, and noticing what's on your mind is in itself worthwhile. It's just not the magic pill some enthusiasts are pushing as the solution to all our problems.

While mindfulness meditation may be the premier route to mindfulness, it takes time. There are other options for enhancing mindfulness. The path I'm advocating is practicing daily mindful moments, which is essentially spreading out your mindful practice throughout your day with purposeful, momentary acts.

While others are recommending brief mindful breaks, they typically offer no strategies beyond a pause to become present. No matter how much you tell yourself to be mindful, it won't happen in a vacuum. You'll need to have tools, strategies, and skills to grow mindfulness. What sets this book apart from the many, many books on mindfulness is taking it beyond present-moment awareness to engagement and action to develop skills for living more mindfully.

There's no one-size-fits-all way to cultivate mindfulness. The best fit for each individual will depend on what challenges life is bringing and what results are most important. If your goal is to slow down, not get carried away by life in the fast lane, and live more in the present moment, a mindfulness meditation practice is your answer. If you're having trouble focusing and concentrating, jumping from one thing to the next, mindfulness meditation is your best choice. If you have a lot of anxiety or tend to get depressed, mindfulness meditation can be a helpful practice. If you're dealing with chronic pain, mindfulness meditation is a good choice to try to get some relief.

On the other hand, if you get caught up in negativity cycles, aren't able to look on the bright side, or just want more enjoyment in your life, practicing brief mood-enhancing activities is a better choice. If you're often stressed-out or overwhelmed, you may benefit most from quick stress-relieving strategies used throughout the day to keep stress from escalating. If you can't seem to stay motivated or thrive on constant variety, pausing for new and different short mindful breaks may work better for you. If what gives purpose to your life is helping others, then frequent, deliberate acts of kindness and generosity can be part of your daily mindful moment practice. If these areas of your life are what's important to you, then adding a mindful moment practice may be the preferred path, as an alternative, or complement, to a mindfulness meditation practice. Practices that serve these purposes can be embedded in your mindful moment practice.

Short of spending hours in meditation and in silent retreat, a daily mindful moment practice offers a way to align with the origins of Buddhist teachings of mindfulness built on the foundation of acting in accordance with our supreme virtues such as kindness, generosity, love, and compassion. Taking frequent mindful moments, designating practices to follow for a day, setting daily intentions, and establishing daily rituals that strengthen your vision of your ideal self can bring you closer to living that vision. When you target some of your mindful moments to support your highest values, the practice can serve a greater purpose and give more meaning to your life. Rather than just being something you think you should do, it can ignite what matters most to you.

Mindfulness meditation is about noticing—noticing your breath, noticing your bodily sensations, noticing when your emotions are bubbling up. But merely noticing doesn't automatically translate into more constructive behavior. If you want mindfulness to be a way of life, it will take simultaneously developing other tools and skills. A daily mindful moment practice is a way to put into practice brief evidence-based strategies coming out of decades of research in positive, cognitive, behavioral, and social psychology, and most currently, in the neurosciences.

How This Book Is Organized

After years of doing research on mindfulness, when I started to put all the pieces together to figure out what a mindfulness meditation practice does and doesn't do for you, I discovered a daily mindful moment practice could fill in the gaps. To make my case, I provide an extensive review of the abundant research related to building a mindful moment practice. The research and resulting practices presented in this book span the science accumulating in many fields. To paint a complete picture of the relevant issues and the range of resources that can be tapped, I draw together the latest scientific research from over the past fifty years. Given my research training, I try to separate the hype from the evidence to offer an accurate assessment of the research findings so readers can benefit from my delving deeper and deeper into the research and make their own conclusions.

The topics of positive psychology, happiness, optimism, gratitude, kindness, compassion and self-compassion all have extensive research bases that provide evidence supporting the importance of cultivating practices related to each of these areas. Enhancing positive emotions, building up defenses against stress, and integrating mind-body pathways are all areas that offer proven practices that can readily be integrated into a mindful moment practice.

This book is organized to present the research necessary to provide the rationale for a mindful moment practice. There are separate chapters for each of the content areas where the research provides relevant background. Because a mindful moment practice encompasses multiple areas, there is a wealth of research. In the format of the book, much of the related research is covered before mapping out the specifics of how to establish a daily mindful moment practice because all of this background and research lay down the foundation for the book.

While I realize there may be way too much research for those interested in practicing mindfulness, I felt compelled to provide a comprehensive review of what we know and don't know to counteract what's being propagated about mindfulness meditation through the mainstream media. To make the research more readable for the average reader, I have summarized the research in a brief statement at the end of each section. The section labeled "Research Recap" offers just a sentence or two highlighting the essence of what the research says. Throughout the book wherever there is extensive research cited, I have compiled and presented much of the research at the back of the chapter in a separate section under the heading, "The Research Findings." (For Chapters 10 and 12 covering two topics, The Research Findings follow each topic.) In some instances, where it has particular relevance to the points being made, I discuss the research in more detail within the chapter.

At the crux of the book are the very practical lists of mindful moment practices. Each of the chapters in Part 2 have lists of practices gleaned from the research. In order to have these lists be brief, they just include the strategies unencumbered with the research. The substantiating research is discussed separately in the relevant sections.

So for those who want to see the data, it's all reported in The Research Findings sections for your own analysis and conclusions. And for those who don't need to be convinced with the research, but may want to just get a sense of the research, you have the Research Recaps available. For those of you who may want to get right to the core of a mindful moment practice, you can skip right to the skill-building chapters in the second half of the book.

What's at the heart of my message is that you can find time to build a daily mindful moment practice regardless of how busy your schedule may be. And when you do, you create the possibility of living a more mindful, less stressed, and happier life.

Based on the many years spent researching and preparing this book, and the compelling research now available, being more mindful and intentional will enrich your life in every arena. It is my hope that this book will inspire you to take action to start creating your own daily mindful moment practice as your path to living more mindfully. Making mindful moments a daily practice can help bridge the gap between *doing mindfulness* and *being mindful*.

CHAPTER 1

My Journey to a Daily
Mindful Moment Practice

The destination is "to be" and not to arrive somewhere else.
–STEPHEN PAUL

For many years, my meditation practice consisted of a daily meditation as soon as I awoke, in fact, even before I got out of bed to make sure I did it before the day got crazy. I would prop myself up with pillows so my spine was straight and meditate for twenty minutes repeating a mantra. Some days, typically about two or three times a week, schedule permitting, I would meditate a second time in the evening.

A few years ago, I began questioning my daily meditation practice because I didn't seem to be reaping the wondrous benefits I kept reading about. After practicing more than a decade, I had yet to experience a blissful state many meditators report experiencing. I never really zoned out to be in that space Deepak Chopra refers to as "the gap." I did, however, sometimes fall asleep.

I started to experiment with my meditation practice. I first tried changing it from a mantra-based meditation practice to breath awareness, paying attention to and feeling my breath. I did notice a slight difference. I seemed to be able to stay focused a bit longer before my mind traipsed off to something. I also tried body scans, but I had trouble sensing and isolating specific body parts. I couldn't seem to "feel" my ankles or other body parts. And when I was done, I didn't feel a whole lot more relaxed.

I then moved to guided meditations, selecting ones that matched my mood or feelings, or the opposite, counteracted my mood or feelings. I also began targeting my guided meditations to align with a character quality I wanted to enhance, like kindness, forgiveness, or gratitude. I found I was enjoying my meditation practice more and looked forward to trying new meditations. As I subsequently learned, and will discuss later in the book, experiencing pleasure along with continuous new experiences is what the brain thrives on. The feeling generated from the kind of meditation practice I did carried into my day, but not for long. It soon dissipated.

While experimenting with guided meditations, I had tried a variety of compassion meditation scripts but none of them seemed to move me to actually feel compassion for myself or for others, or certainly not for "all sentient beings." Somehow, it just didn't resonate with me to wish that everyone on the planet "be happy and live their lives with ease," a common phrase in many compassion meditations. In my research, I learned that my experience was consistent with what the research supports (see Chapter 12). Apparently, you first have to be moved to feel a positive emotion before the compassion meditation practice has a positive impact. There are substantial differences among individuals, pointing to the fact that a particular compassion meditation script will not work for everyone. It may take a lot of trial and error before finding one that moves you to actually feel compassion. I'm still searching for one.

Meanwhile, to try to figure out what I might be doing wrong and how I might improve my practice, I delved deeper into the mindfulness meditation research that I had been following and writing about for several years. With my training and experience in conducting, writing, and deciphering research, I was surprised to find that many of the benefits being touted everywhere were not really substantiated by rigorous research, and that the rewards were often not realized until a practice was in place for quite some time. I was averaging from about 180 to 200 minutes per week, or about three hours. Taking this out to my cumulative number of hours for a ten-year practice came to about 1500 to 1700 hours. I discovered this was a mere drop in the bucket compared to the amount of practice long-term meditators in many of the research studies had done. Often these long-term meditators had accumulated from 9-10,000 hours of practice. I was never going to see that in my lifetime. So I began thinking about other ways to practice.

Around the same time, I found that soon after my morning meditation, a sense of gloom often came over me. And I'm more often than not a "look at the bright side/dig for the good in everyone" kind of person. This also coincided with leaving my university teaching position after many years to concentrate on my writing. As I soon found out, writing can be a lonely venture when you're used to being socially engaged most of the day. My meditation practice wasn't translating into a calmer, sunnier, and gentler way of being. I felt constant angst. So I started to take little pleasure-inducing and stress-relieving breaks during my writing workday to try to shift my mood. I found the effects from a break typically lasted about an hour before I needed another one. And voilà—the birth of my revelation to write this book about getting "a daily dose of mindful moments."

I was also trying out the many research-based practices I was learning about in my research to relieve stress and support a more positive outlook. Some of these included sprinting up and down a flight of stairs, stroking my palms and arms, savoring enjoyable experiences, appreciating my daily accomplishments, and expressing gratitude for the little things that usually fell under my radar.

It was also important to me that my practice go beyond my self-serving need to boost my spirits. And as the research clearly shows, acts of generosity, kindness, and compassion are a direct route to happiness, life satisfaction, and fulfillment. I wanted my mindful moment practice to align with what I held to be dear and the values I wanted to live by. For example, what seemed to work better for me than doing compassion meditations to actually feel compassion was to deliberately practice being more compassionate. I started with setting an intention for the day for my mindful moments to have a designated theme to be compassionate. But that wasn't enough by itself to translate into action. It had to be coupled with a more specific check-in prompt. As a firm believer in it's what you say to yourself that revs up your negativity, one cue I used was to become more aware of when I was assigning someone a negative label like "he's such a jerk" or "she's so self-centered." Then the label itself served as my signal to reconstruct a more compassionate thought or comment.

> My theory is the more you focus on being the person you want to be and how you want to behave toward others, the more mindful you'll become. A daily mindful moment practice can help bring your core values and actual behaviors into authentic alignment. When your inner ideals and outer actions are in harmony, then you are truly mindful.

Searching for Evidence

Given my research background, I began searching to see if I could establish an evidence-base for a mindful moment practice. My predisposition is to have to *prove* or provide evidence for my musings, so I started doing research, more and more research, and it took me far and wide. As it turned out, I wasn't the only one advocating for short, deliberate mindful breaks throughout the day. But typically what others were advocating was a simple "check-in" with body sensations or breathing to reel in a busy mind to be present to the moment, the assumption being that anchoring in the present moment is enough to then act mindfully. The daily mindful moment practice I'm advocating goes beyond awareness to trigger a mindful act.

Because of my personal experience having trouble hanging on to a positive or optimistic outlook, I was especially interested in strategies and practices that might keep me on the sunny side and keep my positivity flowing. I looked again at the positive psychology research that I was already familiar with because I had reviewed it for my previous book intended to help teachers deal with the stress of the job and keep from succumbing to burnout that is common among those in the helping professions. I discovered that some of these practices had an impressive research base and took little time to implement and so could be incorporated as mindful moments.

Then I moved on to the literature on the relaxation response and found that there were many, many practices in addition to meditation that could be used to elicit this response. This took me way beyond the meditation research to some of the research on exercise, touch, and social support...and the list goes on and on. Across all of these domains, there were brief evidenced-based practices that could readily be integrated as part of a mindful moment practice.

Finally, I had to say enough. If I were ever going to get the book written, I had to stop researching and start pulling together the years of research I had conducted and the hundreds of files accumulating on my computer.

At this point, I began sharing my vision for a daily mindful moment practice. My passion and enthusiasm was contagious. I've been practicing what Marcia Wieder, author of *Dream: Clarify and Create What You Want* has dubbed "enrollment."[1] When you have an idea you're fired up about you need to have what she calls "powerful enrollment conversations" to share your ideas in such a way that it inspires others to get on board.

So that is what I've been doing—enlisting others to join me. Nearly everyone I share my idea about mindful moments with gets enthusiastic about it, and some start practicing it right away. Now I've got my friends and family members talking about doing their mindful moments. And we're checking in with each other to support our efforts to get our daily dose of mindful moments. They're sharing with me the new things they've tried. A friend recently shared a body tension-relieving break she takes leaning backwards over an exercise ball for a minute or two. It gives her body just the pickup she needs. Another friend shared how she recently rediscovered *skipping* as a quick mood enhancer. Simply changing your gait to skipping along for a bit makes you feel like you're seven again playing hopscotch. When I tried it, I was amusingly surprised at how quickly it put a smile on my face, not to mention got my heart rate up in no time.

People say yes to what's important to them, and apparently the idea of taking mini destressing, enjoyment, or altruistic breaks throughout the day to amp up their pleasure barometer resonates. A daily mindful moment practice makes sense, it doesn't take a lot of time, it's easy, it's pleasurable, and it's gratifying. And when you integrate practices that extend to others you can get all the benefits that come with practicing compassion, kindness, and gratitude.

I haven't given up my meditation practice, but getting my daily dose of mindful moments allows me, as the saying goes, to "walk my talk" to live and act more mindfully.

What Is a Mindful Moment Practice?

As we're constantly reminded, one route to cultivating mindfulness is a mindfulness meditation practice. An alternate, or complementary, path to being more mindful is the one I'm proposing, a daily mindful moment practice. And the research reported in the coming chapters provides evidence of its promise for enhancing mindfulness, as well as increasing happiness and reducing stress. Spreading mindful moments throughout your day can weave mindfulness into the very fabric of your life.

A *mindful moment* by definition is 1-minute mindful pause, but in practice it can be anywhere from a few seconds to a couple of minutes. A *mindful moment practice* is pausing regularly throughout your day to cultivate mindfulness. A mindful moment takes less than 1-2 minutes and is a deliberate action you take to be mindful. While mindful moments can serve many ends, the core purpose is to accomplish three things: (1) to act with greater mindfulness, (2) to bring more pleasure into your life, and (3) to keep stress from building throughout the day. A mindful moment can be anything that is enjoyable or elicits any positive feeling (including the lift you get from being kind and helping others), triggers the relaxation response to relieve stress, energizes you when you need an energy boost, or is self-soothing or calming. Depending on the juncture in your day, it can fulfill many needs.

Some of your mindful moments can be preventative to offset your acknowledged self-defeating habits, some may be maintenance to keep you tracking when you're tooling along, and some may need to be responsive to deal with the daily onslaught of opportunities for *mindless* moments.

A mindful moment is a deliberate reprieve from business as usual with the intention of being mindful and taking a mindful action, either on your own behalf or for the welfare of others. In my definition, mindfulness takes into consideration how our behavior affects others. Research shows kindness and generosity toward others may make you feel even better than doing something for yourself. So it's crucial to incorporate acts of kindness and generous deeds among your daily mindful moments.

Merely being present-in-the-moment, even if you are aware of your inner landscape, doesn't necessarily translate into acting mindfully. It's not likely that a mindfulness meditation practice will lead to mindful action without simultaneously employing other action-oriented practices. The awareness a mindfulness meditation practice cultivates has to be transported beyond our internal world to infuse the way we treat, interact, and engage with others. A complementary mindful moment practice has the potential to develop skills that actually lead to being more mindful. A mindful moment practice may even work better than a daily mindfulness meditation session if your desired goal is to be happier, more content, and less stressed.

Sometimes during your day what you need is something relaxing to curb mounting stress. At other times when you're feeling beat up, you may need a self-soothing break. If your day has gotten you in a bad mood, you could benefit from something that brings you a little pleasure or conjures up any positive emotion. Or, if someone is getting on your nerves, you can shift your negativity toward the person by spending a mindful moment reflecting on one of the person's good qualities. If you're having an energy slump, you may need a spurt of energy, so you need to do something that is energizing. If your day is clicking along smoothly without too many glitches, that's a good time to spend a mindful moment being generous and doing something that enriches someone else's day. The idea is not only to tailor your mindful moment practice to meet the range of challenges a given day brings, but also to nurture your highest values.

Interspersing preplanned mindful moments throughout your day just may be the fast track route to living more mindfully. While you might be able to actually *be* mindful with a mindfulness meditation practice, it has to be in place for a long time before it permeates your moment-to-moment actions. Until the rewards of an ongoing mindfulness meditation practice gel, dispersing your mindfulness practice across your busy day is a more direct route to managing daily stress and maintaining a positive outlook, two critical life skills for well-being.

While not everyone may be able to allocate sufficient time to see the benefits of a dedicated mindfulness meditation practice, everyone can easily fit mindful moments into their daily routines. While it doesn't take a huge time commitment, it does take acting intentionally. It's not difficult to make mindful moments your practice if you are deliberate about designing your own daily repertoire of practices. You can do this initially by trying out and choosing from over 100 practices provided in this book.

But just as with mindfulness meditation, you'll have to be both intentional and consistent to reap the benefits. A daily mindful moment practice is accessible to anyone and virtually needs no training, although a meditation practice is a valuable companion. Even though minimal time is required, it does take careful forethought and conscious intention. It involves shifting your attention to positive thoughts and experiences, being grateful for what you have and receive, taking time to appreciate run-of-the-mill daily activities, and choosing to act with concern for others in mind.

The key to getting your daily dose of mindful moments is to create your own inventory of mindful moment practices you can tap as needed to offset a hurtful comment, the mounting stress of a never-ending to-do list, or a looming dark cloud hanging over you. And research indicates that our brain is hardwired to seek novelty so you'll want to keep your list varied and novel. It's also important to choose practices you enjoy and motivate you enough to actually do. Over time, you can craft your "personal best" collection of mindful moment practices. Eventually, taking a mindful moment pause will become automatic at the first signs of any form of distress.

Even in the most jam-packed day, you can find a minute in every hour or so to practice mindfulness. Many of the practices offered here can take just seconds. Devoting just one minute most of your awake hours is a minimal commitment with an enormous potential payoff. Because we all have segments of our day where we won't be able to pause for a mindful moment, the target is about 10 in a day. That's only about 1 percent of your day.

The Mindful Moments Path to Mindfulness

A mindfulness meditation practice may not be the right fit for everyone at this point in their lives. Some people aren't able to carve out the time for a mindfulness meditation practice, or think they're too hyper so they don't even try. Others may find the standard ways of meditating too challenging.

Research in the behavioral sciences reveals that when we don't receive sufficient feedback that we are making progress, we tend to disengage from our pursuits.[2] This is a likely explanation for why some people have trouble sticking with meditation. Beginning meditators often succumb to feelings that they just can't seem to settle down their minds the way they *think* they should. Because thoughts are persistently invading their minds, they don't have a sense that they're making any progress. Research also shows that smaller, immediate pay-offs are more motivating than larger, delayed rewards.[3] With a meditation practice, you may not experience any immediate benefits. With a mindful moment practice, you'll not only have a sense that you are making progress, you'll get multiple daily rewards both in the form of feeling less stressed and the chemical surges in your brain that go along with being more grateful, kind, and caring.

I'm certainly not advocating that you give up trying to meditate. Whenever you draw into yourself and bring your attention to your inner world to interrupt the otherwise unconscious flow of your mind's chatter, it's beneficial. But if you're struggling with keeping up a meditation practice, you can still practice being more mindful. Taking brief moments to intentionally be mindful interspersed throughout your day can be your practice. You don't have to keep beating yourself up about not taking the time to meditate. And you just may discover that you start to feel good about your practice, even with just a few mindful moments at first.

Merging a Mindful Moment Practice and a Mindfulness Meditation Practice

While it's not necessary to have a meditation practice to initiate a mindful moment practice, a meditation practice may groom you to take mindful breaks. A mindful moment practice and a mindfulness meditation practice are great partners in cultivating mindfulness. They can go hand-in-hand to advance your mindful practice. My experience after practicing more than a decade was that it wasn't enough. I found I needed to be more deliberate to act mindfully and to align my actions with my core values, which included fairness, kindness, and generosity.

> You actually have to seize opportunities for mindful moments throughout the day in order for your meditation practice to have real staying power so it permeates your day. Even if you do have a dedicated mindfulness meditation practice, it's likely you'll still need to intentionally create openings for mindful practices throughout your day.

After practicing meditation for some time, you may be able to automatically switch in and out of your daily busyness to act with mindful awareness throughout the day, but until that happens, having a repertoire of intentionally-planned, ready-made mindful moment practices will make that more likely to happen. Try adding mindful moments for yourself to see if your day seems to go better than just doing a single meditation session, or even without one.

If with your mindfulness meditation practice you're calmer, more aware, less stressed, less reactive, more positive, kinder, and more generous, then it may be all you need. If you're lacking in some of these qualities, taking brief moments to be intentionally mindful, and specifically targeting your activities, may augment your practice to bring in additional qualities that aren't elicited by your current meditation practice.

The ultimate mindfulness practice is when practice melds into momentary conscious living. Jon Kabat-Zinn says he likes to think of mindfulness simply as "the art of conscious living."[4] When you walk through life mindfully conscious of every step, you no longer have to remind yourself to hold your tongue when anger strikes, prompt yourself to show appreciation for life's little gifts, or remember to do random acts of kindness. The time comes when you can stop *practicing how to be mindful.* You have unleashed your awareness potential to live mindfully in the moment. Until then, you will need many, many orchestrated mindful moments.

CHAPTER 2

Mindfulness and Its Promise

Mindfulness must be engaged. Once there is seeing, there must be acting. Otherwise, what is the use of seeing?
-THICH NHAT HAHN

The challenge of being mindful beckons us to get out of autopilot to live our lives with greater awareness and intention. The call to mindfulness resonates with us all. Does anyone want to be mindless? Of course not—everyone wants to be mindful. It's hard to believe how such a simple notion as paying attention in the present moment can be so compelling.

What Is Mindfulness?
Mindfulness is a quality that we all possess to varying degrees. How often we are able to access it is the real feat. How mindful we actually are depends on how deliberately and consistently we cultivate mindful practices. Mindfulness is developed over time, through dedicated actions or practices, only one of which is mindfulness meditation.

Because of the popular press, mindfulness is routinely associated with mindfulness meditation, and the two terms are, mistakenly, often used interchangeably. Mindfulness meditation is *not* synonymous with mindfulness, it is a path to mindfulness, and there are multiple paths.

Long before mindfulness became a household word and came to be merged with mindfulness meditation, Harvard professor and pioneering researcher in mindfulness, Ellen Langer wrote her ground-breaking book in 1989, *Mindfulness*, applying mindfulness to learning and life.[1] She juxtaposed it to *mindlessness* where one goes through life wearing mental blinders based on past experiences and assumptions, clinging to preconceived ideas about how things *ought to be*. Langer describes mindfulness as:

> *Mindfulness is a state of engagement that draws us into the present and is characterized by being open to new information and consideration of more than one perspective.*

For Langer, mindfulness is being receptive to whatever comes into your awareness, offering a way to disengage from automatic behaviors and habitual responses. The more mindful you are, the more you can access a wider lens for viewing your world, seeing multiple perspectives and refraining from reactive judgments.

In the preface to the recent 25th Anniversary Edition of *Mindfulness*, Langer writes "Regardless of how we get there, either through meditation or more directly by paying attention to novelty and questioning assumptions, to be mindful is to be in the present, noticing all the wonders that we didn't realize were right in front of us."[2]

Mindfulness meditation is one of the most prevalent routes to developing mindfulness as a tool to heighten self-awareness, presumably leading to being more mindful. But, mindfulness extends beyond mindfulness meditation to include many practices that can cultivate the ability to be mindful.

The most quoted definition of mindfulness comes from Jon Kabat-Zinn, esteemed author of many books on mindfulness and developer of the most widely-used mindfulness training program.[3] His definition is:

> *Mindfulness is awareness that arises through paying attention, on purpose, in the present moment, non-judgmentally.*

Amishi Aja, mindfulness researcher and director of the Contemplative Neuroscience, Mindfulness Research & Practice Initiative at the University of Miami, offers a close rendition of his definition.[4] She describes mindfulness as:

Mindfulness is a state of attention to present-moment experience without conceptual elaboration or emotional reactivity.

In other words, mindfulness is being present without being drawn into thoughts that bring on negative emotions and stress. By these definitions, you can still be fully present and non-reactive, yet not act mindfully, nor respond to others or a challenging situation in a mindful way.

A Broader Definition of Mindfulness

Some definitions of mindfulness consider mindfulness as more than paying attention in the present non-judgmentally, adding a kind, accepting component. Master mindfulness meditation teachers Jack Kornfield and Sharon Salzberg, in alignment with its more traditional Buddhist roots, attribute a kind, compassionate, and loving element to mindfulness.[5] But this is referring to the stance we take toward ourselves, the notion being that this attitude toward ourselves builds the self-compassion that helps foster compassion toward others.

My application of mindfulness goes beyond being present and nonjudgmental, taking the position that action should be at the heart of mindfulness. My definition of mindfulness incorporates the conscious consideration of how our behavior affects others. Mindful attention and awareness have to be carried beyond our inner world to acting mindfully in our outer world. It takes both silence and action to make mindfulness a reality.

Being mindful involves awareness, attention, and intention. Acting mindfully takes it to another level. I conceive of mindfulness as having three levels.

Mindfulness encompasses having mindful awareness, holding mindful intent, and taking mindful action.

Paying attention could lead to acting with good intentions, but it doesn't necessarily do so. For most, practicing mindfulness meditation won't translate into what the Buddha has called "the one teaching" which embodies self-sacrifice, generosity, kindness, and compassion. That is, at least not until the practice has been a daily habit for a long time, and even then, there's no guarantee.

Practices that Enhance Mindfulness

Aligning with this broader definition, the term mindfulness would include a very wide scope of awareness-enhancing practices that expand our capacity to live more fully, consciously, and benevolently. Mindfulness can be cultivated through a variety of explicit practices that are awareness expanding and seek to promote self-discovery on some level. There are literally hundreds of kinds of practices, including meditation, relaxation, concentration, visualization, forms of chanting and prayer, as well as movement-based practices such as yoga, tai chi, and qigong.

And I would argue that positive psychology practices, as well as any deliberate practices that elicit positive emotions, such as expressing gratitude, doing acts of kindness, and savoring enjoyable moments, fall into the category of mindful awareness practices. Some practices that have been around many years and are validated by decades of research, under the umbrella of cognitive behavioral interventions, especially those that help us change the messages we tell ourselves, are also mindful practices. In fact, any deliberate practice done with mindful awareness and positive intent could be considered a mindful practice.

Mindfulness Has Multiple Layers

Mindfulness is an umbrella term for a collection of concepts and practices. It has multiple layers, meanings, and purposes. Mindfulness can be thought of in many different ways. It can be:

- *A pathway for personal growth and development*

   Mindfulness can be the pathway for cultivating self-observation, self-inquiry, self-reflection, and self-awareness. This is probably the most prevalent use of the term.

- *A spiritual path*

   Mindfulness for some is a foundation for spiritual practice.

- *A way to enhance functioning*

   Mindfulness can pave the way to improved functioning, such as on the job success, academic achievement, or athletic performance.

- *An avenue for stress reduction*

   Being mindful helps change the way we think and feel about our experiences, especially stressful experiences. This dimension of mindfulness is particularly important because we are living in an age when many of our health challenges are stress-related.

- *A route to cultivating positive qualities*

   Mindfulness provides a gateway to enrich positive attributes such as compassion and kindness.

- *A cognitive capacity*

   Mindfulness can be perceived as a cognitive ability to think in a nonjudgmental way, remaining open to all possibilities. This aspect of mindfulness refers to being able to acknowledge our limiting assumptions, biases, and prejudices.

- *A fixed personality trait*

   On one level, mindfulness is a personality trait, a way of going through life with a general inclination to be mindful. This is also referred to as *dispositional mindfulness,* meaning one has a mindful disposition, a relatively fixed quality. It is a character strength that is partly hardwired, but mostly cultivated through intentional practices.

The Promise of Practicing Mindfulness

Advocates, teachers, and longtime practitioners of mindfulness claim lifestyle benefits that can enhance our quality of life. Over time, the practice of mindfulness creates a way of being in the world that is more accepting and less reactive. When you approach the world with mindful awareness you are more accepting of yourself and others and can assess and respond to situations more purposefully. With mindful awareness, nothing is excluded—all is welcomed in the expansive space of mindfulness. Mindfulness creates a willingness to be present with whatever is unfolding in your life in the present moment. It is a quality of attention you can bring to any experience and apply to any situation, especially those that are challenging.

The promise of mindfulness is all-encompassing. The ultimate goal is to bring mindfulness to every moment and experience, until it eventually becomes a way of life that extends far beyond any particular technique. When you adopt a generally mindful approach to life you participate more fully in life, coming to value the journey along with the destination. You have greater appreciation of the wonder and beauty of life. Practicing mindfulness eventually leads to redefining your relationship to the mundane—from inconvenience to an integral and cherished part of living.

Another promise of practicing mindfulness is that you don't have to tackle your deep-seated demons, or completely revamp your life. You just have to act out of intention, not habit, day in and day out.

Meditation and Mindfulness Meditation

Meditation is a term encompassing a wide range of practices. Meditation practices have been around for thousands of years. Meditative techniques can be categorized as emphasizing mindfulness, concentration, or transcendence. While techniques differ, all types of meditation share the common goal of training attention and awareness so that consciousness becomes more finely tuned to events and experiences in the present.

Meditation can be any activity that keeps attention fixed in the present moment allowing you to transcend your normal state of consciousness. When you block out everything but the focal point commanding your attention, you are in a meditative state. In this state, you are totally engrossed, fully present. You need not be sitting in meditation, you might be walking, dancing, eating, cooking, or praying.

Some forms of meditation require more elaborate techniques than those involved in mindfulness meditation, although they all involve an ability to pay attention and develop insight in some way. Meditation is an active training of the mind to increase awareness, and various types of meditation approach this in different ways. Some meditation practices seek to harness the mind's powers of concentration, contemplation, or visualization, not simply meditation's capacity for quieting the mind.

A large group of practices are included in the category of mindfulness meditation, covering mindfulness-based programs such as Mindfulness-Based Stress Reduction and Mindfulness-Based Cognitive Therapy, Zen or Buddhist meditation, and Vipassana or Insight meditation, all of which emphasize present-focused awareness. These types of meditation primarily involve repeating a phrase or focusing on the breath or bodily sensations as a way of anchoring the mind.

In mindfulness meditation you pay attention to your breath, bodily sensations, feelings and stream of thoughts from a place of nonjudgmental awareness, noting and then letting go of the distractions continuously flowing through your mind. As skill in this type of monitoring develops, you learn to observe the functioning of your mind in a calm and unattached manner.

There are three essential elements of mindfulness meditation:

- The intention to consciously stay singularly-focused (on the breath, bodily sensations, or mantra)
- Sustained attention in the present moment without judging distractions or getting lost in them
- A presence of mind that is both observing and accepting

Two common styles of mindfulness meditation are *focused attention meditation* and *open monitoring meditation*. Most would also categorize the *body scan* as a form of mindfulness meditation.

Focused Attention Meditation. Focused attention meditation entails the voluntary focusing of attention on a chosen object. Focused attention meditation seeks to anchor the mind in attention. As your mind wanders, you keep coming back to the focus of your attention. Focused attention meditation is the most typical type of mindfulness meditation.

Open Monitoring Meditation. Typically, you begin with focused attention and only gradually shift as your practice progresses from monitoring directed attention to monitoring experience as a whole. Open monitoring meditation involves non-reactive moment-to-moment monitoring of what you are experiencing. In open monitoring meditation, practitioners strive to achieve awareness of internal and external experiences as they occur.

During open monitoring, you merely observe the thoughts, feelings, and sensations that occur without reacting or engaging with them. For example, if a memory of a recent argument pops up during open monitoring, rather than getting pulled into the memory along with its emotional tug, you simply observe that the memory is still lingering in your mind and let it pass. You may say to yourself something like, "Okay, that's still on my mind."

Focused attention and open monitoring can bring different benefits. Focused attention helps develop general self-inquiry. Open monitoring, when practiced over time, can lead to changing the way you relate to your thoughts and emotions.

The Body Scan. The body scan is also typically included under the umbrella of mindfulness meditation. It entails systematically paying attention to each part of your body and can be done in a variety of positions. In the body scan you focus on what you're sensing in each part of the body, moving your attention over your body from one location to the next, typically beginning with your feet. You just notice the specific sensations at each body part, such as pressure, tingling, or temperature. You don't think about those parts of the body, you merely experience the sensations in order to cultivate bodily awareness, which is also referred to as "embodied attention." As with any meditation, if you start to get lost in thought or feeling, you come back to re-engaging with progressing through your body areas. The body scan is typically practiced for 5 to 15 minutes.

The Promise of Practicing Mindfulness Meditation

Most teachers of various meditation practice traditions as well as practitioners and researchers alike would concur that many of the benefits associated with meditation may require several years of regular practice to manifest. By regularly practicing mindfulness meditation, you are training your mind to operate in a nonjudgmental, minute-by-minute, completely present mode. When you develop the capacity to be present in the moment, not drawn away by distractions, you can fully experience what's happening in the here and now—good, bad, or indifferent. You simply let experiences occur without attempting to categorize, manage, or direct them. Mindfulness meditation cultivates a mental attitude that there is nothing you can do in the current moment about what has already happened or what might happen.

The promise of mindfulness meditation is that by learning to slow down your thoughts, you create space between the urge to react and action itself, allowing you to make wiser and more considered decisions about how you want to act. When you harness your attention in the moment and maintain a patient, non-reactive response to whatever is occurring, you develop the capacity to recognize emotions as soon as they surface. When you meet your emotions just as they bubble up, you can widen the gap between impulse and action.

By learning to observe your thoughts nonjudgmentally, you can break the mental chain of associations that can keep you reeling in a thought, which causes much stress. While a mindfulness meditation practice won't necessarily make you exercise or eat healthier, it can attune you to your body's signals. You can't change what you're not aware of, but greater awareness can make any change possible.

The potential of a deliberative and consistent mindfulness meditation practice over the long haul is being able to hold steady in times of emotional turmoil. Eventually, an ongoing practice boosts your capacity to manage your emotions, rather than letting them manage you.

CHAPTER 3

What Do We Know about Mindfulness Meditation?

If mindfulness is deeply important to you,
then every moment is an opportunity to practice.
–JON KABAT-ZINN

More and more, we're seeing mindfulness seep into mainstream consciousness as a practical tool for coping with the ailments of modern day society. Mindfulness practices have made their way into businesses, schools, hospitals, prisons, veterans' centers, and beyond as a way to be more present in our lives. Companies such as Google, Apple, General Electric, Ford, General Mills, and many others offer mindfulness coaching and training, meditation rooms and breaks, and other resources to their employees.

The number of empirical publications on the topic is booming. Currently, over 100 peer-reviewed studies on mindfulness are being published every month. As of September 2017, a search for the word mindfulness in Google Scholar yielded 337,000 results. Do a Google search for mindfulness and you'll get a whopping 77,400,000 hits.

Media Mania and Mindfulness

If you just turned on your computer or TV and saw or heard the latest buzz on mindfulness meditation, you'd think research had proven mindfulness meditation was going to make your life better in every conceivable way. Mindfulness has become a media buzz-word. Almost daily, the media cite scientific studies that report the numerous health and well-being benefits of mindfulness meditation and how such a simple practice changes your brain. The findings reported run the gamut from increasing self-control, to regulating emotional turmoil, to enhancing our capacity for tolerance, to making us more compassionate, to engaging in more altruistic behavior. In fact, there isn't much research to support any of these claims.

While the actual benefits of mindfulness meditation are substantial, the claimed benefits embraced by popular media outlets often go far beyond what the research actually supports. While mindfulness meditation is a valuable practice, it is by no means a panacea. That being said, the fact that some of the claims may not be validated with sound research doesn't negate your personal experience which may be the ultimate test. Many of the benefits you experience may not be measurable, and those that are being studied may not be important to you. Just don't expect a mindfulness meditation practice by itself to deliver *everything*. It may not reduce your stress, keep your emotions from getting the best of you, or make you kinder or more compassionate—for these you'll have to add some other deliberate practices.

With greater access to online media, bloggers reporting on research far removed from the original source overstate results, often to the point of misrepresentation of the actual findings. As someone with a doctorate in research methods, it makes me crazy when I read research conclusions that are a gross exaggeration of the data collected in a study. I never like to trust how others cite and interpret research, so when the findings seem exaggerated, I check the original source. When I do, I'm often surprised at how the actual results have been overgeneralized, misinterpreted, or downright misrepresented.

What Don't We Know Yet about Mindfulness Meditation?

With all the research being done, there are still some very basic questions that remain unanswered.

For How Long Should We Meditate?

We really don't have a definitive answer even for the simplest question—what is the ideal length of time for a mindfulness meditation session? Is it 10 minutes as the popular Headspace app promotes, or is it 20 minutes, or two 20 minute sessions as Transcendental meditation advocates support, or a much longer session? Or, is whatever we can manage in a given day good enough as long as we keep doing it day after day, week after week, month after month, year after year? We have yet to determine the ideal dose. We don't know the optimal length, frequency, or regularity of practice required to accomplish the desirable effects.

The renowned Jon Kabat-Zinn, in his chapter in *Wherever You Go, There You Are* addressing how long to practice, begins with this question and answer.[1]

Question: Dr. Kabat-Zinn, how long should I meditate?

Answer: How should I know?

Though I'm sure his answer is really not quite that cavalier, it does give some indication of the lack of definitiveness.

Does Everyone Benefit from Mindfulness Meditation?

We don't know yet for whom and under what conditions mindfulness training is most effective. Not everyone experiences the same level of change as a result of mindfulness meditation training and practice. We know little about what lifestyle, temperamental, or personality differences might contribute to these differences. Many people may be simply relaxing, but not necessarily getting the full range of transformative cognitive and emotional benefits that is the potential of mindfulness meditation practice.

Do Different Types of Mindfulness Meditation Produce the Same Results?

We don't know if repeating a mantra, following the breath, listening to a guided meditation, or doing a body scan have the same effects. The brain is likely doing something quite different depending on whether you are being mesmerized by the voice of the person doing the guided meditation, or zoning out in relaxation mode, or paying attention to the sensations in your body, or following your breath. We really don't know what people are actually getting out of these different types of mindfulness meditation. Some may just be bringing on the body's relaxation response, which does have many benefits.

How Long Does It Take to Reap the Benefits of a Mindfulness Meditation Practice?

We don't know just how much meditation we need to do to make any headway toward achieving the potential long-term benefits. What we do know is that for many of the positive effects of mindfulness meditation to take hold, it takes a lot of practice. It may take persevering with a mindfulness meditation practice for several years to see some of the most desirable benefits.

Would Another Practice Be Just as Effective?

Many studies on mindfulness meditation compare it to a waitlist or usual care, rather than an alternative treatment or practice. This means that the results only indicate that mindfulness meditation is better than waiting, or nothing. So we don't know if mindfulness meditation works better than an alternative practice. And we don't know if another practice might be just as good, or even better, for the particular results we want.

The research findings don't give mindfulness meditation an edge over other practices that have been around for a long time, such as cognitive behavioral therapy, progressive muscle relaxation, or yoga for some desired outcomes. The point is, we don't yet know how mindfulness meditation fares in comparison to interventions and practices that have been shown to produce many of the same effects.

It Takes Time, but How Much?

The research findings tell us that many of the significant changes due to meditation practice take years to emerge. In order to see some of the purported payoffs it could take logging thousands of hours of meditation.

> RESEARCH RECAP: Those with thousands of hours of meditation show increases in brain areas associated with sustaining attention and regulating emotions, and decreases in the normal reduction of age-related gray matter volume. These longtime meditators also develop the capacity to live in a calm state and to be more resilient to stress and adversity. (See The Research Findings)

What Does the Research Say about Mindfulness Meditation?

Much of the research on mindfulness meditation is with those who have received training with the Mindfulness-Based Stress Reduction (MBSR) program. MBSR is undoubtedly the most widely-used mindfulness training program since its development by Jon Kabat-Zinn in 1979. While originally created as a standardized, group-based program for patients with chronic health problems, over the last couple of decades it has gradually become mainstream.

When reading research based on MBSR, it's important to appreciate the scope of this training and to understand how much is really going on that goes way beyond practicing meditation. MBSR integrates three major techniques, mindfulness meditation, body scan, and Hatha yoga. The training consists of an eight-week course in which participants meet once a week for a 2.5-hour session and one 8-hour day, for a total of 28 hours. Participants are also asked to practice approximately 45 minutes per day following guided instructions on a set of CDs. The daily homework assignments include meditation, yoga, and journaling exercises, such as keeping a pleasant and unpleasant events diary to increase their self-awareness, bringing the amount of training up to about 75 hours.

Mindfulness is also encouraged during everyday activities like eating and walking. In addition to mind training, MBSR pays a lot of attention to the body honoring the mind-body connection. Looking at the total picture of the active ingredients, there are actually nine different components in MBSR: (1) breath awareness meditation, (2) walking meditation, (3) body scan, (4) yoga, (5) psychological and social support by group members, (6) instructive communication with the teacher, (7) journaling, (8) attentive listening to inspirational texts such as poetry, and (9) daily homework practice.

A Review of the Significant Research Findings

For those like me who have been studying the research on mindfulness meditation, the evidence is far from conclusive. The next section delves into the research to decipher what a mindfulness meditation practice does and doesn't do. I try to sort out where the evidence is convincing and where it is not, as well as where the research is promising. There are ten areas where there has been considerable research. They include pain, stress reduction, anxiety, depression, regulating attention, regulating emotions, work performance, creativity, immune system response, and sleep.

Below I provide a review of the significant research findings. For the categories where the research is more extensive, so the research is not too overwhelming, a Research Recap is provided with the details of the research placed at the end of the chapter in The Research Findings. In the Appendix, I have also compiled a chart which compares the evidence for mindfulness meditation with the evidence for positive emotions/positive emotion-enhancing activities and for cognitive behavioral therapy for these ten areas, plus an additional ten where there is evidence for any of these categories. The chart shows which of these three categories has the best evidence, and where the evidence is good, limited, and insufficient.

Consensus is building on the effectiveness of mindfulness meditation in specific areas. Those benefits with the greatest research clout include improving attention and concentration, reducing the debilitating effects of chronic physical pain, and lessening anxiety and depression.

Mindfulness Meditation and Pain Relief

With the high prevalence of chronic pain and significant negative side effects of long-term use of pain medication, many sufferers are turning to mindfulness meditation as a self-employed alternative for relieving pain. The majority of the research is with those who have received training with standard MBSR and MBCT programs and focuses more on the psychological aspects of pain that affect quality of life, such as distress, pain acceptance, and functional ability. Comprehensive reviews of research conclude that mindfulness-based interventions have a positive impact on perceived pain control and acceptance, with more limited evidence for benefiting pain intensity.

Those with mindfulness meditation training become significantly better at accepting and managing their pain. Mindfulness meditation produces very different patterns of brain activity, reducing pain by activating regions associated with the self-control of pain to lessen the emotional experience of pain. Actually focusing on the pain during meditation rather than trying to distract yourself is more beneficial because it changes your subjective experience of the pain.

RESEARCH RECAP: Mindfulness meditation has a greater effect on pain acceptance and related quality of life than it has on actually limiting pain intensity. But this can make an immense difference for chronic pain sufferers. Mindfulness meditation reduces pain by changing perceived self-control of pain. It offers a preferable alternative to pain medications given their adverse consequences. (See The Research Findings)

Mindfulness Meditation for Stress Reduction

Mindfulness meditation is often proposed as an antidote to the stresses of today's life. Mindfulness meditation proponents speculate that by engaging in an ongoing mindfulness meditation practice you may come to reinterpret stressful situations in a healthier way, which should lead to substantially less stress. But we know little about how much meditation practice you need for it to reduce stress.

The research findings on the impact of mindfulness meditation on reducing stress are not conclusive. Interpreting the research is complicated by the fact that much of the research relies on self-reports and looks at minor lab-induced stress which may bear little resemblance to what causes stress in real life. The research is also limited because there are few long-term studies. By far, the evidence is strongest for MBSR which has several additional components also likely to affect stress.

In my review of the findings, I found they ranged from increasing stress reactions, to no differences whether compared to either no treatment or an alternative treatment, to reducing self-reports of stress but not actual physiological stress measures like cortisol levels (an indication the power of positive expectations may be influencing perceptions), to reducing both self-reports of perceived stress levels as well as physiological measures. In most reviews of research, the majority of the studies included are based on the more comprehensive programs, MBSR and MBCT. The rigorous review published in the *Journal of the American Medical Association* determined that mindfulness meditation had little impact on improving stress.

RESEARCH RECAP: Those who have MBSR training typically report experiencing less stress, especially those with chronic health conditions. When compared to alternative training or interventions, mindfulness meditation is generally not any better at reducing stress. While people often report feeling less stressed, actual physiological stress measures are seldom affected. (See The Research Findings)

Mindfulness Meditation and Anxiety and Depression

There is a growing body of research indicating that meditation reduces negative symptoms related to anxiety and depression. The evidence for mindfulness meditation for anxiety and depressive symptoms is as good as the evidence for many standard medical treatments. The effectiveness is comparable to what would be expected from an antidepressant.

Recent reviews support that mindfulness meditation training has a moderate effect on depression and anxiety, which is a strong finding for research in this area. With the typical treatment of depression with drugs, only one third fully recover after one treatment period. After a second treatment period, still only 50% recover, leaving half of those suffering from depression still agonizing from their symptoms.[2] Alarmingly, the rate of depression has increased roughly tenfold over the last two generations. The average onset of depression is now 13, where it used to be 42.[3] The World Health Organization reports depression is the leading cause of disability in midlife and for women of all ages.

With mindfulness training, those suffering with anxiety and depression learn to experience their symptoms with less emotional reaction, coming to realize that the awful feeling that springs up and can engulf them is just their overactive brain circuitry. They learn to think, "It's just my brain producing another obsessive thought, just static from a faulty circuit. I know it's not real and I can resist this message."

RESEARCH RECAP: The effectiveness for mindfulness-based and mindfulness-based cognitive programs for treating anxiety and depression are comparable to standard treatments and the use of antidepressants. While generally not better than traditional cognitive behavioral treatments, they offer an effective alternative. Some resent research suggests combining with an antidepressant may be better initially with gradual withdrawal of medication possible. (See The Research Findings)

Mindfulness Meditation and Regulating Attention

Research shows that ongoing mindfulness meditation practice alters brain circuitry to enhance our ability to stay focused and not get hijacked by the endless stream of negative chatter parading through our minds.[4] More hours of mindfulness meditation practice translate into greater capacity for regulating our attention. Basically, the mental training mindfulness meditation provides reduces background babble to allow you to direct your attention to selected information. While earlier research focused on studying more experienced meditation practitioners, some recent research shows that brief training in a mindfulness practice can also produce similar increases in the ability to regulate our attention.[5]

While practicing mindfulness is associated with enhanced ability to control and sustain attention, short-term and long-term mindfulness meditation training seem to induce different brain responses.[6] The early phases of mindfulness training involve developing focused attention and are associated with improvements in controlling attention. In the more advanced stages where little or no effort is needed, meditation is associated with improved ability to sustain attention.[7]

Mindfulness Meditation and Regulating Emotion

Daniel Siegel, New York Times best-selling author of several books on the brain and mindfulness and co-director of the Mindful Awareness Research Center at UCLA, maintains that regular mindful awareness practice strengthens brain connections to support self-reflection and self-monitoring which leads to less emotional reactivity.[8] Reviewing brain imaging studies of meditators, researchers report brain regions consistently altered in areas important for self-awareness of thoughts and emotions, body awareness, self-regulation, emotion regulation, and communication between parts of the brain.[9] Mindfulness training increases brain size in regions which are primarily responsible for self-awareness and emotional control.[10]

Neuroscientists at Stanford and Harvard report that the area of the brain that sounds the alarm for threat and danger shrinks in meditators while the more thoughtful response region of the brain grows.[11] The connections between the fear-responsive amygdala and the rest of the brain weaken, while those between the emotion-regulating prefrontal cortex and the rest of the brain are strengthened. These changes suggest that mindfulness can lessen reactive and fearful responses to allow for more thoughtful assessment of events and situations.

While one of the key outcomes for practicing meditation is better regulation of our emotions, brain scans show that not everyone reaps this benefit from meditation. The way it is often measured is to look for a reduction in reactivity of the amygdala. With the amygdala quieted, the more rational parts of the brain take over to allow us to tame our emotional response. When researchers look at the actual brain scans to compare meditators with non-meditators, they see that some meditators don't show less reactivity in the amygdala, while many non-meditators do show less reactivity.[12] Interpretation of these results means not only that everyone isn't getting the same results from meditating, but also that having less reactivity can be accomplished from practices other than meditation.

Interestingly, *positive reappraisal* (also called *cognitive reappraisal* or just *reappraisal*), a core coping strategy of cognitive behavioral therapy that has been used for decades and is one of the most well-validated strategies, also produces similar changes in the brain. In reappraisal, you learn to recast a negative or stress-producing experience or event as in some way positive, beneficial, or meaningful. Brain imaging studies show using reappraisal leads to lesser reactivity in emotion-regulating regions of the brain, such as the amygdala.[13]

While brain scans show greater activation in areas of the brain that are associated with processing emotions, we don't yet know how these brain changes actually effect behavior. When scientists report greater *activation* what this really means is that more oxygen is flowing to that brain area. It does make intuitive sense that mindfulness meditation training would help to regulate emotions by allowing for that brief pause to let the thinking mind catch up with the habitual reactive part of the brain, it really hasn't been validated. There aren't studies comparing how meditators regulate their emotions in real life situations compared to non-meditators.

Mindfulness Meditation and Work Performance

Because mindfulness training may enhance self-awareness and emotional control, such skills can contribute to better teamwork and conflict resolution, as well as better relationships with colleagues which are key to success in the workplace. There is some evidence that mindfulness meditation improves areas related to work performance and productivity. The ability to stay on task without distractions is certainly a desirable skill related to work performance. Research indicates that mindfulness meditation practice enhances the brain's working memory.[14] Improved working memory helps to keep attention engaged in the task at hand over an extended period of task engagement, instead of mind-wandering to task-unrelated thoughts. One study found that after a two-week mindfulness training course, participants improved both their GRE scores and their scores on a measure of working memory, while simultaneously reducing the occurrence of distracting thoughts while completing the GRE.[15]

It's estimated that our mind wanders roughly half of our waking hours and mindfulness meditation practice can help stabilize our attention in the present. Mindfulness training reduces mind-wandering based on both self-reports and task performance.[16] Research shows those who receive mindfulness meditation training can stay attentive longer on both visual and listening tasks.[17] While mindfulness training may reduce mind-wandering, that's not always what the task at hand may require. Some problem-solving tasks may be better performed when the mind is wandering.

Mindfulness Meditation and Creativity

The evidence linking mindfulness to greater creativity is limited and the findings vary considerably. The research indicates that it is important to distinguish between different aspects of mindfulness training because they may have varying effects on creativity. Some research shows that open monitoring meditation can increase creativity, whereas focused-attention meditation has no effect on creativity.[18] Other research shows that the ability to focus attention and act with full awareness is associated with decreased performance on a creativity task.[19] Yet, a different aspect of mindfulness, the ability to observe and attend to various stimuli, is associated with increased creativity.

Mindfulness Meditation and the Immune System

While a few studies have shown differences in markers of immune system response for meditators, the results are not consistent and are most pronounced for more experienced meditators. In the first comprehensive review of randomized control trials (RCTs) recently published, the researchers concluded that while the findings suggest possible effects of mindfulness meditation on some markers associated with immune system response, the results are tentative and require further replication.[20]

Mindfulness Meditation and Sleep Problems and Treatments

About one third of us will experience insomnia at some point in our lives.[21] With the latest research indicating that sleeping pills on average give you only 11 extra minutes of sleep a night and come with significant side effects,[22] many are trying mindfulness meditation. While improving sleep is often promoted as a benefit of mindfulness meditation, the research does not support this claim.

> RESEARCH RECAP: Mindfulness meditation may increase self-perceptions of sleep quality and daytime fatigue, but has no significant effect on total sleep time, how long it takes to get to sleep, or waking up during the night. While the research evidence isn't there, it's worth exploring different mind-body approaches as individual experiences with such approaches vary greatly. But these strategies may not be enough for more chronic sleep problems. (See The Research Findings)

What is the Best Treatment for Sleep Problems?

Cognitive behavioral therapy for insomnia, or CBT-I, is the most effective treatment.[23] Whether delivered in person or online, it has impressive research results.[24] The American College of Physicians in its guidelines advises its members that CBT-I should be the first treatment they offer patients with chronic insomnia.[25]

What Challenges Does Mindfulness Meditation Research Face?

Despite the media blitz and blog craze, those at the forefront of the actual research are much more cautious about the proven benefits with foremost authorities at mindfulness research centers around the globe calling for more rigorous research to substantiate findings they view as preliminary. Much of the research has been wrought with methodological weaknesses. Recently, there have been a number of summaries of the research with major systematic reviews and meta-analyses published in esteemed journals bringing into question some of the claimed benefits. These review sources that base their conclusions on both the quality as well as the quantity of the evidence provide an unbiased view of what the research shows.

A recent special issue of the *American Psychologist* journal was devoted to research challenges mindfulness meditation faces. These experts in the field concluded that while much progress has been made over the past decade, this area of research is "still in its infancy" and leaves many questions yet to be addressed.[26] Richard Davidson, preeminent researcher on mindfulness meditation, in a recent article reported: "There are still very few methodologically rigorous studies that demonstrate the effectiveness of mindfulness-based interventions in either the treatment of specific diseases or in the promotion of well-being."[27] In a 2016 talk he gave to the National Center for Complementary and Integrative Health (NCCIH), he reported that methodological concerns about meditation research are at the forefront now with recent pushback about the rigor of mindfulness meditation research reported in reviews in two prestigious journals.[28]

In the Journal of the American Medical Association (JAMA) review, the researchers found that when various meditation practices were compared to other interventions, there was no evidence that meditation practices were more effective than other treatments, including exercise, in changing any of the outcomes they studied.[29] In the PLOS ONE review, researchers found that positive findings were reported 60 percent more often than is statistically likely based on the small sample sizes, suggesting that negative results are going unpublished.[30] The team also examined another 21 registered trials and found 62 percent were unpublished 30 months after they were finished.

Research Issues Affecting Mindfulness Meditation

While some issues are common to any type of research, there are some that pose a particular problem for studying mindfulness and mindfulness meditation.

1. **Defining Mindfulness**

   One of the main issues is the inclusion of many practices under the heading of mindfulness. Although they are frequently used interchangeably by the popular press as well as researchers, mindfulness and meditation are *not* the same. Most often the term *mindfulness* is used synonymously with *mindfulness meditation* where much of the research has focused. It is also used synonymously with meditation in general, even though there are many types of meditation. There are also plenty of practices that cultivate mindfulness other than mindfulness meditation.

With no general agreement on the meaning of mindfulness, it is hard to know what is being studied. Lumping everything together and assuming diverse meditation and mindfulness practices are all doing the same thing and have the same outcomes makes the conclusions drawn questionable.

2. Meditation Practitioners Engage in Many Other Related Practices

Many people who practice meditation use more than one style of meditation as well as other contemplative practices. When this happens, you can't isolate the benefits of each individual practice.

For example, David Hamilton, author of several mind-body books, reported that he regularly uses three meditation practices.[31] One is mindfulness meditation, another is the Buddhist loving-kindness meditation, and the third is a contemplative practice involving asking deep probing questions (like what is the nature of consciousness or what is reality) and being receptive to what answers come to him.

My daily practice, in addition to taking mindful moments throughout the day, includes practicing mindfulness meditation mostly in the form of a personal mantra, but also sometimes focusing just on my breath, or my heart. I also use guided meditations that focus on a wide variety of feelings, virtues, and intentions depending on my mood. In addition, I have a longtime yoga practice. To help me fall asleep, I sometimes use a body scan, progressive muscle relaxation, self-hypnosis, or other guided meditations specifically targeted to induce sleep.

If our two brains were examined, we wouldn't be able to say what it was that led to our current brain structure or other capacities. The problem this creates is that while the researchers may be studying one variable, the participants are doing other things as well that are affecting the outcome being studied.

3. Mindfulness Meditation May Not Be the Cause

Some of the beneficial effects associated with meditation may be due to other correlated factors so causal links cannot be made. Many studies linking mindfulness meditation to specific outcomes just show a relationship—that doesn't prove it's the cause. It may not be just the meditation practice, but the conglomerate of healthy behaviors that accounts for the differences. Meditation practitioners are also likely to lead healthy lifestyles. It's possible that the other things a person has been doing are responsible for the differences found.

A new study published in June of 2017 surveyed 34,525 adults during the 12 months prior and collected information on three common meditation styles—mantra, mindfulness, and spiritual meditation.[32] Looking at mindfulness meditators specifically, they were more likely than non-meditators to use other complementary health approaches, including getting acupuncture and chiropractic treatments and practicing yoga. The general results showed that meditators were more likely than non-meditators to:

- Be middle-aged, white, female, and college-educated
- Have a heathy body weight
- Be physically active
- Eat vegetarian diets
- Engage in preventive health practices, such as physical activity, not smoking, and having their cholesterol checked

4. **How Mindfulness Meditation Compares to Alternative Practices**

Another issue is the need to compare mindfulness meditation to other interventions, treatments, or practices that have some similar benefits in order to determine if it works better than an alternative. Many studies compare mindfulness meditation to being on a waitlist to get the training or getting just usual care rather than a different, but similar treatment. Including an "active" control group is necessary if we want to determine if mindfulness meditation works better than an alternative practice.

In the JAMA review that paired down thousands of meditation studies to just 47 considered well-designed, the researchers found little evidence that any of the mindfulness practices studied were more effective in changing any of the outcomes if they were compared to other interventions likely to produce similar benefits. The outcomes studied included anxiety, depression, stress/distress, positive mood, mental health-related quality of life, attention, substance use, eating habits, sleep, pain, and weight.[33]

Similarly, in a recent comprehensive review of 25 studies of loving-kindness meditation (LKM), the majority of comparisons with an alternative treatment, including those that have been practiced for a long time, such as emotion regulation, progressive muscle relaxation, and music therapy, found no significant differences.[34]

One relevant comparison is with cognitive behavioral therapy (CBT) which has an extensive body of research spanning decades that supports its effectiveness.[35] We know that CBT works and we also know it works when combined with mindfulness training, Mindfulness-Based Cognitive Therapy, what we don't know yet is whether this combination is necessarily better than CBT alone.[36]

5. **Mindfulness Meditation Programs Have Multiple Components that Affect Findings**

Much of the research findings are based on two systematic meditation programs, Mindfulness-Based Stress Reduction

(MBSR) and Mindfulness-Based Cognitive Therapy (MBCT), designed based on MBSR with an added cognitive component. These programs have multiple components that have little to do with meditation. And these different features all have their own research indicating they are effective strategies independently producing similar benefits as mindfulness meditation.

So the challenge is to determine how much the mindfulness component contributes to the overall results participants achieve. We need to know the separate impact of each practice, or if it is the combination, that leads to the results. As described earlier, these programs have as many as nine individual components. Because the majority of studies and reviews of research are based on these two programs, we can't assume that other meditation practices where individuals have had little training and guided practice will achieve the same results.

We don't have the answer to the question of whether mindfulness meditation is making the difference. In the two studies where the controls have been truly matched to MBSR or MBCT, allowing them to determine whether mindfulness meditation is the distinguishing active ingredient, differences have not been found.[37]

6. Measuring Mindfulness

Researchers measuring mindfulness use self-report assessments. As is always the case, it is questionable what can and cannot be inferred from self-report measures. The major problem with any self-report is that there is a tendency to *overestimate* aspects viewed as positive, while underestimating aspects viewed as negative. A problem unique to measuring mindfulness with self-reports is that there is an inherent paradox in using frequency of attention lapses as an index of mindfulness because the ability to detect such lapses is contingent on one's overall level of mindfulness.[38]

Depending on self-reports with no external confirmation or investigation of differences between self-report and external measurements (i.e., actual observations of behavior, others' perceptions) renders them entirely subjective. We don't know how well self-reports of mindfulness correspond with actual daily life mindful behavior. When someone participates in a mindfulness or meditation study, they are already primed to expect benefits and then when you assess how mindful they think they are, they're likely to report being more "mindful."

The self-report questionnaires that have been developed to assess mindfulness vary greatly. While some researchers consider mindfulness to be one-dimensional, referring specifically to paying attention to the present-moment experience,[39] others argue that qualities such as curiosity, acceptance, and compassion are inherent to mindfulness.[40]

In my review, I identified ten scales or questionnaires. Five of them define mindfulness as having a single dimension, while five others define mindfulness and having from two to eight dimensions. The two most-commonly in use also have the best validity, the Mindful Attention Awareness Scale (MAAS) and the Five Facet Mindfulness Questionnaire (FFMQ).[41]

The MAAS assesses a core characteristic of mindfulness as a receptive state of attention and awareness of what is occurring in the present.[42] The FFMQ assesses the ability to (1) pay attention to both internal and external sensations, (2) describe thoughts, feelings, and perceptions, (3) focus un-divided attention on the present, (4) experience events and thoughts without judgments, and (5) non-reactivity to inner experience.[43] Those studying different dimensions often find different results.

7. Small and Non-Representative Samples

Many studies have small sample sizes, or are *pilot* studies, which typically means the sample is not representative of the general population. Studies with smaller sample sizes are more affected by chance making them worse at detecting statistically significant results. This means that new, larger, better quality studies could change the conclusions.

Those willing to participate in a meditation study may be different from the average population. Research indicates that they are more likely to have tried at least one type of meditative practice before participating in a study.[44] Studying a sample that is not representative of the general population means the results may not be true for those who are different from the sample.

8. Changing Real Behavior

There are no studies that observe life practices, so we don't know if mindfulness meditation actually leads people to be more mindful in their daily lives. The true test would be whether or not having a mindfulness meditation practice leads to treating ourselves and others mindfully.

9. Assessing Placebo Effects

In medical studies, the *placebo effect* is the effect of no treatment, but the patient does not know whether or not he or she is getting the real thing or a fake. The placebo effect has particular relevance to the study of mindfulness meditation. Studying mindfulness meditation interventions or trainings, the power of suggestion, expectation, or belief is an important variable.

Because we are inundated with positive reports of the benefits of meditation, preconceived notions regarding expectations for improvement can be a source of bias. This is especially a problem when self-reporting perceived changes, such as stress levels. People who believe in the benefits of meditation are more likely to enroll in a meditation program and report that they benefited. Participants in studies may have already tried meditation and/or come into a study believing in the results of meditation which may bias their results. And biases of the researchers may be transferred to participants. Variables such as the trainer's confidence, expectation for results, and support provided may all have an impact.

The Placebo Effect: Mind over Matter

Many of the measured outcomes of mindfulness studies evaluate symptoms that are largely subjective, such as perceived stress, anxiety, and pain. When participants in mindfulness studies experience relief from such symptoms, there's no objective measurement to quantify or prove what they are actually experiencing and reporting.

More and more research verifies the power of the placebo effect. While nearly every clinical trial demonstrates a placebo effect, placebos are especially effective for mental-health conditions, such as anxiety and depression.[45] Many studies demonstrate that nearly all of the happy responses patients experience as a result of antidepressants can be attributed to the placebo effect.[46]

In more recent trials from both antipsychotic medications as well as pain medications, positive placebo responses have increased considerably in pain clinical trials conducted in the United States over the past several decades.[47] There is ample research indicating that placebos are most effective when treating pain. Placebos for pain have powerful effects, often comparable to a variety of other treatments.[48] When compared to morphine, placebos are almost equally effective at treating pain.[49]

Harvard researcher Ted Kaptchuk who has been studying the placebo effect for many years has conducted research showing that placebos actually activate specific areas of the brain such as the prefrontal cortex, anterior insula, and amygdala.[50] And these are some of the same areas affected by mindfulness meditation. Many common medications also act through these pathways. Such findings have greatly enhanced the credibility of placebo effects. Recent research has provided compelling evidence that these effects are genuine phenomena, revealing objective neurobiological pathways and correlates of placebo responses.[51]

Interestingly, the three areas where the research is most substantial for the effectiveness of mindfulness meditation are pain, anxiety, and depression, and these are also the areas that are most susceptible to the placebo effect. In these three areas where a person's experience is subjective, placebos can be as, or even more, effective than an actual treatment.

THE RESEARCH FINDINGS

For Meditators with Thousands of Hours of Meditation Practice

- **Thicker Cerebral Cortexes/Increased Gray Matter**
  Meditators with an average of 9 years meditation experience who averaged 6 hours of practice per week had thicker cerebral cortexes compared to non-meditators in brain areas associated with self-regulatory processes, including the ability to sustain attention and regulate emotions.[52]

- **Brains Aging at a Slower Pace**
  A recent UCLA study found that the brains of long-term meditators seem to age at a slower pace than those of other people. The expert meditators studied had a mean practice of close to 20 years. Brain scans revealed that these meditators showed less age-related reduction of gray matter volume. Gray matter is a layer of tissue critical to cognition and memory storage that tends to begin shrinking in a person's 20s.[53]

- **Ability to Live in a Calm State**
  While much research is conducted during meditation, or shortly after, some research also looks at meditators when they are not meditating to try to determine carryover effects. Research on expert meditators, those with 40,000 or more hours of meditation practice under their belts, shows that their resting brains when they are not meditating look similar to a normal person's brain when he or she is meditating. They have a "new normal" which is like the experience most of us have only during meditation. They have honed the ability to live in a calm state. Of course, 40,000 plus hours of meditation means they're not doing much of anything else. Doing the math and spreading these many hours over a 30-year period, these longtime meditators would be averaging about 25 hours of meditation a week.[54]

- **Lower Stress-Induced Cortisol and Inflammatory Response**
  Comparing experienced meditators, with an average of 9000 hours of meditation practice, to a matched healthy control

group with no meditation experience, the experienced meditators had lower stress-induced cortisol and a smaller inflammatory response. This study involved 31 experienced meditators after a day of intensive practice of mindfulness meditation. The control group engaged in leisure activities. When these experienced meditators were put in a stressful situation afterward, the genes and hormones that typically flare up in response to stress remained quiet. The stress response spiked in the control group with no meditation experience.[55]

- **Slower Resting Heart Rate**
  The goal of meditation is that the practice will have enduring effects outside of the time spent meditating. Recent research looked at whether longtime meditators, when not meditating, would show a slower resting heart rate, a measure which correlates with many aspects of well-being.[56] They found that in order for them to have significant differences in resting heart, longtime meditators who had practiced many hours, averaging 6 hours of practice per week, also needed to have spent time in an intensive meditation retreat. They needed a minimum of an additional fifteen days of intensive meditation retreat practice for their heart rates to be lower when they were not meditating. Just practicing meditation for a long time was not enough to affect resting heart rate.

- **Greater Resilience**
  Richard Davidson and colleagues at the Center for Healthy Minds have been able to isolate the neural circuitry related to resilience. They say mindfulness meditation is a key practice because it directly strengthens those circuits over time. Their recent research looked at how rapidly the neural brain circuitry used to recover from adversity can return to baseline. Their preliminary data suggest it would take 6,000 to 7,000 hours of cumulative practice before brain changes associated with resilience occur.[57]

  It sounded like a long time, so I did the math: 6000 hours is 360,000 minutes. So even someone with a dedicated practice doing 20 minutes a day for seven days a week would log only 140 minutes a week, about 120 hours per year. It would take about 50 years at this level of practice to accumulate 6000 hours. Assuming the average person may not meditate 20 minutes, or every day, pushes the timeline even further.

THE RESEARCH FINDINGS
Mindfulness Meditation and Pain

The majority of the research is with standard MBSR and MBCT programs. The research indicates the effects of mindfulness-based programs on pain may vary depending on the type of chronic pain condition.

- The JAMA review of randomized control trials (RCTs), concluded there was moderate evidence that mindfulness meditation can improve pain, based on 8 studies in their sample.[58]

- In the 2017 RAND Corporation review, researchers conducted a meta-analysis with 38 RCTs and only 11 received a "good" quality rating. They found low-quality evidence that mindfulness meditation is associated with a small decrease in pain compared with all types of controls. They also noted possible publication bias and the need for additional rigorous and large-scale RCTs to decisively determine the effectiveness of mindfulness meditation for chronic pain.[59]

- Previous comprehensive reviews with RCTs have similarly revealed that mindfulness-based interventions may have a positive impact on perceived pain control or acceptance with a moderate effect size, but there is limited evidence of a benefit in pain intensity. Individual studies included in the reviews are generally small and results for many outcomes are not statistically significant.[60]

- Studies with active control groups show smaller effects, with the effect of mindfulness meditation generally equivalent to the alternate treatment. Studying adults with chronic low-back pain who received either MBSR training, cognitive-behavioral therapy (CBT) or usual care, there were no significant differences between the two treatments.[61] Participants in the MBSR and CBT groups had significant improvement in back pain and functional limitation compared with those who had usual care at 26 and 52 weeks.

- MBSR effects on pain may vary as a function of chronic pain condition. A longitudinal investigation of 133 chronic pain patients found that patients with back pain and arthritis demonstrated a significant change in pain intensity and functional limitations due to pain following meditation training. Patients with chronic headache/migraine experienced the smallest improvement in pain and health-related quality of life.[62]

- Mindfulness meditation diminishes pain intensity, distress, and related quality of life in unique ways. Chronic pain patients become better able to view thoughts about their pain, such as *It's killing me* or *This will never end*, as just thoughts and not statements of truth. When chronic pain patients were randomly assigned to either MBSR training or a wait list, researchers found that while there were no significant differences for pain measures, those having the training were significantly better at accepting and managing their pain.[63]

- Brief mindfulness training may also be effective in reducing feelings of acute pain. A recent study found that mindfulness meditation reduced pain more effectively than a placebo or morphine in healthy and pain-free volunteers.[64] The participants' brains were scanned before and after their training while a heated probe was pressed against their skin until it reached a level of heat most people find very painful. The mindfulness meditation group, who had 20-minute sessions of mindfulness meditation for 4 days, reported pain intensity was reduced by 27 percent and pain unpleasantness by 44 percent. The placebo cream reduced the pain intensity by 11 percent and unpleasantness by 13 percent. Research indicates that morphine reduces physical pain by about 22 per cent. Brain scans showed that mindfulness meditation produced very different patterns of activity than those produced by the placebo. Mindfulness meditation reduced pain by activating regions associated with the self-control of pain, while the placebo cream lowered pain by reducing brain activity in pain-processing areas.

- A similar small study found that mindfulness meditation helps to control pain but doesn't use the brain's naturally occurring opiates to do so. Researchers examined pain responses in healthy volunteers during mindfulness meditation in response to applying painful heat along with both intravenous administration of an opioid inhibitor or saline placebo. Meditation during saline infusion significantly reduced pain intensity and unpleasantness ratings compared to the saline only group. What was most surprising, there were no significant differences in pain intensity or unpleasantness reductions between the meditation plus opioid inhibitor and the meditation plus saline groups. These results lead the authors to conclude that treating pain may not only be more effective with meditation, but in combination with pain medications, may be even more effective for reducing pain.[65]

- In studies comparing the pain perception of long-term meditation practitioners and those naïve to meditation, the long-term practitioners report less pain in response to a pain stimulus administered while meditating.[66] Meditators have much less activity in regions of the brain that interpret sensation and emotion suggesting that mindfulness may lessen the emotional experience of pain. Advanced meditators don't fit any of the classic models of pain relief, including drugs. They seem to be blocking the experience by reframing the thought processes that make it painful.

THE RESEARCH FINDINGS

Mindfulness-Based Stress Reduction (MBSR) for Reducing Stress

- Corresponding with the purpose for its development, there is much research showing that for those suffering from a variety of physical and psychological diagnoses, including cancer, cardiovascular disease, chronic pain as well as depression and anxiety disorders, MBSR can bring about significant improvements in psychological distress.[67]

- In a meta-analysis of 10 studies, researchers concluded that MBSR is an equally effective program for reducing stress in healthy people.[68]

Although the effectiveness of MBSR for reducing stress and anxiety is more conclusive for those coping with symptoms of chronic illness, some findings are mixed, as indicated in the meta-analyses reported below.

- A meta-analysis of 8 randomized control trials (RCTs) considering different chronic diseases concluded that MBSR has small effects on psychological distress.[69]

- A meta-analysis of 23 RCTs considered the combined evidence for MBSR and MBCT for different patient categories on several outcomes. MBSR and MBCT significantly improved stress based on only 2 reviews compared to a waitlist and to treatment as usual. The reviewers acknowledged this meta-analysis was limited due to lack of comparisons with other treatments and long-term follow-ups.[70]

- Another meta-analysis considering 8 RCTs of both MBSR and MBCT on psychological outcomes for people with vascular disease found significant reductions in self-reported stress. But the effects on physical outcomes related to stress, such as blood pressure and stress hormones were mixed.[71]

Because of the increased stress and potential burnout inherent in health care professions, the effects of MBSR for reducing stress for this population is often studied. Results from multiple studies suggest that MBSR can be effective for reducing stress and related symptoms.

- Reduced stress after MBSR training has been reported in separate studies for a variety of health care professionals, including nurses, doctors, clinicians and therapists.[72]
- A review of 10 empirical studies concluded that MBSR is effective for reducing stress for health care professionals.[73] But 9 of these studies utilized self-reports to measure stress.
- In the one study measuring cortisol, there was no significant change.[74]
- The only study comparing MBSR training with an alternative training found no significant differences for reducing stress between meditation training and progressive relaxation training.[75]

THE RESEARCH FINDINGS

Other Mindfulness Meditation Training for Reducing Stress

- Because many reviews of research combine stress, distress, and anxiety, it is difficult to interpret the findings. Considering stress and anxiety separately, the comprehensive JAMA review concluded there was little evidence that mindfulness meditation improved stress/distress.[76]
- Another review of 17 studies where they did not differentiate stress from anxiety reported that 16 showed positive changes in psychological or physiological outcomes related to stress and anxiety.[77]

Many studies have not found mindfulness meditation training results in lower stress, or improves stress more than other alternatives.

- Following brief mindfulness meditation training, participants showed greater levels of cortisol while completing a stressful performance tasks.[78]
- As part of the Shamatha Project, even after participating in an intensive, 3-month meditation retreat, levels of cortisol were not affected.[79]
- Mindfulness meditation training compared to a wait-list, showed no changes in two stress-related measures, salivary cortisol and heart rate variability for older adults aged 50-85.[80]
- Following training comparing MBSR and the Health Enhancement Program, an 8-week training including all the elements in MBSR except the mindfulness meditation, there were no differences in general distress or anxiety.[81]
- A 3-day mindfulness meditation retreat compared to a "scam" meditation focusing on relaxation found no differences in self-reported stress reduction.[82]
- After a weeklong mindfulness meditation and yoga retreat, comparing experienced meditators and novice meditators with those who simply vacationed at the retreat center, all three groups showed the same significant improvements in self-reported stress.[83]

THE RESEARCH FINDINGS

Mindfulness Meditation and Anxiety and Depression

- The comprehensive JAMA review of randomized control trials (RCTs) found that there was moderate evidence that mindfulness meditation can improve anxiety and depression.[84]
- The 2017 RAND Corporation meta-analysis with 38 RCTs also found significant effects for depression symptoms.[85]
- Another meta-analysis of 23 RCTs reviewed the evidence of the effectiveness of MBSR and MBCT for a variety of outcomes in different patient categories. The researchers concluded that MBSR and MBCT significantly improved depressive symptoms based on 5 reviews and anxiety based on 4 reviews in comparisons with wait list controls and treatment as usual.[86]
- In general, mindfulness-based cognitive therapy interventions, while not superior to traditional cognitive behavioral treatments, are effective alternatives.[87]
- Mindfulness-based cognitive therapy (MBCT) is as effective as antidepressants in preventing relapse in patients with recurrent major depression. In several studies MBCT combined with antidepressant withdrawal was comparable to MBCT plus antidepressants in preventing relapse.[88]
- Recent findings from a large, real-world sample showed MBCT is more effective when antidepressant treatment continues.[89] The combination lead to lower risk for relapse in patients with partially- or fully-remitted recurrent depression. Researchers in this multisite Netherlands study assessed outcomes quarterly for 15 months with 249 patients. Relapse rates were 69% for MBCT alone versus 46% for MBCT plus antidepressants.
- In a randomized, controlled trial comparing the MBSR with an active control for generalized anxiety disorder (GAD), 93 individuals with diagnosed GAD were randomly assigned to an 8-week group intervention with MBSR or to an attention control, Stress Management Education (SME).[90] Both interventions led to significant reductions in anxiety rating scores, but did not significantly differ. MBSR was associated with greater reductions than SME in anxiety and distress ratings in response to a laboratory social stress task and a greater increase in positive self-statements.

THE RESEARCH FINDINGS

Mindfulness Meditation and Sleep

- The comprehensive JAMA review which included 9 randomized control trials (RCTs) found mixed evidence concluding that there was insufficient evidence of any effect of mindfulness meditation on sleep outcomes.[91]
- A more recent meta-analysis of 6 RCTs with systematic mindfulness meditation programs found that these programs significantly improved only two of eight measures, total wake time and sleep quality. But mindfulness meditation had no significant effect on total sleep time, how long it takes to get to sleep, waking after falling asleep, sleep efficiency, insomnia severity, and on a scale of dysfunctional beliefs and attitudes about insomnia.[92]
- In the two studies that included alternative treatments, mindfulness meditation was not significantly better.[93]
- A recent small study in *JAMA Internal Medicine* included 49 middle-aged and older adults with moderate sleep disturbances. Half were randomly assigned to either a mindful awareness practice, MAPs for Daily Living, or a sleep hygiene education (SHE) program. Results showed that while those in the MAPs group showed no significant differences for total sleep time, they did show significant short-term improvements in other measures of insomnia and fatigue symptoms at the end of the training compared with those in the SHE group.[94]

CHAPTER 4

Times They Are A-Changing

If I can not do great things, I can do small things in a great way.
—MOTHER THERESA

While the traditional recommendation for a meditation practice has long been to meditate from 30 to 40 minutes or longer, research is now accumulating that indicates we may get some of the same benefits by meditating for as little as 20 minutes. But even this benchmark is being chipped away. Andrew Newberg, co-author with Mark Waldman of their latest book *How Enlightenment Changes Your Brain: The New Science of Transformation*, reports that people chanting a mantra for just 12 minutes had the same types of neurological changes as those who practiced longer meditation sessions.[1]

Similarly, recently Jack Kornfield and Tara Brach, preeminent mindfulness meditation teachers and authors, are offering a new online training sponsored by Sounds True, headlining *Mindfulness Daily: Create a Life-Changing Meditation Practice in Less than 15 Minutes a Day!* And Headspace guru Andy Puddicombe is promoting "meditation made simple" with his app and advocates meditating for just 10 minutes a day.

Not only has the amount of time been decreasing, the amount of training suggested for learning meditation has also decreased considerably. The latest message is that you don't need to enroll in a formal program, or even spend a lot of time practicing, 10 to 15 minutes a day will do, but consistency is the key. The range that Herbert Benson, who coined the term the *relaxation response*, suggests is to practice meditating for 10 to 20 minutes, once or twice a day. This translates into a range of 10 to 40 minutes a day—a huge range coming from one of the best-known experts.

Jon Kabat-Zinn writes: "Forming the intention to practice and then seizing a moment—any moment—and encountering it fully in your inward and outward posture, lies at the core of mindfulness."[2] In the Mindfulness-Based Stress Reduction program he developed, the recommendation is to practice for 45 minutes a day given that it was initially intended for patients with chronic health problems. His recommendation is for far less of a time commitment for a more general audience. He says that when he teaches those who are not patients, he suggests practicing every day for 15 minutes at a time, or twice a day if that's manageable. In addition to a dedicated practice, he also encourages giving undivided attention to normal activities like walking, eating, or cooking as another way to practice mindfulness.

Can Less Be Just as Beneficial?

After more than 50 years of research endorsing the benefits of exercise, we're finding out that the assumption we have been operating under for what was good for us actually turns out not to be so. We're discovering that the ideal quantity and type of exercise is shifting. We also learned recently that less may be better. Compelling research shows that the ideal form of exercise is short bursts of high-intensity exercise. A couple of years ago, *The New York Times* reported evidence that high-intensity interval training for just 7 minutes provides the same fitness benefits of prolonged endurance training but in much less time. They dubbed this new exercise regimen "The Scientific 7-Minute Workout."[3] Not only does it beat conventional cardio as the most effective and efficient form of exercise, it also provides health benefits you cannot get from regular aerobics, such as a boost in the human growth hormone, also called the "fitness hormone."

Regular exercise also affects some of the same brain areas as an ongoing mindfulness meditation practice. Recent research shows with exercise, brain changes can be evident within months. For older adults, walking for 30 minutes, four days a week for 12 weeks, strengthened connectivity in a region of the brain where weakened connections have been linked with memory loss.[4] Regular exercise of moderate intensity done just two days a week over six months, significantly increased gray matter density in several areas of the brain which affect memory.[5]

Just like with exercise, we're starting to see some evidence that it may also be the case with mindfulness meditation that briefer periods are just as beneficial for some of the desired outcomes. With yoga too, there is research indicating that shorter sessions done consistently may be as beneficial as the typical hour-long sessions.[6]

The Benefits of Brief Mindful Breaks

The idea of taking brief breaks to be more mindful is fueled by mounting research evidence that very brief practices, ranging from doing aerobic bursts to deep breathing to viewing nature scenes, can produce significant results, especially for reducing stress. Some of the convincing research findings that support the effectiveness of momentary practices are presented below. As you will see in the coming chapters, many of these are incorporated into the mindful moment practice advocated in this book.

Brief Aerobic Exercise

- Just two minutes of exercise that raises your heart rate can change your mood. According to Dr. John Ratey, Harvard medical school professor and author of *Spark: The Revolutionary New Science of Exercise and the Brain*, anything from jumping jacks to a quick sprint works like an antidepressant to release a surge of dopamine and serotonin.[7]
- Bouncing around raising your arms up and down moves your lymph nodes to get toxins out of your body. Our lymphatic system doesn't have muscles to get it moving; it works when we move other parts of our body and allow gravity to massage it.

Deep Breathing

- Because our body is designed for self-preservation, it gears up to face danger within one heartbeat. By increasing the depth and decreasing the rate of your breathing, you signal your body that threat has passed and the body can calm down. That's why the simplest and most direct form of stress management is to change your shallow, rapid breathing to deep, slow breathing.

- Deep breathing shuts down the stress response within 10 seconds, typically this takes about three to four breaths.[8]
- Based on their research conducted at the Stanford University School of Medicine, Fred Luskin and Ronald Pelletier created the Stress Free for Good program. Of the ten "life skills" in this research-based stress reduction program, they consider deep breathing to be the most important.[9]
- In their book, *The Healing Power of the Breath*, Richard Brown and Patricia Gerberg report that our heart beats faster when we breathe in than when we breathe out.[10] This means lengthening your exhales will slow your heart rate quicker. Slowing down your rate of exhalation so you're breathing out twice as long as you're inhaling (e.g., counting to 3 or 4 on your inhale and 6 or 8 on your exhale) for about a minute relaxes your nervous system.

Yawning

- According to Mark Waldman, best-selling author of several book on the brain, of the many quick and easy physical actions that can trigger the relaxation response, yawning is the fastest route for most people. He says yawning is the quickest way to relax and simultaneously become more alert. It interrupts worry, procrastination, and neurological stress. He suggests yawning with your whole body for a minute, about 10 to 12 yawns.[11]

Music/Silence Breaks

- Luciano Bernardi found that music affects participants' physiology. Slower music reduces heart rate, blood pressure, and breathing rate.[12]
- To Bernardi's surprise, so did the moments of silence he had only included as a means of comparison. In fact, he found

that periods of silence inserted between tracks of music were much more relaxing than the soundtracks designed to induce relaxation. Physiologically, taking a "silence break" had the most profound relaxing and calming effect.

- A recent study found that both the experience as well as the anticipation of listening to pleasurable music induces release of dopamine, a neurotransmitter associated with more tangible rewards such as food, drugs, and sex. When people listened to music, their brains released more dopamine. In fact, even just thinking about listening to music caused the dopamine to start flowing.[13]

- Research also reveals that dopamine release is greater for pleasurable versus neutral music, and that levels of release are correlated with the extent of emotional arousal and pleasurability ratings.[14]

Micro-Breaks during Tasks

- Research reported in the journal *Cognition* shows that taking brief mental breaks, at approximately 20-minute intervals, improves performance on a prolonged task.[15] Those who took two momentary divergences twice during a repetitive computerized task lasting 50 minutes showed no drop in their performance while those with no breaks showed a significant decline in performance over the course of the task. Simply taking two brief breaks from the main task sustained the ability to stay focused during the entire time. Working continuously, performance fell off dramatically.

- Taking a 40-second micro-break to view a flowering meadow rooftop during a computerized task both decreased subsequent error rates as well as sustained attention levels.[16]

Brief Views of Nature

- We have all felt the therapeutic and restorative effects of being in nature. It creates a sense of being away from everyday concerns. A recent review of research found that views of nature can boost attention and mood, over minutes to hours.[17]

- Being in, or just viewing, natural environments can bring

about significant increases in mood. Studies suggest that being in natural spaces, just looking out the window onto a natural scene, or merely looking at pictures, can be soothing and stress relieving.[18]

- Even looking at a picture of a natural scene for just 40 seconds can maintain attention and improve performance.[19]

- University of California at Irvine researchers found that participants who gazed up at towering eucalyptus trees for as little as one minute not only experienced increases in awe, they also demonstrated more helpful behavior than participants who spent the same amount of time looking up at high buildings.[20] When they had someone pass by and drop some pens, those who looked at the trees were significantly more likely to help pick up the pens.

Reflexology

- Reflexology involves applying pressure to specific points on the feet, hands, and head which correspond to different body organs and systems. Robert Thursday, editor of *Yoga Journal Presents Your Guide to Reflexology*, reports that "Similar to the way anesthesia can numb certain zones of the body, stimulating certain reflexology points can affect very specific organs, nerves, and zones of the body to decrease pain and increase functioning." Holding these pressure points for about 30 seconds can reduce tension and release feel-good hormones.[21]

- Numerous studies funded by the National Cancer Institute and National Institute of Health show reflexology can be effective in reducing pain, improving physical functioning, and treating psychological symptoms, such as anxiety and depression, as well as enhancing relaxation and sleep.[22]

- For example, if you store your stress in your upper or middle back as is often the case, applying pressure to the arch of your foot, the spot that corresponds to your spinal vertebrae, can release tension.

- Pressing into the back of your neck right below your head by interlacing your fingers and bringing your hands behind your head, thumbs pointing down, helps reduce tension.

- Applying pressure to the fleshy part of the hand between your thumb and index finger, by pinching this area from both sides with your opposite thumb and index finger, relaxes the nervous system when you're stressed.

Taking Regular Breaks Improves Concentration and Productivity

Herbert Benson, author of the legendary *The Relaxation Response* first published in 1975, has conducted research showing that as soon as you start to feel stress when you're working you need to take a break otherwise your concentration and productivity will start to falter.[23] Usually this is after 20 to 30 minutes of intense work or concentration. During your break, you need to do something that is utterly different and that you find pleasurable or relaxing. Your brain needs constant replenishing to keep your motivational circuits working. A short break to do something that is enjoyable or calming recharges a stressed-out brain.

As mentioned above, more recent research shows that taking less than a minute mental break at about every 20 minutes as a divergence from the task at hand just to do something different, not necessarily something enjoyable or calming, can also lead to improved performance and increase the ability to stay focused on a task. These findings support the contention that prolonged attention to a single task hinders performance. Because the brain is built to detect and respond to change, the old "I have to stick with this until I get it done" mentality actually works against us.

Benson's more recent book, *The Breakout Principle* with William Proctor, explains how managers can learn to use stress productively by applying the "breakout principle—a paradoxical active-passive dynamic."[24] They show how using simple techniques to regulate stress can boost productivity at work and avoid burnout, writing "We found that by taking the stress level up to the top of the bell curve and then effectively pulling the rug out from under it by turning to a quieting, rejuvenating activity, subjects could evoke the relaxation response, which effectively counteracts the negative effects of the stress hormones." By taking the brain to a peak point of activity and then suddenly moving it into a passive, relaxed state, you can stimulate much higher neurological performance than would otherwise be the case. Benson and Proctor maintain that over time, those who learn to do this as a matter of course perform at consistently higher levels.

The stress response is an essential response and can provide a competitive edge, such as before a race or an important meeting. You become more focused, alert, and efficient. But if you push it beyond a certain level, stress compromises your performance, efficiency, and eventually your health. Two Harvard researchers, first identified the relationship between stress and performance over a hundred years ago, showing that performance increases with physiological or mental arousal (i.e., stress), but only up to a point.[25] Later research found that performance levels decrease earlier for complex tasks than for simple tasks.[26] Simpler or well-learned tasks are better performed with higher levels of stress to increase motivation. For difficult or unfamiliar tasks, the relationship between stress and performance becomes inverse, with performance declining as stress increases. In fact, performance takes a nose dive after it reaches a critical point. This means if you are doing a relatively simple task, you are capable of dealing with higher stress levels. If you are doing a much more complex task, your performance is much more heavily influenced by a high stress level.

You can tell when you're nearing the top of your performance curve because you stop feeling productive and start feeling stressed. You may start to feel anxiety or become fearful, or conversely, you may become bored or feel like procrastinating. Often this feeling is accompanied by physical symptoms such as a headache or a knot in the stomach. This is where you need to walk away from the problem or task and do something completely different that produces the relaxation response. The relaxation response can be brought on by engaging in any repetitive mental or physical action which essentially breaks the chain of everyday thinking by intentionally slowing down the mind.

Benson's research shows that by completely letting go of a problem or demanding task at the point you feel stressed, the brain actually rearranges itself so that the hemispheres communicate better. Then the brain is better able to solve the problem.[27] As the brain quiets down, another phenomenon that Benson calls *calm commotion*, a focused increase in activity, takes place in areas of the brain associated with attention, space-time concepts, and decision making.

How Low Can We Go?

The timeline may be dwindling down even more. Mark Waldman, faculty at the NeuroLeadership Program at Loyola Marymount University along with colleagues have been developing, testing, and implementing a new strategy. They began by asking "What would happen if instead of meditating for 12-20 minutes, you spent one minute each hour during your day doing a different type of meditation or mindfulness exercise?" By taking 60 seconds an hour, by the end of the day you would have done about 12 to 16 minutes of mindfulness practice. They were interested in studying whether shorter, more frequent mindfulness practices would be just as beneficial.

The NeuroLeadership Program

They began having those in their Executive MBA program set a mindfulness bell to ring three times every hour, or at 20-minute intervals corresponding to the time research indicates it takes for your brain to start to get fatigued. On two of those occasions they took just a few second break to relax or stretch. Then once per hour they took 60 seconds to do a deliberate mindfulness exercise that commanded their attention and was also pleasurable and/or relaxing, like running in place, self-massaging, or a doing a brief meditation.[28]

Neuroscientists have shown that anything that brings pleasure activates the motivational centers of the brain.[29] Waldman refers to pleasure as the "neurological antidote" for stress. Brain research also shows that our brain thrives on novelty, increasing dopamine levels. Waldman reports in his latest book, *NeuroWisdom: The New Brain Science of Money, Happiness, and Success*, anything that is new, different, and enjoyable causes dopamine to be released which wakes up the consciousness centers of the brain.[30] The NeuroLeadership Program incorporates novelty by providing activities that are varied and novel to keep dopamine flowing.

In more than ten years of teaching MBA students these strategies, 90% of the students every year report that their work productivity increases and their stress level diminishes drastically. Research on the program also showed the same neurological benefits from these brief, 1-minute mindfulness practices interspersed hourly throughout the day as shown with meditators. These included seeing more activity in social awareness areas of the brain and less activity in parts of the brain that detect threat to initiate the body's stress response.[31] Their findings and those of others led Waldman to assert that the old model of meditating for lengthy sessions is no longer necessary to see similar results.

Short Mindfulness Breaks Are Catching on in the Workplace

The concept of short mindfulness breaks is catching on, especially in the workplace, with mindfulness programs starting to spring up that are more amenable to the workplace than lengthier mindfulness meditation sessions. In her best-selling book, *Finding the Space to Lead: A Practical Guide to Mindful Leadership*, Janice Marturano attempts to bring the concepts of mindfulness into the workday of those in leadership roles, or any worker for that matter, through specific mindfulness practices that address practical issues, such as scheduling, meeting times, phone usage, and responding to email.[32] The strategies she recommends for promoting mindfulness are targeted to fit into the busy executive's working life and to not require any major upheaval of the work day. She advocates finding moments throughout the work day to pull the mind away from spiraling into the future or rehashing the past by anchoring in the present moment.

Marturano's mindful leadership training cultivates leaders' capabilities to be more intentional about how they spend their time by targeting logical transition times, like coffee or lunch breaks, walking to and from their destinations, or crossing thresholds to enter into new spaces. She says one of the most powerful tools is a "purposeful pause," taking a little space to reset and re-center to break the autopilot fog we often operate from. In a purposeful pause, you simply take a few moments to intentionally guide your attention back to the present to pay attention to your inner and outer sensations.

One of the purposeful pause strategies is "use the door" where just entering into a new room serves as the cue to shift into present moment awareness. Another is using the simple act of walking from one place to the next during the work day as a prompt for using walking as an opportunity for a brief meditation where you keep shifting your attention from thinking back to the experience of walking. Marturano's emphasis is clearly present-moment awareness without suggesting setting any specific intention beyond that—a missed opportunity from my perspective.

Geoff Soloway's organization, MindWell, recently launched an online program called the 30 Day Mindfulness Challenge, geared toward making mindfulness both less time-consuming and less disruptive to the daily work routine. His approach called "Take Five" involves short mindfulness breaks that can be as little as two minutes and don't require participants to remove themselves from their desks or meeting rooms.[33] Take Five encourages participants to find certain "cues" to begin a practice. Much like Marturano's, the cues could be anything from a coffee or lunch break, walking through a doorway, or even during a meeting or conversation with a co-worker. From there, participants follow a five-step process that requires them to focus their attention on whatever they may be experiencing in that moment.

Similarly, Aetna, a large health insurance company, has developed a program called *Mindfulness at Work* in collaboration with Duke Integrative Medicine and e-mindful. The program teaches brief mindfulness practices, 5 to 15 minutes, targeting workplace stress and work-life balance.[34] Results show that employees taking the training either online or in person had a 36 percent reduction in perceived stress. Search Inside Yourself (SIY) Leadership Institute offers mindfulness and attention training suited to the workplace developed and tested at Google. Participants report reduced stress levels, greater ability to focus, and increased work production.[35]

Shawn Achor, founder of the corporate strategy firm Good Think, reports research published in the Harvard Business Review showing that engaging in just one brief positive exercise every day for as little as three weeks had lasting impact.[36] In December 2008, just before the worst tax season in decades, he asked tax managers to choose one of five activities to perform daily, most of which took only one to two minutes: (1) Jot down three things they were grateful for; (2) write a positive message to someone in their social support network;

(3) take two minutes to describe in a journal the most meaningful experience of the past twenty-four hours; (4) meditate at their desk for two minutes; or (5) exercise for ten minutes. The participants performed their activity every day for three weeks. Following their training, they scored significantly higher than a control group in optimism and life satisfaction. Four months later, those who had performed their one daily activity still showed significantly higher scores. Doing a quick daily exercise for just a few weeks was enough to maintain optimism and life satisfaction for months later.

RESEARCH RECAP: Shorter, more frequent mindful breaks may be just as beneficial as longer mindfulness meditation sessions. Taking brief breaks is restorative in many ways, including reducing your stress level, boosting your mood, and keeping you more alert and focused to improve your performance.

CHAPTER 5

Three Key Ingredients in the Recipe for Well-Being

You can either live in a surviving space or in a thriving space.
–HELEN KELLER

Mindfulness meditation is well on its way to becoming an accepted component of our daily health regimen to complement a healthy diet and regular exercise. There is no doubt that mindfulness meditation does produce some desirable results. But it doesn't do everything—it's not the do-all and end-all for a life worth living. In fact, there are areas that are crucial to well-being that are not linked to a mindfulness meditation practice.

Everyone seems to have different recommendations for best practices for maintaining well-being. After decades of research, my three essential ingredients overlap with what other best-selling authors are advocating while representing a unique combination. Nearly everyone contends that tending and strengthening social networks is among the top pathways. My take is that the way you do this is to stay in a positive or optimistic state of mind more often, my first ingredient. When you're feeling upbeat, you are more likely to be social, generous, and altruistic. And a genuine smile, a hearty laugh, or a pleasant mood has the added benefit of recruiting others to join in. An optimistic outlook enhances your capacity for kindness, gratitude, forgiveness, and compassion, for yourself and for others.

My second indispensable ingredient is staying out of the stress response as much as possible, and when you're in it, trying to recover quickly. Reducing stress is probably one of the major goals people have for a mindfulness meditation practice. But mindfulness meditation doesn't take the place of stress-buffering strategies needed in the moment stress strikes. Without deliberate calming mindful practices used throughout the day as stress accumulates, the stress response causes unhealthy cortisol spikes all day long.

In my recipe for well-being, the third ingredient is staying motivated with practices that offer variety and novelty to keep your brain stimulated. To realize these three intentions, you'll have to expand your mindfulness meditation practice with congruent mindful actions. The complementary practice I'm advocating is taking brief mindful breaks interspersed throughout your day specifically geared to fulfill each of my essential ingredients for sustaining well-being.

> Mindfulness as a way of life will require simultaneously developing other skills and capacities beyond meditation to advance awareness into action.

I recently asked a friend who had been meditating twice a day for over forty years how the practice affected her self-acknowledged tendency to be impatient. She reported that her meditation practice had increased her capacity to notice she was being impatient (*oh—I'm being impatient again*) while acknowledging it had not had much impact on her feeling impatient and acting impatiently. There is a big difference between bringing awareness to experiencing impatience and feeling its jitteriness, being able to recognize it and name it, and having the awareness carryover to not acting on the sense of urgency. This takes yet another step.

The mere act of noticing will not be enough to change your behavior. You have to keep chipping away at what drives the feeling that results in the behavior. In the example with my friend, if she believes she has to be at "full throttle" to get everything done that she thinks needs to be done, she may tell herself, "I'm never going to be able to keep up if I don't keep moving." This feeds the tense energy to be in perpetual motion, scurrying to the next thing that needs to get done.

Mindfulness meditation is a passive practice where you just notice, but you have to take it one step further with active practices. What I mean by an "active practice" is simply a plan you make with yourself to take deliberate action in a specific way. It could be either making a commitment to take a different action to break a self-defeating pattern, or embarking on a new practice. You can notice all you want, but the mere act of noticing by itself doesn't automatically change behavior. You have to do something with that awareness.

For only the most dedicated will a meditation practice by itself equip them to live a mindful life without complementary intentional practices. Perhaps after years of meditating we might be able to stay cool, calm, and collected in the face of any storm, whether it's tangible, physical, or emotional. But for the many relatively new meditators who haven't yet logged thousands of hours of practice, they will need to access other tools to live mindfully now. By most estimates, the amount of time needed for the major benefits of a mindfulness meditation practice to kick in is several years.

My intent is not to challenge the many benefits of a mindfulness meditation practice, rather to point out its limitations as a sole practice. What I am advocating is an extension of your daily meditation practice (that is, if you have one), not a replacement, in several areas where the research favors other practices that likewise promote mindfulness. Taking daily mindful moments offers a plan to put into practice key findings of decades of research in the neurosciences, the behavioral sciences, and the social sciences, including positive psychology and cognitive behavioral therapy.

A mindful moment practice can complete the formula for well-being if you want to:

1. Counteract your brain's negativity bias with deliberate brief mood-enhancing practices
2. Keep your daily stress at bay with momentary stress buffers
3. Prime your brain to create new connections and stimulate reward pathways with mindful practices that are varied and novel

The next sections provide an introduction to these three essential ingredients in my recipe for well-being. They are covered in greater detail in chapters to follow.

1. Counteract the Brain's Negativity Bias by Increasing Positive Emotions and Experiences

The brain has a built-in negativity bias that scientists believe evolved to help our early ancestors survive constant threat. We pay attention to and remember negative experiences more vividly than positive ones because we evolved from a world full of imminent dangers. Rick Hanson writes in *Hardwiring Happiness: The New Brain Science of Contentment, Calm, and Confidence*, the brain's negativity bias makes it "like Velcro for bad experiences but Teflon for good experiences."[1] Negativity attracts negativity but positivity doesn't stick around for long. Negative thoughts and events dwell in our mind while positive ones just flit away. That's why we all need to develop an inventory of strategies to counteract the brain's predisposition to look for trouble.

As we all know, the happiness generated by a positive change or experience gives us only a temporary rush while the gloominess of a negative experience can ruin the whole day. After years of graduate school culminating in passing the oral exam for my doctorate, I still remember being surprised that my surge of exhilaration and sense of accomplishment felt like a fleeting moment after all those years in the making. And the research supports my experience that we quickly revert to our normal setpoint even after very significant life changes, like getting married or landing the job of our dreams.

Feeling positive sends a signal to the brain that things are going well and we can carry on. In contrast, negative emotions warn of possible peril or unpleasantness that we need to respond to by taking some action, such as fighting or fleeing. Because survival is much more dependent on urgent attention to potential dangers than on passing up opportunities for positive experiences, our brain has evolved to make bad much stronger than good. Barbara Fredrickson, in her book *Positivity: Top-Notch Research Reveals the 3-to-1 Ratio that Will Change Your Life*, presents convincing evidence that positive to negative ratios need to be at least 3-1 to gain enough impetus to prevail over negativity.[2] Below this ratio, positivity is overwhelmed by the greater potency of negativity. The blow of one bad emotion, comment, or event can match or undo that of three or more positive ones. At or above a 3-1 ratio, positivity gains enough momentum to overcome negativity. But advocating for more time spent feeling positive emotions is in no way meant to invalidate the need to fully process our negative emotions when they grab hold of us and won't let go. A ratio of 3-1 still leaves a lot of room for the other side.

Research shows the positivity ratios that distinguish flourishing individuals, couples, and groups generally range from 3-1 to 5-1.[3] Happily married couples have ratios of approximately 5-1 in their positive verbal and emotional expressions to each other compared to very unhappy couples who display ratios of less than 1-1.[4] The same optimal ratio of 5-1 characterizes the verbal comments of profitable and productive versus less profitable and productive business teams.[5] In classrooms, a ratio of at least 5-1 positive to negative comments to students, but preferably closer to 10-1 to nurture a developing sense of self, has long been advocated to cultivate a supportive climate.

In actuality, we have three times more positive than negative experiences, making a positivity bias more reality based.[6] But our reality is skewed because our brain wants to focus on what danger might be lurking, what problem needs to be solved, what's not working, what we wish we had, and why we're not quite good enough.

Because of our brain's negativity bias, we are not only less likely to pay attention to positive experiences, we also have weaker emotional reactions to them. Because of this, we need to stop to soak up our positive experiences to prevent them from fading fast. Besides making the most of positive experiences when they occur, we also need to use intentional practices that will increase the amount of positive emotions we have if we want to keep our negative emotions from trumping our positive emotions. Positive emotions can be derived from our actual life experiences, from deliberately practicing positive-emotion enhancing activities, or from mere thoughts intentionally initiated to reminisce about or savor our positive experiences. All three of these avenues need to be tapped to do battle against the brain's negativity bias.

Our brain takes its shape from our prevailing thoughts. If our mind is filled with ill thoughts about ourselves and others, then our brain will be primed for greater anxiety and stress. If we keep dwelling on our worries, problems, and disappointments, then our brain will be molded into one that is more vulnerable to negativity, pessimism, and distrust. On the other hand, if we keep focusing on the good stuff, such as the pleasant feelings emitted by someone else's or our own kind deeds and good intentions, then over time our brain reconfigures itself to one groomed for positivity, optimism, and resilience. The key to overshadowing negativity is to increase the quantity of our positive experiences, especially the little ones.

The path to enhancing positive emotions is via implementing practices that are directly related to experiencing more positivity, happiness, and satisfaction. Positive emotions are realized not just by enjoying pleasurable experiences, but also from having a sense of meaning in your life that comes from serving something greater than yourself and being engaged with the things and people you care about. As you log more time aligning with what gives purpose to your life with intentional daily practices that increase your proportion of positive experiences, you counterbalance your brain's tendency to dwell on negative events and thoughts, and you can eventually tip the scale.

When you direct your attention to doing a kind act for someone in need, appreciating a compliment from a stranger, savoring a fond memory, or experiencing the awe of a beautiful nature scene, you come out of that moment with a little glow of pleasure. Feeling pleasure stimulates the motivational centers of the brain.[7] Our brain is programmed to seek pleasurable experiences, and it doesn't matter if they are big or small, brief or enduring. Every time we feel pleasure, dopamine is released in the brain which activates the reward system. When the reward system is activated, it increases motivation while putting a damper on the brain's fear system. Our brain needs constant renewal and frequent pleasure is its replenishing source. A sense of play, enjoyment, or pleasure is a strong motivating force.

There is ample research to support both the long-and short-term effects of deliberately cultivating positive emotions for enhancing well-being (see Chapters 6, 7, 10, 11, 12). On the other hand, there is little evidence that practicing mindfulness meditation will generate positive emotions. The training of your mind that a mindfulness meditation practice provides can facilitate focusing attention and improve your ability to regulate your emotional responses by honing your capacity to take that brief pause before reacting, the first step to responding mindfully. A mindfulness meditation practice may also help you cope better with chronic pain and symptoms of anxiety and depression. But practicing mindfulness meditation doesn't cultivate happiness, sustain optimism, or give a sense of meaning or purpose to your life. These are all vital elements for thriving in life.

2. Interrupt the Body's Stress Response throughout the Day

It's alarming how often in a day we feel stress. In her book, *Mind Over Medicine: Scientific Proof That You Can Heal Yourself*, Lissa Rankin reports that we typically experience the stress response about 50 times a day.[8] Those who are lonely or overly stressed, experience it even more often. To rein in the runaway physiological and psychological effects unleashed by stress, we need to have our own repertoire of strategies we can use.

Today many people live in a chronic state of mild to moderate stress. Over time, filling our body with stress hormones manifests as physical symptoms, predisposing our body to illness. Chronic stress makes us more likely to get sick, and more often. If we already have a health problem, stress makes it worse. After years of medical practice, Dr. Rankin concluded that there are so many people living in chronic stress that it ought to be an actual diagnosis. Everyone has had the experience themselves or knows someone suffering from multiple symptoms where doctors have no diagnosis. I experienced my own meltdown when the overpowering grief of losing my mother collided with the onset of menopause to set in motion a whole host of debilitating symptoms. And one doctor after another had no clue what was going on.

Just as the stress response exists as a survival mechanism designed to help us stay alive in emergency situations, the body also has a counterbalancing response to calm the body. Herbert Benson, Harvard Medical School cardiologist, back in the 1970s identified the relaxation response as a deep physiological shift in the body that's the opposite of the stress response.[9] Research shows that eliciting the relaxation response brings about coordinated biochemical changes, characterized by decreased oxygen consumption,[10] the elimination of carbon dioxide, and lower blood pressure, heart, and respiratory rate.[11]

When the relaxation response is elicited, stress hormones drop, relaxation hormones are released, and the parasympathetic nervous system takes over.[12] The parasympathetic nervous system is responsible for calming the body and returning it to its natural state of equilibrium.

Benson's early research identified a smorgasbord of techniques that can evoke the relaxation response. These many different techniques include several types of meditation (mindfulness, mantra-based, Transcendental, and Zen meditation), various yoga practices (for example, Vipassana and Kundalini), repetitive prayer, self-hypnosis, progressive muscle relaxation, and deep breathing.[13] Other mind-body approaches that elicit the relaxation response include tai chi, qigong, biofeedback, visualization or guided imagery, as well as touch and self-touch. Research also shows that the relaxation response can be elicited during exercise because it leads to decreased oxygen consumption for a given heart rate.[14]

Given that daily stresses occur frequently and often, it's unlikely that a morning and/or evening meditation practice will have the staying power to sustain you throughout the day. You need to be able to turn on the relaxation response when stress strikes to restore an inner state of calm. And you need to do it soon before your body floods with toxic hormones. It's so easy for the day to go dismal as stress piles up without practices to keep you, as the song goes, "bouncing back like a rubber ball." If you can follow little stressors that come at you all day long with a brief mindful moment practice to clear it before the next one hits, minor hassles won't snowball into full-blown wipeouts by the end of the day.

Generally, the stress response lasts about 90 seconds, that is, unless you feed it.[15] As long as the threat is over and you don't keep revving yourself up ruminating about it, it moves through your body quickly and naturally resides. Yet keeping your mind from prolonging your stress experience is no easy feat. That's what cognitive behavioral therapy (CBT) is all about, and it has a comprehensive body of research, spanning more than fifty years, supporting its effectiveness for curbing stress-producing thoughts. An outgrowth of this therapeutic approach is the now well-accepted notion that one of the most important life skills you can learn is to take charge of the self-sabotaging thoughts continuously parading through your mind. The daily mindful moment practice I'm advocating incorporates some of these evidence-based strategies that can take just seconds.

More recent brain research substantiates the intricate dance between thought patterns and emotional states. Thoughts materialize in the form of self-talk and shape the reality you perceive. So you have to choose the words you use to talk to yourself mindfully because they become as real as the ground you walk on.

The research on the impact of mindfulness meditation for reducing stress often has conflicting results (see Chapter 3). There are many other research-based brief strategies that have an immediate effect on reducing stress and can be used inconspicuously if necessary. The research findings on the beneficial role that positive emotions plays in tempering stress is much more convincing. If you are able to access positive emotions while experiencing negative emotions during stressful situations, you can diminish the impact of stress, recover from stress more quickly, and build up enduring resilience against future stress (see Chapters 6).

3. Infuse Daily Mindfulness Practices with Variety and Novelty
We have a natural inclination to shift our attention to things that are new and novel.[16] One of the fastest routes to creating new neural connections is through novelty. Neuroscientists have shown that

our brain's capacity to create new connections between neurons is increased not only during the process of exploring a novel environment or stimuli, but also for 15-30 minutes afterwards.[17] This means that the impact of novelty lingers for a while, making the brain ripe for learning following an experience that is novel.

We are even drawn to novelty without being conscious of it because seeking out novelty is hardwired into our brains.[18] Being exposed to novelty activates neurological reward pathways. The brain reacts to novelty by releasing dopamine, which makes us want to go exploring in search of a reward. Dopamine is a reward chemical that is part of the brain's reward system. The most recent research shows that novelty is actually more closely related to our motivation to seek rewards rather than being a reward itself.[19] This accounts for why a new level or world to explore in a video game motivates people to play longer—seeking the reward of unlocking a code and gaining more points. Each new incentive induces a little rush of motivation to explore because it makes us anticipate a reward. When we experience something new, the brain is activated to seek its potential for rewarding us in some way. The potential that lies in new things motivates us to explore our environment for rewards. Variety is innately stimulating and rewarding.[20]

Taking multiple mindful moments throughout the day offers greater opportunity than a routine mindfulness meditation practice for keeping your practice novel, new, and varied. Variety and novelty not only stimulate your brain's reward system, they also enhance your brain's capacity for learning. That old saying, "Variety is the spice of life," is a motto that has significant scientific support.

RESEARCH RECAP: Supplementing mindfulness meditation with complementary intentional practices will take mindful awareness to mindful action. Research shows explicitly cultivating positive emotions reduces stress, helps you recovery more quickly when stress strikes, and builds up your resilience to future stress. You have to keep your mindful practices varied as novelty is what sparks new neural connections to keep growing your brain.

CHAPTER 6

Sustaining Authentic Happiness and Positive Emotions

Happiness is like a butterfly which, when pursued,
is always beyond our grasp, but, if you will sit down quietly,
may alight upon you.
–NATHANIEL HAWTHORNE

How Happy Are We?

The relationship between happiness and life circumstances, including income, relationship status, and health is not as strong as you might think. The fulfillment of psychological needs— autonomy, competence, and sense of connectedness—is a better predictor of daily positive and negative emotions than one's income.[1] Once basic needs are met, greater income does not significantly boost happiness.[2] Economist Richard Easterlin first introduced this "happiness-income paradox."[3] His research showed that within a given country, happiness aligns closely with income, but only up to the point at which basic needs are met. Richer countries aren't happier then poorer ones, unless the poor people are very poor and struggling.

Fewer than 20 percent of adults in the United States report that they are flourishing.[4] Many of us are languishing, feeling as if we're "stuck in a rut" or "wanting more."[5] Data show that even though our life conditions are improving, we haven't ' actually gotten any happier.

In 2012, the United Nations issued its first *World Happiness Report*, a global survey of well-being and happiness ranking countries from the most happy to the least. The primary data come from the *Gallup World Poll*, which surveys about 1000 residents per year from each of 158 countries around the globe. The rankings are based on the main life evaluation question, which asks respondents to rate their life on a scale of 0 (worst possible life) to 10 (best possible life). In the latest 2017 report, America ranked 14th.[6]

This report found huge variations across individuals in their happiness and in their misery. Key factors accounting for this variation include economic variables (such as income and employment), social factors (such as education and family life), and health (mental and physical). In all three Western societies, diagnosed mental illness emerges as a more important factor than income, employment, or physical illness. In every country, physical health is also important, yet in no country is it more important than mental health.

Happiness Fluctuates over Our Lifespan

A recent study reporting on 1.3 million survey responses spanning 1972 to 2014, found that today's American adolescents are happier than teens were in the past, but adults over age thirty have become less happy.[7] Those in their late teens tend to say they are fairly happy, but people in their eighties rank their psychological well-being even higher.

Happiness tends to go up and down over the course of a lifetime. Most research indicates that happiness falls dramatically in middle age and then gradually increases as we enter our senior years. A large database in the behavioral and social sciences has found that well-being follows a U-shape over age. The predominant theory is that this is due to unmet expectations that are felt painfully in midlife but beneficially abandoned and experienced with less regret during old age.

The trajectory toward greater satisfaction is far from a straight line according to a study reported in the *Proceedings of the National Academy of Sciences* relying on a poll of more than 340,000 people.[8] The poll included questions to gauge well-being in which respondents were asked whether they experienced the following feelings during much of the previous day: enjoyment, happiness, stress, worry, anger, or sadness. The results showed that stress and anger decline as people grow older. Happiness and enjoyment drop gradually until age fifty, after which they rise steadily for the next twenty-five years. Interestingly, when ranking their happiness during their daily activities, mothers report being happier eating, exercising, shopping, napping, or watching TV than when spending time with their children.

Authentic Happiness

Martin Seligman, author of *Authentic Happiness*, originally used this term to extend the meaning of happiness beyond the "feel-good" connotation of the term *happiness* itself, to include *engagement* and *meaning* as elements of a contented and satisfying life.[9] His years of previous research and that of colleagues revealed happiness actually boils down to a single dimension, *life satisfaction*. This is mainly because of the measurement used in most studies that simply asks people to rate how satisfied they are with their lives (on a 1 to 10 scale). Researchers report that, averaged over many, many people, the mood you are in determines more than 70 percent of how much life satisfaction you report. This finding led researchers to begin to clarify the multiple dimensions of happiness and well-being.

As defined by Seligman, the term *authentic happiness* refers jointly to (1) positive emotion, (2) engagement, and (3) meaning.[10] Subsequently, research on happiness has explored these three distinct routes to happiness. The most obvious and original meaning of happiness referred to feeling good, having positive emotions and pleasurable experiences. The second, engagement, is the gratification that stems from doing activities we like, that engage us fully to create what Csikszentmihalyi called a "flow" experience—a state of concentrated attention where we are so absorbed in the activity we lose our self-consciousness.[11] This kind of deeply involving and gratifying experience depends on our capacity to develop our authentic talents, strengths, and virtues. Research in positive psychology has shown that recognizing, honoring, and developing our character strengths is the most effective way to instill a true sense of engagement.[12]

The third essential element that contributes to our feelings of happiness and well-being is finding a sense of meaning or purpose in life, belonging to and serving something greater than ourselves. Developing such a sense rests on our ability to use our strengths and virtues in the service of something beyond our own self-interest. This might be focusing on children, family, spirituality, social justice, disease, or the environment. Such altruistic actions are also deeply tied to our sense of satisfaction and fulfillment.[13]

In his book, *Gross National Happiness*, Brooks argues that what is crucial to well-being is not how cheerful you feel nor how much money you make, rather it is the meaning you have created and your sense of "earned success"—the belief that you have created value in your life or in the lives of others.[14] Seligman asserts that if happy feelings were all we wanted our species would have died out long ago.

> The most satisfied people are those who orient their pursuits toward all three elements of happiness. You might be surprised that pleasure is the least consequential pathway to a contented, satisfied life. Meaning carries the greatest weight, with engagement a close second.[15]

From Authentic Happiness to Flourishing

Seligman now defines well-being as a state of human functioning where you are not languishing, rather you are flourishing in life. His research has led him to extend his original conception of *authentic happiness* and to now advocate for *well-being*. In his latest book, *Flourish: A Visionary New Understanding of Happiness and Well-Being*, he identifies five distinct elements that contribute to a sense of well-being.[16] They include two dimensions that have been added to the original three that comprised authentic happiness, which were having positive emotions and experiences, being fully engaged using your unique talents, and pursuing your life's purpose. These new dimensions are achieving your creative or professional goals and maintaining positive relationships. He refers to these as the five pillars of his latest version of positive psychology and they are what it takes to flourish or lead what he calls a "life of profound fulfillment."

The five pillars of positive psychology are:
- Enjoying positive emotion
- Being fully engaged with what you care about
- Having meaning in your life
- Achieving your work and life goals
- Sustaining positive relationships

Seligman has coined the term "PERMA" as a label for these skills necessary for well-being or flourishing. This acronym stands for positive emotion, engagement, relationships, meaning, and accomplishment.[17] Well-being is typically defined for research purposes as a global self-report of happiness, satisfaction, or mood, as much research has shown that these measures tend to be interchangeable.[18] The term *well-being* is thrown around loosely so it's hard to know what is actually being studied. At one extreme well-being may refer to any measure that is considered positive. At the other extreme is Seligman's definition as a compilation of five distinct elements that all contribute to a sense of well-being. The bottom line is when you see the term well-being you can't assume anything until you decipher what is actually being referred to, and more importantly what yardstick is being used to measure well-being.

Emotional Setpoint

You are probably under the assumption that there is a fixed, genetically-determined setpoint for happiness—a "feel-good" gene that you either have or you don't. Actually, that's about half true. We all do have a "happiness setpoint," but it is only partially driven by our DNA, our genetic endowment from our parents. Increasingly we are discovering that it's possible to shift our emotional setpoint in a positive direction. Only 50 percent of our tendency toward being happy and optimistic is genetic. Roughly 40 percent is influenced by attitudes and behaviors, and the remaining 10 percent by circumstances.[19] With nearly half of our happiness quotient determined by the way we think and act, by exerting intentional effort we hold the power to become happier.

Whether we win the lottery or lose a bunch of money with a bad investment, whether we get married or divorced, or whether we have fame or humiliation, we will inevitably return to that setpoint. With only 10 percent of our happiness directly related to our circumstantial changes, whether we drive a luxury car or a beat-up pickup truck, live in a mansion or a shack, or make millions or just enough to get by, it will have little to do with our happiness.

Researchers Richard Davidson and Sharon Begley report in *The Emotional Life of Your Brain: How Its Unique Patterns Affect the Way You Think, Feel, and Live—and How You Can Change Them*, the ratio of left-to-right brain activity predicts our usual mood range.[20] Our typical mood, which they refer to as our "emotional style," is the result of brain circuitry laid down in our early years by the genes we inherited and by the experiences we have. But that circuitry is not fixed. Although emotional style is quite stable over time, it can be altered by serendipitous experiences as well as by intentional effort at any point in our lifespan.

Emotional style also affects physical health. Its physiological consequences have downstream effects on the function of our respiratory, immune, cardiovascular, gastrointestinal, and endocrine system. In fact, they go so far as to assert that the most powerful influence on our physical health is our emotional life.

Davidson and Begley differentiate among an emotional state, mood, trait, and style. A state is a fleeting moment, whereas a mood may last minutes or hours. A trait is a propensity to think and act in a certain way and can be lifelong. They characterize emotional style as a consistent way of responding and assert that we are very capable of altering aspects of our emotional style to strengthen those that serve us well, and modify those that work against our well-being.

Sustaining Positive Emotions

We all know that both the joys of loves and triumphs in our lives, and the sorrows of disgraces and losses, fade with time.[21] But we may not realize that although both positive and negative emotions do not sustain themselves, the positive emotions fade much more quickly.[22] In other words, when you get knocked down you are more likely to stay down than you are to stay up when you get uplifted.

The impact of everyday negative events is more powerful and longer-lasting than that of positive events.[23] Ordinary negative circumstances, like just having a bad day, tend to carry over into the next day, where as positive feelings are much more fleeting with far less potential carryover. I am often surprised to wake up the next morning feeling anxious after having had a great previous day.

Maintaining happiness and well-being then calls for activating or accelerating recovery when our fortunes have turned for the worse and slowing down the return to neutral when they have turned for the better. So the trick is to work on increasing the duration of your positive emotional experiences while shortening the duration of your negative ones. In other words, intentionally speeding up bouncing back so you're not languishing in negativity, while stopping to relish in your positive experiences.

> As a general strategy, you want to intentionally try to delay the normal, brief time a positive emotional experience lasts by developing active practices to keep that feeling going a bit longer. You need to take time to pay "appreciative attention" by savoring an enjoyable moment.

According to Rick Hanson, if we don't stay with a positive emotion to let it sink in, then its impact will be lost on the brain.[24] His research shows it takes staying with a positive experience an extra ten to twenty seconds, otherwise it doesn't get "encoded" by the brain. In other words, the positive experience doesn't get hardwired as negative experiences do.

As discussed in the previous chapter, because of the brain's negativity bias, we are less likely to attend to a positive versus a negative experience. We also have a weaker emotional reaction to a positive event than to a negative one.[25] This means in addition to savoring positive experiences that happen, we also need to develop intentional practices to increase the extent to which we experience positive emotions to keep from being overpowered by our negative emotional experiences.

Positive Emotions Activate Our Reward System

Back in the 1950s, scientists identified what they referred to as a "pleasure center" in the brain. After decades of research, neuroscientists now believe the brain responds to a pleasurable sensation by activating a more complex "reward system" that includes a chemical component.[26] When the brain receives something that feels good, it sends a signal that releases the neurotransmitter dopamine. Dopamine activates the reward system and is associated with positive emotions and desire. Another group of opiate-like chemicals, called endorphins, are also associated with pleasurable feelings, such as those created by eating chocolate or a "runner's high." When endorphins are released in the brain they increase the release of dopamine. Neuroscientists have found that positive emotions activate this reward system, and with continued activation, they can enhance feelings of well-being as well as reduce levels of stress hormones.

Positive emotions that have been widely studied include love and affection, hope and joy, inspiration and awe, along with what Mario Martinez, author of *The MindBody Code: How to Change the Beliefs that Limit Your Health, Longevity, and Success*, has called the "exalted emotions."[27] The five exalted emotions include kindness, generosity, empathy, compassion, and gratitude. Based on his research, these emotions provide the bonding that allows our immune system "to shine during our most challenging times." Scientists say we are both the most loving and the most social species on the planet, but we do need to nurture and cultivate these qualities.

Positive Emotions Create an Upward Spiral

Barbara Fredrickson asserts that our daily experiences of positive emotions compound over time to build up enduring personal resources that may be psychological, social, or physical.[28] According to her so called "broaden-and-build" theory, positive emotions set in motion more expansive thinking that opens up a greater repertoire of options for action.[29] On the other hand, negative emotions lead to narrow and fixated thinking and a limited range of possible actions. In other words, when negativity is in charge, we're stuck doing the same old things, whereas with a positive mindset we can access a range of options. With positive emotions at the helm, we have a panoramic view rather than tunnel vision.

Actively cultivating positive emotions in everyday life produces potentially lasting increases in well-being. But, just as with mindfulness meditation, for that potential to be realized you need a steady diet. A constant flow of positive emotions creates an upward spiral that puts you on a positive trajectory of well-being.

Happiness Is the Key to Success

Success is not the key to happiness, happiness is the key to success.
−ALBERT SCHWEITZER

While you may assume that successful outcomes in important areas of life lead to greater happiness and well-being, the reverse is also true. Greater happiness leads to more successful life outcomes. Ample evidence has accumulated in support of the association between happiness and successful outcomes in personal, social, health, and work domains.[30] Greater happiness leads to success in nearly every life domain, from health and longevity to workplace performance, creativity and relationships.

Experiencing positive emotions and feeling happiness promotes numerous successful life outcomes.[31] Some of these are:

- Greater life satisfaction
- Better mental health
- Superior physical health
- More satisfying marriages and relationships
- Longevity

In the work environment, greater experience of positive emotions has been linked to:

- Improved work productivity
- Greater work success
- Higher income
- Stronger interpersonal relationships
- Enhanced creativity

Positive Emotions Increase Work Performance

Contrary to what you might think, happiness fuels success, not the other way around. According to Shawn Achor, who was one of the instructors for years of the most popular class at Harvard on happiness, when we stay positive, we are more engaged, motivated, enthusiastic, resilient, creative, and productive at work. He cites decades of research in management, psychology and, more recently, neuroscience, to substantiate his claim. Writing in *The Happiness Advantage: The Seven Principles of Positive Psychology that Fuel Success and Performance at Work*, Achor maintains that those who cultivate a positive mindset perform better in nearly every desirable business outcome, coining what he calls the "happiness advantage."[32]

Research provides strong evidence that happiness and life satisfaction lead to successful business outcomes. Happy employees have on average 31% higher productivity and 37% higher sales.[33] Co-workers who are happy, friendly, and supportive tend to be more engaged with their jobs[34] and build higher-quality relationships at work.[35]

Positive Emotions Drive Creativity

Positive emotions can prompt a creative frame of mind enabling us to come up with more creative and novel ideas. When we're feeling good, we're more able to see the bigger picture and new ways of doing things to solve problems more creatively. Because our thinking is more expansive, we are receptive to more options. This broadening aspect of positive emotions is also beneficial to decision-making.[36]

Positive emotions spark neural connections that facilitate greater mental flexibility and creativity.[37] In a review of studies on specific moods and creativity, positive moods produced more creativity than neutral moods.[38] Another review of research found happier employees had three times greater creativity.[39]

Positive Emotions Build Resilience for Coping with Stress

Cultivating and sustaining positive emotions not only promotes successful life outcomes, it plays an important role in moderating stressful experiences.[40] Until more recently, most approaches to reducing emotional stress focused on a "negative pathway" using coping or emotion regulation strategies to try to limit the harmful effects of negative emotions such as hostility, anger, despair, and guilt. Now, with the mounting science of positive psychology, coping strategies target a "positive pathway" by cultivating positive emotions that can serve to protect, sustain, and even restore well-being during periods of stress.

Fredrickson's broaden-and-build theory of positive emotions extends to coping with stressful situations. Positive emotions not only help during the process of recovering from a negative experience, they also can help sustain efforts to cope with ongoing stress.[41] This is because experiencing positive emotions can widen the range of potential coping strategies that come to mind so you enhance your resilience against stress.[42] Being able to access a broader array of possible actions allows you to consider different behaviors and actions for responding to stressful situations.

This broadening role of positive emotions helps develop a reserve of coping strategies to be kept in store until needed to cope with stress and hardships. For instance, experiencing gratitude heightens your feelings of connectedness to those you love and appreciate. When you feel a sense of gratitude, you think about the many ways people are important in your life. The outgrowth of feeling a positive emotion, like gratitude, is a greater breadth of action alternatives as coping resources when you need them.

Positive emotions provide a short breather from stressful experiences, giving you the momentary pause necessary to help you restore and replenish after experiencing stress. Deliberately cultivating positive emotions and taking the time to appreciate the many little things that put a smile on your face help you cope with daily stresses. Positive emotions accumulate over time to create a lasting "undoing effect" on negative emotions.

Research by Fredrickson and others shows that being able to access positive emotions helps you recover from stress more quickly.[43] Even brief positive emotions, thoughts, or experiences marshaled in the face of adversity can build resilience to help you bounce back from stressful experiences.[44] Strategies that maintain positive emotions don't have to be directed at what is causing the immediate stress, they can be directed elsewhere at other positive events or situations in your life that might be past, present or anticipated. Accessing positive emotions helps you recuperate more rapidly from negative emotions so you spend less time feeling bad. Over time you build up a reservoir to deal with stressful situations.

Resilience is our ability to flexibly adapt to the ever-changing demands of life and to bounce back quickly from negative experiences. Resilience is a key factor in well-being. Those who are resilient are able to learn from adversity and are better equipped to handle challenges down the road.[45] Being resilient can also lessen the full impact of the adversity and protect us from the destructive impact of stress. Although it is often reported as one of the main benefits of a mindfulness meditation practice, the amount of practice it would take is out of reach for most of us. Mindfulness meditation training may make you more resilient when faced with adversity, but as mentioned in Chapter 3, this could take from 6,000 to 7,000 hours of cumulative practice before brain changes associated with resilience occur.[46]

The research indicates that cultivating positive emotions is a faster route to developing resilience. With a mindful moment practice, you will be having more pleasurable experiences throughout your day, and as these accumulate, you'll be building your resilience.

Positive emotions can and do occur alongside negative emotions during stressful circumstances.[47] Positive emotions can buffer negative emotions in the aftermath of crises. In one of Fredrickson's studies, those who experienced more positive emotions were able to cope better and recover sooner from the stress of the September 11th attacks.[48] Following the attacks, depressed symptoms were held at bay for individuals who reported fleeting experiences of gratitude, love, and other positive emotions in the midst of considerable distress.

Research reveals that positive emotions can set in motion a chain of reactions that protect against the harmful effects of stress.[49] Lending support for the broaden-and-build theory, researchers found experiencing positive emotions leads to greater resilience, use of more positive coping strategies, and reduced anxiety and depression.

Intentional practices that elicit positive emotions done over time actually build enduring resilience.[50] While we may initially use positive emotions strategically to cope with a stressful situation, to the extent that we do this repeatedly, over time, the conscious strategy becomes automatic.[51] Using positive emotions to cope eventually requires only minimal attention or effort. Because of our brain's ability to change with new experiences throughout our entire lifespan, as we develop new habits we're changing our brain. Frequently calling forth positive emotions in stressful times can expand your outlook in ways that, little by little, rewire your brain so you become more resilient.

Positive Emotions Lead to a Healthier and Longer Life

Positive emotions and health are inextricably linked. Research convincingly demonstrates that experiencing positive emotions is associated with a multitude of health benefits. These benefits include less likelihood of becoming sick, and slower disease progression if you do, as well as a longer life.[52] People reporting higher levels of positive emotions can live up to ten years longer than those experiencing fewer positive emotions.[53]

Researchers hypothesizing why positive emotions may influence physical health identify three possible reasons, or pathways: biological, psychological, and social. The biological pathway is through the direct influence on the body, for example, the immune or cardiovascular systems. The more psychological route has to do with stress and how we cope. Positive emotions over time build enduring resilience so they help sustain efforts to cope with ongoing stress. This pathway leads to increased coping resources that facilitate coping better with stress in a variety of ways to buffer the effect of stress on physical health. The third possible pathway is by way of social support. Positive emotions facilitate social support leading to greater social connectedness which is associated with a multitude of positive consequences.[54]

RESEARCH RECAP: People who have more positive emotions live longer, regardless of whether they are healthy or suffering from chronic diseases. They have stronger immune systems, less inflammation, fewer cardiovascular diseases, and greater heart rate variability, an indication of a more balanced and resilient stress response system. (See The Research Findings)

THE RESEARCH FINDINGS

Positive Emotions and Longevity

Multiple large studies across many countries provide convincing evidence that experiencing more positive emotions is associated with a longer life.

- A landmark longitudinal study called the Grant Study, which followed 268 exceptionally gifted Harvard sophomores, mostly from the classes of 1942, 1943, and 1944, who were believed to be the pinnacle of physical fitness, mental health, and hope for the future. Researchers studied them for the rest of their lives. Those who reported being extremely satisfied with their lives had one-tenth the rate of severe illness or earlier death compared to their unhappy counterparts.[55]

- In the now famous Nun Study conducted by researchers at the University of Kentucky, young women entering the order wrote a one-page autobiography. Analyzing these essays years later when the nuns were between the ages of 75 and 95, researchers found a very strong association between longevity and the expression of positive emotions. Women who expressed the most positive emotions lived 10.7 years longer than those who expressed the fewest.[56]

- The researchers found that 90 percent of the most cheerful nuns were still alive at age 84, compared to only 34 percent of the least cheerful. In fact, 54 percent of the most cheerful nuns were still alive at age 94, compared to 11 percent of the least cheerful. In general, happy nuns lived seven and a half years longer than their unhappy counterparts.

- In a large study of 3500 individuals between the ages of 65 and 105 in the United States, the researchers found positive emotions predicted a reduced risk of all causes of death over a 10-year period.[57]

- Examining average reported positive emotions over the course of a day for over 3500 individuals ages 52 to 79 living in England, researchers found a high level of positive emotions was associated with a 35% decreased risk in mortality over a 5-year follow-up period.[58]

- In a large Dutch study of elderly patients, upbeat mental states reduced an individual's risk of death by 50 percent over the study's nine-year duration.[59]
- In a study in the Netherlands of over 4000 adults between the ages of 61 and 102, for only those aged 61 to 70 at the start of the study did positive emotions predict greater survival over about seven years. The results were not significant for those over the age of 70.[60]
- With a sample of over 3000 German adults between the ages of 40 and 85, researchers found that positive emotions as well as life satisfaction had a significant positive relationship with longevity. The effect was stronger among those aged 65 and older.[61]
- Examining positive emotions for 2673 individuals in the United States with no chronic conditions, researchers found no association with mortality. However, restricting the sample to the 334 participants over the age of 65, positive emotions were significantly associated with longevity.[62]

THE RESEARCH FINDINGS

Positive Emotions and Cardiovascular Health

A growing body of research indicates that a sense of well-being fueled by positive emotions makes people less likely to have strokes, heart attacks, and other cardiovascular diseases.

- Examining over 2500 individuals age 65 or older in the United States, researchers found that positive emotions reduced the risk of having a stroke over a 6-year period.[63]
- Examining over 1500 individuals, researchers found positive emotions were related to a lower incidence of heart disease over a 10-year period.[64]
- In cardiology outpatients, positive emotions were significantly associated with lower risk of mortality over a 6-year follow-up.[65]
- Positive emotions produced faster returns to baseline levels of cardiovascular activation following negative emotional arousal.[66]

THE RESEARCH FINDINGS

Positive Emotions and the Immune System

Those experiencing more positive emotions have stronger immune systems and less inflammation.

- An increased proportion of positive experiences and emotions predict resistance to the common cold.[67] In studies where researchers expose healthy volunteers to a cold or flu virus, those reporting more positive emotions during the two weeks prior are less likely to develop a cold up to five days after exposure.[68]

- Happy people develop about 50 percent more antibodies in response to flu vaccines and mount stronger immune responses.[69]

- Those who experience high levels of positive emotions in general have significantly lower levels in their bodies of pro-inflammatory proteins associated with type-2 diabetes, heart disease, Alzheimer's, depression, and other health problems.[70]

- Positive emotions produced a significant increase in S-IgA levels.[71] S-IgA is the predominant antibody class in mucosal secretions, the first line of defense against pathogens in the upper respiratory tract, the gastrointestinal system, and the urinary tract. Higher levels of S-IgA are associated with decreased incidence of disease and susceptibility.

- Greater levels of positive emotions are associated with reduced inflammation.[72]

THE RESEARCH FINDINGS

Positive Emotions and Heart Rate Variability

Having higher heart rate variability (HRV) is associated with a healthier, more flexible cardiovascular system and overall greater health. Studies show the following results related to the association between positive emotions and HRV.

- Measuring positive emotions by asking participants to rate how happy they felt in each episode of their day, researchers found positive emotions were related to greater HRV.[73]
- Measuring feelings of appreciation generated by the HeartMath "freeze-frame" practice increased HRV.[74]
- Studying those practicing loving-kindness meditation for 61 days, only those who reported an overall increase in positive emotions and felt more socially connected as a result of focusing on compassionate thoughts about themselves and others showed improvements in HRV.[75]
- Studying couples, experiencing positive emotions measured daily for three weeks was related to greater resting HRV for women, but not for men.[76] This result is consistent with other findings showing that emotions in general have a greater influence on the health of women than they do for men.

CHAPTER 7

The Emergence of Positive Psychology and Positive Psychology Activities

*Things work out best for those who make
the best of how things work out.*
–JOHN WOODEN

The positive psychology movement marshaled in by the then in-coming president of the American Psychological Association, Martin Seligman, in 1998 marked a turnabout in psychology. What triggered the birth of positive psychology was Seligman's contention that the majority of efforts in psychology since the 1940s had focused on human problems and how to remedy them, neglecting the study of what makes life most worth living. At that time, he began asking why the field of psychology shouldn't be putting as much energy into studying what makes us thrive, what sustains our hopes and desires, and what spurs our motivation and creativity as we do studying what drags us down and makes us miserable.

Traditionally, the goal of psychology has been to relieve human suffering. Positive psychology attempts to shift the assumptions of psychology away from embracing a disease model of human nature which views people as flawed and fragile, victims of bad environments and/or genetics.

> Challenging the established disease model, positive psychology calls for as much focus on strengths as on weaknesses, as much interest in building the best things in life as in repairing the worst, and as much attention to fulfilling the lives of healthy people as healing the wounds of the distressed.[1]

Positive psychology is forging an alternative route to mental health and well-being. Psychological well-being is now viewed as not only the absence of mental disorder, but also the presence of "positive psychological resources," some of which include positive emotions, life satisfaction, happiness, purpose in life, self-acceptance, positive relations, and autonomy.

Positive psychology was originally conceived as a way to advance well-being and optimal functioning in healthy people, focusing on enhancing positive emotions and building character strengths. The emerging field of positive psychology explores and analyzes conditions and actions that lead to thriving and flourishing human beings.[2]

Supporting Character Virtues and Strengths

One of the central themes of positive psychology is that we can function better in life and become happier if we bolster and use our inherent character strengths and virtues.[3] Just as athletes exercise to stay strong, by using a variety of strategies that encourage identifying, regularly using, and further developing our character traits, we can enhance our well-being.

Based on research across forty countries, Peterson and Seligman were able to devise a classification scheme that identified six categories of virtues with twenty-four corresponding character strengths.[4] Virtues are broad, overarching characteristics such as wisdom and courage that are universal, perhaps grounded in biology through an evolutionary process. These virtues are endorsed by almost every culture around the world. These are what allow human beings to struggle against, and to triumph over, what is darkest within us. The late cultural anthropologist, Angeles Arrien describes virtues as the qualities that support the inherent goodness that resides in each of us.[5]

Character strengths represent the psychological ingredients or processes that define the virtues. In their research, Peterson and Seligman found that the five most commonly endorsed strengths are kindness, gratitude, fairness, authenticity, and opened-mindedness.[6] Seligman and colleagues also found that strengths "of the heart," namely, zest, gratitude, hope, and love, have greater association with life satisfaction than the more cerebral strengths like curiosity and love of learning.[7]

Virtues with Corresponding Character Strengths

1. Wisdom and Knowledge
Creativity
Curiosity
Open-mindedness
Love of learning
Perspective

2. Courage
Authenticity
Bravery
Persistence
Zest

3. Humanity
Kindness
Love
Social intelligence or emotional intelligence

4. Justice
Fairness
Leadership
Teamwork

5. Temperance
Forgiveness

Modesty
Prudence
Self-regulation

6. Transcendence
Appreciation of beauty and excellence
Gratitude
Hope
Humor
Religiousness

In a milestone study, five positive psychology interventions were tested with hundreds of participants.[8] One of these exercises was geared to building character strengths. It turned out that it was one, of only two, that achieved real staying power. Those completing the following character strengths exercise were significantly happier and less depressed than the control group, not only following the week-long intervention, but even up to six months later.

Personal Exercise: Using Your Signature Strengths

Identify your top five strengths (by taking an inventory of character strengths online at www.authentichappiness.org). Then use one of these top five strengths in a new and different way daily.

Subsequent research has shown that finding ways to use your character strengths in all areas of your life, including emotional, social, cognitive, physical, and spiritual areas, boosts happiness and well-being while also decreasing symptoms of depression.[9]

A current rendition of the Using Your Signature Strengths exercise is to recraft something that you don't like doing so you do it using your highest signature strength. It could be something in your personal life or some task at work you dislike but have to do. The way it works is you first take the online assessment, then to shift your attitude, you do your undesirable task in a way that utilizes one of your highest strengths. Seligman presented the example of a college student working as a bagger at a local grocery store. She hated the job and was miserable. She completed the Values in Action Survey of Strengths to identify her five top character strengths, finding that social intelligence was her top strength. The way to use this strategy is taking something you don't enjoy and doing it in a way that activates one of your core strengths. So what the student did was make an attitude adjustment where she tried to make everyone's interaction with her the highlight of their day. She did this by deliberately setting the intention to be pleasant, friendly, and supportive with every customer. With this conscious intention first and foremost in her mind, she was able to transform the negative experiences she was having to a continuous stream of positive emotions. Can you think of some area in your life where this strategy might make things better?

Each of us has a unique combination of relative strengths and weaknesses. According to Seligman, each of us typically has anywhere from three to seven character strengths that represent our personal bests.[10] Successful, happy people dwell on their strengths, not their weaknesses and this is what you should be doing. As you become more adept at recognizing and expressing your own strengths you will also be more likely to recognize and acknowledge the strengths of others. This will help you see another as a whole person and to transfer this holistic view to finding others' strengths, especially when they may be exhibiting a weakness.

While some strengths are innate, most strengths are acquired. Whatever thoughts you frequently have become habits of the mind. By consistently thinking positive thoughts, you are creating millions of new connections in your brain to form a new groove that eventually becomes your preferred route. For example, the way to become kinder is by doing more kind acts and thinking kind thoughts of others. When kindness becomes a habit, whenever you see another person, your first thought will be one of kindness toward that person. When kindness is a prevailing thought, even when someone does something unkind, you can still think well of the person and extend kindness. With more and more experiences of positive thoughts and emotions, they become lasting traits.[11]

Evidenced-Based Positive Psychology Activities

Because research had shown that naturally happy people are grateful and optimistic, positive psychology researchers set about devising practices meant to mimic the myriad of healthy thoughts and behaviors of happy people with the idea in mind that when used intentionally they would increase happiness.

By examining the characteristics of "dispositionally" happy people, that is, those with inherent tendencies to exhibit optimistic thinking, be grateful for what they have, and engage in positive behaviors, researchers initially conceived of activities likely to increase happiness if they were deliberately practiced. But there is more to happiness than racking up pleasurable experiences. Research shows that happy people in addition to enjoying and savoring joyful events and finding ways to stay optimistic, tend to express gratitude on a regular basis, engage in frequent acts of kindness, and practice forgiveness.

The idea was to create brief positive practices intended to mirror the various thoughts and behaviors that happy people naturally draw on. The field now offers numerous simple and easy to implement practices that when used intentionally are linked to a positive impact on happiness and well-being. As an outcome for positive psychology activities, the term *well-being* could be referring to greater happiness, increased life satisfaction, higher levels of a variety of positive emotions, fewer negative emotions, reduced depression, or some combination of all or some of these.

What is especially advantageous about positive psychology activities is that they don't require making any major shifts in current lifestyle. And unlike most interventions that require change, people actually enjoy doing them, often continuing the activities long after they participate in a study.

While originally labeled *positive psychology interventions*, more recently they have been referred to in the literature as *positive psychology exercises*, or *positive psychology activities*, to change the more clinical connotation the word intervention carries because these activities are intended for anyone wanting to have more positive experiences and bring greater happiness into their lives. As a general strategy, the idea is to engage in explicit practices to actively elicit positive emotions. Such practices include cultivating gratitude, taking time to savor enjoyable moments, deliberately reminiscing, and recasting challenging situations in a more positive light. Other practices are more overt, such as performing acts of kindness and compassion.

Through a multitude of studies, researchers have zeroed in on specific actions and practices that build happiness and cultivate optimism.[12] Such activities and practices can instill new ways of thinking and behaving to produce significant increases in well-being. The many strategies that are now accumulating have three things in common:

1. They direct attention to positive aspects and away from negative aspects of experiences.
2. They keep positive experiences fresh, that is, varied and novel.
3. They produce a stream of positive emotions, thoughts, and experiences to thwart negative emotions.[13]

In their landmark study, Seligman and colleagues developed a series of personal exercises intended to create positive emotions and build character strengths.[14] They conducted extensive research online with 411 adults, ranging in age from thirty-five to fifty-four. The participants were asked to record their responses to five exercises done every night for just one week. The study used random assignment with a control group writing about early memories every night. Participants also completed both baseline and follow-up assessments to gauge the impact of these exercises.

The results showed that three of the positive exercises led to participants' being happier and less depressed, even after several months. Those recording three good things that happened daily and those using their character strengths in different ways daily were significantly happier and less depressed than the control group. These results were sustained six months later even though participants had discontinued recording their responses. In the third exercise, participants wrote a letter of thanks to someone and also reported being significantly happier and less depressed. This often-cited study put positive psychology "on the map" and inspired research on a multitude of positive emotion-enhancing interventions.

Over the past two decades, the effectiveness of numerous positive psychology exercises have now been tested empirically in thousands of studies. Such activities boost mood and/or well-being, and in many cases, maintain these effects for up to several months after doing the exercises. In several meta-analyses researchers have found that those engaging in positive intentional activities experience significant increases in well-being, including positive emotions, hope, life satisfaction, and happiness, as well decreases in depression.[15] Positive emotions also build inner resources such as character and virtues, hardiness, resilience, and an optimistic outlook.

These very simple positive psychology activities have had some very impressive results. There are five general types of activities that have the most research validating their positive impact:

1. Reflecting on your daily accomplishments
2. Acknowledging and aligning with your core values or character strengths
3. Expressing gratitude for what you are thankful for and appreciate
4. Performing acts of kindness
5. Savoring your positive experiences

Savoring pleasurable experiences helps sustain a positive attitude. The idea is to focus your attention on something pleasing as it occurs, consciously pausing to enjoy the experience as it unfolds. Otherwise, everyday little pleasures can slip by without notice.

Research demonstrates that greater happiness and well-being result when prompting people to engage in such activities as:

- Expressing gratitude[16]
- Specifically writing letters expressing gratitude[17] (Some re-

searchers encourage delivering their letters[18] whereas others
specify that the letters remain unshared[19])

- Counting their blessings[20]
- Performing acts of kindness[21]
- Pausing to appreciate and savor the good things in their lives[22]
- Practicing optimism[23]
- Replaying their happiest days[24]
- Using their personal character strengths[25]
- Contemplating their "best possible selves" also sometimes
  referred to as "ideal future selves"[26]

The activity referred to as contemplating "best possible selves"
is particularly thought-provoking and involves asking people to
imagine themselves in the future, after everything had gone as well
as it possibly could, thinking of their future as the realization of their
lives' dreams and reaching their best potential. Study participants
are asked to identify the best possible way that things might turn
out in their lives in order to help guide their decisions in the present.
They write about their ideal lives in the future, choosing different life
domains and imagining their best possible selves, related to those
areas of their lives. Typically, they do this for seven days, choosing a
new domain each day. In a study where participants first performed
this activity during a laboratory session, they experienced both
increased positive emotions and reduced negative emotions. Those
who continued performing the activity at home over the next four
weeks sustained their increase in positive emotions.[27]

Positive psychology activities currently being studied include
activities that target not only positive emotions, but all of the components of Seligman's PERMA model of well-being, namely, pleasure,
engagement, meaning, positive relationships, and accomplishment.[28]
(See discussion in Chapter 6) The latest trend is to leave it up to the
individual to design his or her own activities related to what would
be pleasurable, engaging, have meaning, build relationships, and
fulfill a sense of accomplishment. The idea is that each person is the
best judge of what kinds of activities would work best.

Variety Is the Spice of Happiness

Sonia Lyubomirsky, author of *The How of Happiness* and *The Myths of Happiness*, asserts that variety is not only the spice of life, it's the spice of happiness as well.[29] Variety plays a special role in increasing how long the effects of happiness activities last. Variety allows you to maintain the initial boost you get from performing a mood-enhancing activity.

Among the many factors that influence the effectiveness of positive activities, variety is one of the most significant. To the extent the positive activities engaged in are diverse, novel, surprising, or unexpected, they prolong initial feelings of well-being.[30]

As discussed earlier, one of the major obstacles to sustaining increases in happiness is our remarkable capacity to adapt to almost all positive changes regardless of their significance.[31] But we adapt more slowly to positive changes that are varied than those that are stable.[32] Given this tendency, it's no surprise that the impact of a positive activity would diminish over time. Keeping your positive activities varied will enhance their effectiveness.

New and different activities contribute to greater satisfaction and happiness over time because they have more potential to continue to keep elevating our well-being.[33] By keeping our positive activities fresh and stimulating we can stay happier over a longer period. Varying what, how, when, and where we do a positive activity can be decisive in determining whether that activity continues to increase our happiness and well-being. Practicing only one activity, such as counting our blessings or doing acts of kindness, is likely to lead to tiring of the activity over time and experiencing fewer and weaker positive emotions each time we subsequently do it.

Results from many studies show that practicing multiple positive-emotion enhancing activities concurrently yields greater benefits than practicing one single activity.[34] For example, participants in an online study obtained the greatest benefits when they practiced two to four positive activities at the same time.[35] Those who voluntarily purchased a happiness-increasing iPhone app saw greater increases in mood and overall happiness if they practiced multiple positive activities as opposed to just one.[36] Investigating how people pursue happiness in the real world, that is, without participating in a study, researchers found people perform between seven and eight activities to improve their own happiness at any one time.[37]

Studies show when participants are asked to perform different acts of kindness, they show larger gains in well-being than those asked to do the same acts of kindness over and over.[38] Those varying their acts of kindness report significantly increased happiness compared to those doing the same acts. Similarly, when researchers asked participants to make positive life changes over 2-weeks time, those who reported doing their change (e.g., start walking to work) with greater variety (e.g., walking a different route to work every day this week) were more successful at maintaining their initial boost in well-being than those who did not report variety.[39]

What Makes Positive Activities Effective?

Due to our individual differences in preferences, personality characteristics, beliefs, and values, any particular activity will not work equally well for everyone. Research findings are based on averages, so a positive result doesn't mean that the practice worked for all the participants, or that it will necessarily work for you. It's always important to honor your own experience.

To explain how and why performing positive activities may make people happier and increase their well-being, researchers have put forth the "person-activity fit" model.[40] Variety along with how often the activities are done are key factors for determining how long the effects of positive activities last. Similar to most interventions, social support often increases the impact of positive activities.

As with any behavioral change, you have to be motivated, persevere, expend effort, and believe that your efforts will pay off. According to the person-activity fit model, greater gains in well-being will come from practicing positive activities that match our preferences and characteristics. The theory holds that the optimal person-activity fit will produce the greatest increases. Characteristics of the individual, such as baseline emotional state and specific personality traits, influence the effectiveness of a particular positive activity. The degree to which one enjoys a positive activity is also an important factor.

Other variables which distinguish positive activities may also cause certain activities to work better for some than others. Aspects of the positive activities themselves, such as whether the activities are self-oriented, like practicing optimism, or other-oriented, like expressing gratitude, may be more or less effective for certain individuals. Some positive activities are more overt, like being kind, while others are more reflective, like savoring happy times. Positive activities also differ in their time orientation, focusing on the past, present, or future. These variations will also influence how effective an activity is for a particular individual.

The emotional state that you go into an activity with can also be a determining factor in how much success you will experience performing a particular positive activity. As is often the case, it's easier to move along the continuum of progress if you don't start out at the very bottom. In other words, it takes less effort to make change once you get over that initial hump. In fact, there seems to be a "sweet spot" where interventions typically work best, and that is if you start out somewhere within the middle range.

RESEARCH RECAP: You'll reap the most benefit trying out multiple mood-enhancing practices to find those best suited to your personality and preferences. Doing a variety of positive activities and enlisting social support will increase your success. (See The Research Findings)

THE RESEARCH FINDINGS

The Person-Activity Fit Model for Performing Positive Activities

- How diligently or successfully one performs an activity influences how long the effects on happiness will last. Participants who are motivated to be happier and invest effort into positive activities experience enhanced well-being.[41]

- Exerting high levels of effort to practice a positive-emotion enhancing strategy, and continuing to practice it even after the study is over, results in greater improvements in well-being as well as depression.[42] Seligman and colleagues found that the durability of the beneficial effects over a 6-month period was affected by the degree to which participants continued the positive activity on their own.[43]

- Belief in the efficacy of positive activities also affects their success.[44] Participants who wrote about their "best possible selves" once a week for four weeks, and were led to believe that this activity was effective in improving well-being by reading a peer testimonial, experienced greater increases in positive feelings and flow than those who did not read a peer testimonial.[45] The no-testimonial participants still showed greater increases in positive feelings and flow than those in the control group.

- How well the chosen activity fits one's personality and interests affects outcomes. People who indicated a preference for certain positive activities, reporting that they enjoyed them, thought they benefited from them, or did not find them difficult, were more likely to adhere to those activities and to show greater increases in well-being.[46]

- Perceiving an activity as natural leads to greater happiness. Participants who reported that specific happiness-increasing activities were more natural and enjoyable to them showed greater boosts in happiness and were more likely to continue to engage in the activities after the study was over.[47]

- The frequently that the positive activity is performed influences the effect on happiness. Performing five acts of kindness every week for six weeks resulted in a significant boost in happiness only if they were performed in a single day rather than spreading them out over each week.[48]

- Engaging in positive activities can be more successful with social support. Even virtual social support can bolster the benefits of positive activities. Participants who received autonomously supportive messages from a peer while performing a kind act had greater improvements in happiness than those who did not receive social support or who performed a control activity.[49]

- Participants who read an empathetic peer testimonial about the challenges of an optimism-boosting exercise experienced greater increases in positive feelings compared to those who did not read a peer testimonial.[50]

CHAPTER 8

Seizing Opportunities for Mindful Moments

You don't have to see the whole staircase, just take the first step.
–MARTIN LUTHER KING, JR.

Get creative and find opportunities for mindfulness in all your everyday activities. Go through your day and identify the best times to fit in mindful moments. Intentional brief practices can be done without interfering with your daily schedule. No matter what your situation, or how overwhelmed you feel, you can free up a minute or two at various points throughout your day. It's the incessant pushing yourself without a break that wears you down so you're frazzled by the end of the day. We've come to think being overwhelmed and exhausted gives us some bragging rights, as if it's a good thing. It seems to have become the new status symbol.

A good way to start to add mindful moments to your day is to begin with something you are already doing, like eating, driving, or walking. You can often do "double duty" by using routine actions as your prompt for being mindful. Simple, everyday acts like walking to and from your destinations throughout the day can be opportunities to be more mindful. This can also help you make smoother transitions from one thing to the next. Just something as simple as opening a door or entering a room can be a chance for a real "opening." Your hand on the doorknob acts as your cue to shift your attention—to switch out of autopilot into conscious action. For example, if you're dealing with a testy teen, stepping over the threshold to enter his or her room can serve as your reminder to respond to that haughty comment with mindful intention.

> While many others are recommending that all you need is a cue to be present in the moment, I argue you need more than attention—you need to formulate your intention and you need a strategy to take action.

We each have our own daily rhythm. It's important to become aware of your own cycle of peaks and valleys. When is your energy high? When does your energy or motivation start to plunge? Start paying attention to the times of the day you are most annoyed or frustrated, or antsy or unfocused. These present opportunities for mindful moments. Experiment to notice which sense is your fastest route to pleasure or relaxation. Is it sight, touch, smell, sound, or taste? Is it feasting your eyes on the beauty of nature, or feeling the soft fur of your cat? Maybe it's the smell of lavender or rose, or the sound of trickling rain or breaking ocean waves. My top two are touch and smell. Caressing my face with a feather, gently stroking my arms, rubbing some of my favorite essential oil on my forearms, or walking out to my garden to smell some flowers are my best pick-me-ups.

Daniel Siegel, author of *Mindsight: The New Science of Personal Transformation*, uses the saying "Where attention goes, neurofiring flows, and neuroconnection grows," to illustrate that what we focus our attention on grows.[1] Every day we experience up to 70,000 thoughts according to research from the University of Southern California's Laboratory of Neuro Imaging.[2] And most of these are negative. Other research identified that we make approximately 50,000 self-talk utterances a day,[3] with 77 percent being negative.[4] Stopping for just a brief moment interrupts our endless negative chatter that goes on "behind the scenes."

If you can take ten mindful moments a day, after a month you will have had about 300 mindful moments you would have otherwise not experienced. These experiences will go a long way toward reorienting your mind away from dwelling on negative experiences and thoughts. As you log more and more mindful moments, you'll be stimulating the growth of literally countless new neural connections. Of course, we don't know exactly how many intentional mindful moment breaks taken throughout the day are optimal, but what we do know is that consistent action, done time after time, is what it takes to reshape our brain.

Getting Started

There are several routes you can take. Setting a specific intention will boost your likelihood of actually taking mindful breaks. One obvious approach would be to set a reminder on your smartphone or watch, or on your computer, at whatever schedule you've determined may work for you. Another option is to take a mindful moment at regular intervals throughout the day. One plan could be to pick a number from 0 to 59 corresponding to the minute each hour you will take your mindful moment break. You might pick a number that has some significance for you, such as a birthday, anniversary, or a landmark event. Then use that date to create an awareness of that time. For example, my anniversary is June 23, so I try to take my mindful moments around 23 minutes after the hour for the hours I take them. I may not take my mindful moment break at exactly that time, it's just a way to enhance my awareness and give me a target.

While you may want to start slow and keep adding more mindful moments gradually, my plan is to shoot for 10 mindful moments daily. My first mindful moment is soon after I get up. I make it a daily ritual to think about my day and find something that I can look forward to in my day among all the things I have to do to remind myself to do at least one thing I enjoy, no matter how small. I try to take my mindful moments pretty much hourly throughout the day until dinnertime, then do a nightly ritual which I change after a while. My favorite is making a mental "I did it list" of what I got done. I also like to scan my day for the accomplishment I'm most pleased about, things I'm grateful for, or kindnesses others did for me. The idea is to have your last thoughts be positive ones, ending your day by taking a moment to be appreciative. I consider getting in 8-10 mindful moments a good day. And I don't stress if my daily schedule doesn't allow for consistent hourly mindful moments. Some days I get in very few. I just start each day with a renewed intention. It's the cumulative effect that's going to matter.

You could get even more specific and plan the mindful moment practices you intend to do the evening before, or in the morning. You can pick and choose from the many lists provided here, adding some of your own, to create endless possible combinations. Planning your schedule and sequence of mindful moments could be your first mindful activity of the day. When you couple prompting yourself with ready-to-go practices, you'll greatly increase your odds of achieving whatever goal you set for yourself.

When you take a mindful moment break, you can do something from your preplanned list, something spontaneous, or something tailored to where your head is at or what your body needs at that moment. Most of us experience an energy dip between 2 and 4 in the afternoon and stress takes its toll as the day progresses, so you should plan accordingly. If you're feeling drained, you may choose something energizing, like a few jumping jacks or running up a flight of stairs. If you feel rejected or inadequate, do something self-soothing. If someone just said something and the anger monster rears its ugly head, you might choose to take a few deep breaths to calm yourself down, and if you lengthen the exhale the relaxation response will kick in faster. If you're feeling unappreciated, switch your focus and try expressing your appreciation for something someone else has done for you. If you're facing a difficult conversation, you might take a mindful moment to visualize the conversation going exactly the way you want it to go, or think about what you like best about the person to get you in an open-hearted frame of mind.

As the saying goes "An ounce of prevention is worth a pound of cure." You'll want to pause at the earliest signs of fatigue or stress. One plan is to mix up the many variations of mindful moments, interspersing the different types when they will be most beneficial.

A mindful moment can serve your fluctuating needs throughout the day, using practices that relieve stress, release body tension, elicit positive emotions, or are relaxing, calming, self-soothing, or energizing.

It's also a good idea to keep a record so you can track your progress. One option is to do it the old-fashioned way by making a tally mark every time you actually do take the time for a mindful moment. Or, you could even get creative and do something like setting aside 10 (or whatever your target is) pistachios, or the nuts of your choice, and eating one each time you break for a mindful moment. You might choose blueberries, blackberries, strawberries, raspberries, or grapes. I have a sweet tooth so I sometimes opt for those little red cinnamon hearts they sell around Valentine's Day or m&ms which have the added benefit of the association with "mindful moments" and the taste of chocolate will give your mood a little boost. At the end of the day, if there are none left, you'll know you met your goal of how ever many mindful moments you were striving for, unless of course you cheated! You can also eat them all at once as a mid-afternoon mindful moment break when your energy takes a dip, eating them slowly and savoring the taste and texture. You can probably come up with an even more clever plan.

You might want to do a few of your mindful moments with coworkers at lunch or family members at joint meals, or any time you have together for that matter, by enlisting whomever you're with to join you in a mindful moment practice. Research shows social support is a strong predictor of many desirable results. And it's true not only for how much social support you receive, but also for how much social support you provide. When you enlist others to join in a mindful moment, you're both providing and receiving support.

You can also engage others by posing questions that prompt reflection to spark a positive feeling such as "What's the best thing that's happened to you so far today?" or "What do you like most about this job?" Or, on your drive home from work, go over your day to find something you're pleased about and make that your day's story to share with your family or household members. This is a refreshing alternative to the usual reporting of all of the hassles you had and who ticked you off. This also poses an opportunity to invite others to join in.

Try an "If X, Then Y" Plan

The more specific you get, the more likely you are to carry through. There are hundreds of studies on everything from diet and exercise to negotiation and time management showing that deciding in advance when and where you will take specific actions to reach your goal enhances your likelihood of succeeding. It can double or even triple your chances for meeting your goal. One form of planning that has been widely researched is the "if-then" format.

For example, "If it is 4:00 p.m., then I will return any phone calls I need to return today."

A recent review of results from nearly 100 studies that used the if-then formula found significantly higher success rates for just about every goal you can think of, including test preparation, using public transportation instead of driving, buying organic foods, being more helpful to others, not drinking alcohol, not smoking, losing weight, recycling, negotiating fairly, avoiding stereotypic and prejudicial thoughts, and better time management.[5]

Why is this type of plan effective? It's written in the language of your brain—the language of contingencies. We're particularly good at encoding and remembering information in "if X, then Y" terms, and using these contingencies to guide our behavior, often without our awareness. Once you formulate your if-then plan, your unconscious brain will start scanning the environment, searching for the situation in the "if" part of your plan enabling you to seize the critical moment.

Applying my previous example of taking a mindful moment at 23 past the hour, the if-then statement would be:

"If it's 23 past the hour, I will pause to take a mindful moment."

Creating a New Habit

We are indeed creatures of habit. Our habits provide the comfort of familiarity and define who we are. But we can become slaves to our habits, bestowing them with the power to rule our lives. According to

Charles Duhigg, author of *The Power of Habit: Why We Do What We Do in Life and Business*, habits are not born, rather they are created.[6] Habits follow a three-step pattern in the brain called a "habit loop."

> **Step 1:** Every habit starts with a *cue*, the trigger that tells our brain to shift into automatic mode.
> **Step 2:** Next comes the *routine*, or the behavior that happens when we take action based on the cue.
> **Step 3:** Lastly, comes the *reward*, something pleasing or satisfying that strengthens the connection between the cue and the response, reinforcing the routine, to help our brain remember the habit loop.

Over time this loop becomes automatic and a habit is formed. The cue and reward become so entangled they generate an intoxicating sense of anticipation and a craving emerges.

Once we've formed a habit, it's hard to break because we're often doing it unconsciously. The habit becomes hardwired into our brain and we perform it automatically. Our brain is always searching for patterns to work more efficiently. Converting some things to operate on auto pilot liberates our brain to ponder other things.

Because of this habit loop, more brain power is freed up so we are able to go about our business without thinking about our habit. Research shows that a habit is never really eradicated, it is merely replaced with a new one.[7] When a habit is broken, it is not forgotten. It will always be there, but it can be overridden. It's lingering in the background ready to reassert itself.

Duhigg maintains "Habits are most malleable when the Golden Rule of habit change is applied: If we keep the same cue and the same reward, a new routine can be inserted." So the way to change a habit is to find an alternative routine. His message is that if we want to change, the way to do it is by examining our cues, cravings and rewards, the driving forces for our behavior, and then finding ways to replace the routines they set in motion with better alternatives. But he says that's not enough, we must also believe change is possible. And like most other things, our odds are markedly increased when we enlist the help of a comrade or group.

Making Mindful Moments a Habit

If you apply what Duhigg is advocating to making mindful moments a habit, you start with your behavior cues—your body's subtle (at first) signals that it's time for a break. Instead of trying to push through these times, you pause for a mindful moment. Or if you're not that in tune with how your body "talks to you" you can establish another cue such as setting a bell to ring at regular intervals. You'll get the immediate reward of being reenergized to face the task at hand.

The first cue many people have as soon as they open their eyes is their phone sitting right there on the nightstand. The idea is to replace your first cue with something that will start you thinking about your mindful moment practice. You might put some little reminder right on top of your phone like a special rock. This will be your cue to set your intention for your mindful moment practice for the day. Then you can be thinking about the specifics as you shower or have breakfast.

The small changes a mindful moment practice takes are so simple you won't have any trouble believing you can make them. You'll notice how gratifying this practice can be, even with taking just a few mindful moments at first. And finding a pal to partner with, or someone who will support your efforts, will prod you to follow through.

How Long Does It Take to Create a New Habit?

You've probably heard it takes 21 days to change a habit, but it turns out that's a myth passed down since the '60s. Here's how it became sort of folk history. Maxwell Maltz, a plastic surgeon in the 1950s started noticing a pattern. When he performed an operation, a nose job for example, he found that it took the patient about 21 days to get used to seeing a new face. Similarly, when a patient had an arm amputated, the patient took about 21 days to adjust. In 1960, Maltz published his observations and other thoughts on behavior change in a book called *Psycho-Cybernetics*, writing "These, and many other commonly observed phenomena, tend to show that it requires a minimum of about 21 days for an old mental image to dissolve and a new one to jell."[8] He clearly was not talking about habits of the mind which have a much stronger grip on us.

The book sold millions of copies. In the decades that followed, major "self-help" gurus picked up on this message and started spreading the word that "It takes 21 days to form a new habit." And it's understandable why this myth caught on—it's short enough to be encouraging, yet long enough to be credible. But it's not true.

Based on their knowledge of how the brain and nervous systems function, Fred Luskin and Ronald Pelletier, pioneers in mind-body medicine, and authors of *Stress Free for Good: 10 Scientifically Proven Life Skills for Health and Happiness* report it generally takes from ten to twelve weeks to change or replace a behavior with a new one.[9] This timetable has proven accurate for many aspects of life in which you may want to learn a new skill or develop a new habit, whether it's physical fitness, dieting, changing a behavior pattern, or putting a new plan into place. It could take longer to change a behavior if you have a more ingrained or dysfunctional way of thinking or behaving.

Investigating habit formation in everyday life, a team of UK researchers support this timeline finding it generally takes a little less than ten weeks to form a new behavior.[10] They had volunteers chose one new habit to develop over the next twelve weeks. Some chose simple habits, like drinking a bottle of water with lunch, while others chose more difficult ones, like running for fifteen minutes before dinner. Analyzing the data to determine how long it took each person to go from starting the new behavior to doing it automatically, they found it took anywhere from 18 to 254 days. (They were able to statistically estimate the longer timelines to form a habit.) On average, it took 66 days for the new habit to be in place.

Missing an occasional opportunity did not significantly impact the habit-formation process. But people who were very inconsistent in performing the behavior did not succeed in making their behavior a habit. It doesn't matter if you mess up every now and then. Building better habits is not an all-or-nothing process. You just have to start each day anew.

Of course, how long it takes to form a new habit will vary widely depending on the person, the behavior, and the circumstances. This research focused on the time it takes to create a habit, but if you're trying to kick an old one while picking up a better one, it's likely to take longer.

Based on this study, it can take anywhere from about two weeks to eight months to build a new behavior into your life. Because it can be so satisfying, I would speculate that making mindful moments a daily practice would fall on the low end of this range. While establishing a mindful moment practice will take some time, you'll start to notice the difference it makes in your day right away. Feeling a sense of satisfaction will speed up the timeline for making mindful moments an integral part of your day.

CHAPTER 9

How to Launch a Mindful Moment Practice

Your actions are your only true belongings.
–ALLAN LOKOS

There are at least four ways to get started with your mindful moment practice. The options provided in the next sections include individual lists of mindful moments, as well as daily practices, intentions, and rituals. You will want to make sure your practice stays fresh and novel to keep you motivated. You can do this by alternating among individual mindful moments, following daily practices, setting daily intentions, and establishing daily rituals. By far, the easiest way is to begin with picking from my lists and tweaking them a bit to personalize them. There are also more lists in each of the chapters to follow. These mindful moment daily practices cover gratitude, kindness, as well as other high-need areas, such as managing stress and coping with moods by bringing more smiles into your day and combating the blues.

These lists of practices have been amassed from scouring the abundant research available across many fields. The specific research findings are discussed in the related sections of the book, in both previous and subsequent chapters. I chose to present the research throughout the relevant chapters so that the mindful moments lists themselves would be brief and not encumbered with describing the specific research.

Some of your mindful moments may be designed for people you care about and are trying to support through a particularly rough patch. Recently one of my dear friends had a serious bout of depression and so my first mindful moment of the day was to find something uplifting, inspiring, encouraging, or funny to include in a text I sent to her every morning. I did this for forty-nine days—until she told me she finally was coming out of her "dark night of the soul." It took me only a minute or two, but she keeps telling me how much that little act of kindness meant to her.

Because I seem to always have someone in my close circle who could use a boost, I started a folder on my smartphone. I labeled this collection my "inspiration" folder and it has in it what I sent to my friend plus others I've been adding. I now have more than 100 inspiring quotes and other items I can flip through and usually find something just right for whatever challenge someone I care about may be facing.

Applying Individual Mindful Moments

This general list of 50 mindful moments runs the gamut of strategies to cover a wide range of your fluctuating daily needs and includes practices that are for the benefit of others. The idea for making this long list is so that you might find some mindful moments you could see yourself doing, acknowledging some will not be your cup of tea. I have no doubt that you will resonate with, enjoy doing, and actually do many from this list.

To get feedback, I asked one of my sisters to review this list of mindful moments. Although, as I had anticipated, she did find many she really liked, the one she really hated and could never see herself doing is getting a large feather and stroking herself with it—way too hokey for her. Coincidentally, that happens to be one of my favorites for when I'm sitting and writing for hours. I find it so comforting. It makes me smile and in a minute I'm ready to get back to my writing.

Perhaps it's that I'm more tactile, or maybe it's just the fact that I found this huge, soft, bright blue feather in New Orleans when I was presenting at a conference.

The best way to use this list is to think about your typical day and what might be feasible and manageable to get you going with a mindful moment practice. If you're anticipating, or having, a stressful day, then most of your mindful moments can be stress relief practices taken from this list or the Instant Stress Busters list in Chapter 13. If you're feeling generally sad or having a melancholy day, the mindful moments you choose can be ones that will boost your spirits as well as be self-soothing. You also can choose from the more specific lists provided in Chapters 12 and 14. If you wake up feeling angry, frustrated, or resentful, then your mindful moments can be tailored to bring about calm, forgiveness, or acceptance. Remember that song "Fifty Ways to Leave Your Lover"? Well, here's fifty simple ways to add mindful moments to your day.

50 Ways to Pause for a Mindful Moment

1. Start the day by visualizing your day going really well. Go through the sequence of your day in your head and get a mental picture of everything working out the way you want it to.

2. Make one genuinely kind comment to the first person you have contact with.

3. Decide on something nice you can do for yourself today. Make sure you do it.

4. Tighten every muscle in your face, head, and upper body. Hold it for 20 seconds. Then relax these muscles and shake out your arms and hands.

5. Take a moment to daydream about a pleasurable past event. Try to recapture how you were feeling.

6. Give someone your full attention. Maintain eye contact and if your mind wanders repeat to yourself, "I am fully present here with (name)." Offer only non-verbal, and minimal verbal, acknowledgement and support.

7. Stroke your palms and arms for 60 seconds.

8. Think about your day and note something in your schedule to be grateful for. Remind yourself throughout the day that you have this to look forward to.

9. Pause to acknowledge yourself for something you did to help someone in need. Stay with that good feeling for 30 seconds.

10. Take a mental spotlight and scan over the day and make a list of everything that went right.

11. Rub your hands together rapidly to create some heat. Then place your hands on both sides of your face and hold them there for 30 seconds.

12. Give something away. It could be something tangible, or as simple as giving someone your spot in line.

13. Think about something you really enjoy and haven't done lately and make a plan to do it soon. Decide when, where, and how.

14. Bring to mind an accomplishment you had recently that you are especially proud of and dwell in that feeling of self-pride for a minute.

15. Take a power pose by standing erect, hands on hips, chest out, head up, and shoulders back. Hold this pose for 2 minutes to decrease stress and boost your confidence.

16. Recount your day by remembering someone else's act of kindness toward you. Think about how you might "pay-it-forward" tomorrow.

17. Run in place as fast as you can or sprint up and down the stairs for 2 minutes.

18. Listen to your favorite soundtrack of relaxing music for a few minutes.

19. Let your tongue go limp in your mouth and open your mouth slightly to loosen up your jaw which turns off the stress hormones signaling your body to restore to a calm state.

20. Scroll through pictures on your smartphone of your most enjoyable times and pick one picture and spend a moment recreating the feeling you were having at the time. This works best if you have first selected your pictures and created a folder of your special times for ready access.

21. When you are walking to or from your car or wherever you're going, consciously slow down to a very slow pace and pay attention to your surroundings. Concentrate only on walking with awareness. Focus on your senses noticing how the air feels on your face and what sounds and smells are present.

22. Acknowledge one of your attributes, like compassion or acceptance, and recall the last time you expressed it.

23. Instead of the usual "to do" list, compile an "I did it list" at the end of the day.

24. When something brings a smile to your face, linger in the moment. Think about what it is specifically that's making you feel good.

25. Think of two words, a positive quality you want to bring in and the other a negative state you want to release, to complete the phrase "I breathe in _____, I breathe out _____." Repeat the phrase to yourself for 30-60 seconds. For example if you're feeling stressed, unworthy, or frustrated, say: "I breathe in calm, I breathe out stress," "I breathe in confidence, I breathe out self-doubt," or "I breathe in composure, I breathe out frustration."

26. Yawn with your whole body for 1 minute, usually that's about 10-12 times.

27. Review your day to find at least one thing that went well and make that your day's event to share at dinner as a mindful alternative to rehashing all the things that went wrong.

28. Caress your face, neck, hands, and arms with a large soft feather.

29. Place your hands on your belly. Slowly inhale and watch your hands rise. Then slowly exhale and watch your hands fall. Keep your attention on the rise and fall of your belly and take 3 more slow, deep breaths.

30. Stand up straight and imagine a vortex spiraling from the top of your head through to your toes and back up again. Feel the energy surging through you.

31. Take a brief relaxation break with the Meditation Jar app which simulates a snow globe. You just set a time (from 10-50 seconds), shake your phone, and watch the spots float and sink to the bottom of the jar. Here's the link: https://itunes.apple.com/us/app/meditation-jar/id528913221?mt=8.

32. View beautiful natural scenery like a starlit sky or a spectacular landscape. Nature can inspire an experience of awe slowing down your perception of time and bringing you into the present moment.

33. Use a tennis ball or foam roller to massage away tension. Put the ball between your back and the wall. Lean into the ball and hold gentle pressure for up to 15 seconds. Then move the ball to another spot and apply pressure.

34. Recount your day by remembering 5 things you are grateful for.

35. When you're feeling overwhelmed, make a list of all the things making you stressed. Then review your list to find one thing where you can exercise some control and come up with a small, concrete step you can take now.

36. Imagine your best friend describing your qualities to someone else. Relish in that feeling of knowing how much you are appreciated.

37. Listen to an upbeat, happy song. According to a recent UN survey, the world's three happiest songs spanning multiple decades are: (1) "I Got You (I Feel Good)" by James Brown and His Family (1964), "(Your Love Keeps Lifting Me) Higher and Higher" by Jackie Wilson (1967), and "Three Little Birds (Everything's Going to be Alright)" by Bob Marley and the Wailers (1977).

38. Rub some essential oil on your wrists or take a few sniffs. When you're feeling mentally exhausted, try peppermint or basil for a quick boost.

39. Think about a memorable trip engaging as many senses as you can. Stay with that feeling 30-60 seconds.

40. Give yourself a hug. Wrap your arms around yourself and hold it for 30 seconds.

41. Count backwards from 100 by sevens (100, 93, 86...). This distraction helps interrupt feelings of frustration or irritability.

42. Read an inspirational poem or quote. You can keep a folder on your smartphone with some of your favorites, or keep your collection on a board at Pinterest.

43. Sip some green tea taking time to experience the warmth of the cup in your hands.

44. Apply pressure to the base of your skull by interlacing your fingers and bringing your hands behind your head, thumbs pointing down. Press into the back of your neck right below your head. Holding this pressure point for about 30 seconds can help reduce tension.

45. Take time to think about the best thing that happened to you today. Share it with someone and then ask them to do the same.

46. Take a "silence break" and just be quiet for a minute or two. A period of silence can be even more calming than music designed to be relaxing.

47. Do 2-1 breathing for a minute by slowing down your rate of exhalation so you're breathing out twice as long as you're inhaling. Try counting to 3 on the inhalation and 6 on the exhalation, or 4 on the inhalation and 8 on the exhalation, whichever feels more comfortable. This is especially helpful if you're feeling anxious.

48. Bounce around raising your arms up and down. Our lymphatic system doesn't have muscles, so it works when we move other parts of our body allowing gravity to massage it.

49. Look at photographs of greenery. Better yet, look out a window or step outside if you can. Just 40 seconds is enough to give you a boost and increase your attention level. You might set your phone's wallpaper to a forest or other nature scene.

50. Meditate for 1-2 minutes repeating to yourself "here" on the in breath and "now" on the out breath.

The Daily Plan

In my mindful moment practice, I like to cover all the different categories including doing things for others and eliciting a positive feeling (these are not mutually exclusive), as well as practices that are stress-relieving, energizing, self-soothing, or calming as the moment commands. I try to do things for others early to set the tone for the day, followed by things that give me pleasure. As the day goes on, my mindful moments are targeted to what's needed. I shoot for getting in about 10 mindful moments.

Below I've provided an example of a general plan for taking individual mindful moments rather than following a daily practice, intention, or ritual. This sample plan is compiled from the list of 50 above along with some from the more targeted lists from subsequent chapters. It includes practices from each category spread out throughout the day. This daily mindful moment practice has two mindful moments that extend to others, two that generate positive emotions, two that are stress-relieving, two that are self-soothing, one that is energizing, and one that is calming. As the day goes on, you may find you need more stress relief if you're feeling frazzled, or self-soothing if you're feeling beat up as the day unfolds.

This list of 10 mindful moments can get you thinking about how you might create your own list. Try some of these and mix and match with some from all the other lists provided as well as from your own list. Because our brain needs novelty to stay motivated, keep varying your list. At the end of every day or so, replace something on your list with something new and different, or even do a completely different list. One way to do this is to share the idea of daily mindful moments with your friends and challenge them to come up with their lists. Then you can share lists and get lots of ideas you wouldn't have considered on your own. This is a great way to add variety to your practice and keep it fresh.

You likely won't get them all in at first—or maybe ever. Even if you do just one thing on your list the first day, it's a beginning. And having a ready-made list will nudge you to keep up with your mindful moment practice.

A Daily Sample Practice of 10 Mindful Moments

1. Map out the sequence of your day in your head and 'see' your day working out just the way you want it to.

2. Express appreciation to someone for something the person did that was helpful to you or to others.

3. Put your hand on your heart, take a few deep breaths and think about someone who loves you.

4. Tighten every muscle in your body. Hold it for 20 seconds. Then enjoy the feeling of relaxation.

5. Rub your hands together rapidly to create some heat. Then place your hands on both sides of your face and hold them there for 30 seconds.

6. Listen to an upbeat, happy song. "Good Vibrations" by The Beach Boys should give your mood a jolt.

7. Slow down your breathing so you are exhaling twice as long as you are inhaling. Count 3 on the inhalation and 6 on the exhalation, or 4 and 8, whichever is most comfortable. Take about 3-5 breaths when you need to calm down.

8. Make a kind or supportive comment to a stranger.

9. Bounce around raising your arms up and down, or skip swinging your arms to your next destination.

10. Gently caress your palms and arms for about a minute because self-stroking is as soothing as being touched by others.

Implementing a Mindful Moment Daily Practice

An option for taking your daily mindful moments is to institute a practice that you follow for the day. A daily practice is a specific action you take throughout the day related to your selected theme or topic.

You may pick a person to be the focus of your practice for a day. Or, you might choose to have all your mindful moments for a day be ones that you find pleasurable. Another option is to select a situation or circumstance and implement a designated practice each time the situation presents itself. For example, you might want to change your reactive responses whenever you feel criticized, put down, or dismissed. Maybe you have a "fast draw" and usually retort with a sarcastic or caustic remark and you want to make a plan to respond more mindfully. When you decide on your focus, that's your mindful moment practice for that day. The majority of my examples are actions taken on behalf of others.

10 Mindful Moment Daily Practices

1. Select one person to be the object of your mindful moments throughout the day—the object of your attention and affection. You might be more tolerant of a pet peeve, do a little favor for the person, send thoughtful texts, or bring the person a small gift.

2. Spend each of your mindful moments recalling and getting a visual image of a time when you felt really happy and content. Actually recreate the feeling and stay with it for 15-30 seconds.

3. Check in with your posture throughout the day. Notice if you're slouching, hanging your head down, or walking in a non-confident stride. Then make the required body shifts.

4. Be aware of every time you assign a person a negative label whether out loud or in your self-talk—he/she is a jerk, know-it-all, stupid, inconsiderate, lazy, boring, needy, or self-centered. Pause for a few seconds and construct a more mindful thought or comment. If you actually made the comment, follow up with your revision. You may want to offer an apology, or say something like *Let me try that again...*

5. Make a list of all the activities you can think of that give you pleasure and take less than 1 to 2 minutes to do. Do one each time you take a mindful moment.

6. Make a kind or supportive comment to everyone you have contact with at your first encounter.

7. Whenever you're feeling criticized or unappreciated because of someone's comment or action, respond with a mindful clarifying question rather than a nasty retort or passive aggressive behavior. Just focusing on formulating a non-blameful question will keep you from reacting immediately. For example, you might ask *Is there something you think I should have done differently?* or *What would you like to have happen now?*

8. Have your practice for the day be looking for opportunities to give out compliments. It could be for a job well done or a nice smile, or expressing appreciation for a kind deed you noticed someone doing. You might even keep a tally throughout your day so you can aim for more the next time you do this daily practice.

9. Take whatever action you can that would "do no harm." It might mean taking a timeout in a difficult conversation, or refraining from making a sarcastic comment when you're frustrated with someone.

10. Implement an "if-then" practice such as: If it's half-past the hour, I will take a mindful moment.

Setting an Intention-for-a-Day

Another approach is to set an intention-for-a-day as your mindful moment practice. Intentions can focus on behaviors, thoughts, or feelings. An intention sparks an awareness that you carry with you for the day. Setting an intention primes your mind to be focused throughout the day as you shift among your many activities. It's a way to purposefully cultivate mindfulness, such as remembering to take one breath before responding to something you didn't like.

Setting an intention also can be a way to prompt you to activate a particular quality or strength, such as patience, generosity, or kindness. Although many others are recommending setting intentions, it's not enough to merely set an intention and think that it will actually come to fruition. That won't work without a strategy.

Let's say you set your intention-for-a-day to be appreciative. Now you have to think about what that means for you and how it will translate into action. So your mindful moments might include just bringing to mind what you are appreciative of, telling others what you appreciate about them or something they have done, or appreciating yourself for your good qualities and deeds.

Rather than setting a more general intention, you are more likely to actually follow through if you set a specific intention. Give yourself details which include how and when you will apply the intent. For example, instead of setting a broad intention to be patient today, set an intention to be patient with a particular person who tends to press your buttons and then specify what you are going to do to actualize your intention. Rather than setting an intention for the day to stay calm, set an intention to take a minute or two to do deep breathing at the slightest sign of stress setting in.

To get started, it's better to set more achievable intentions where you are more likely to be successful. As you log more experience and success setting daily intentions, you can keep shifting your attention to intentions requiring more and more effort. When you set an intention for the day, you check in with that intention regularly and that's your mindful moment practice for that day.

10 Intention-for-a-Day Mindful Moment Practices

1. Set an intention for the day to prompt yourself to activate a positive quality, such as generosity. Go through the day with a generosity mindset. Be generous in your thoughts as well as your actions. Decide what you will do to convert your intention into action.

2. Have a "no-complaints" day. Every time you catch yourself complaining about something that is not going right, follow up with something that is going right.

3. As your daily intention, ask yourself an open-ended question that would be the theme of your mindful moments for that day. You might ask yourself *What would (name of someone you admire) do in this situation?* Each time you break for your mindful moment you would ponder your question.

4. Spend the day responding to everyone and everything with a "yes" attitude instead of our normal tendency to lead with a "no" attitude most of the time. Get in a yes-saying frame of mind and lead with yes unless it is really not possible.

5. Dedicate a day to acts of kindness and challenge yourself to come up with novel actions to surprise others.

6. Listen from the heart. As your daily practice, just listen whenever someone speaks to you. Don't add anything unless you are specifically requested to do so. Don't analyze, diagnose, advise, judge, or provide solutions. Give nonverbal support by nodding, smiling, and leaning forward. Offer encouraging, acknowledging, and accepting feedback. Ask questions that help expand the person's thinking and discover new possibilities about an issue, such as *Have you thought about...?*

7. Set the intention for a day to be a kind voice in your head. Each time you take a mindful moment ask yourself *Is my self-talk being a friend to me?* Think about the monologue running in your head and consciously shift to using "terms of endearment" for yourself. Try addressing yourself with your nickname, or as *honey* or *buddy* or whatever term connotes loving kindness.

8. Pick a positive attribute such as being patient and then make your daily mindful moment practice to reflect on this quality throughout the day by asking yourself these questions at each of your mindful moment check-ins.

    Did I show patience? Take a few seconds to reflect back on those moments.

    Did I miss any opportunities when I might have shown patience but did not? For those instances, think about what you might have done differently.

9. Each time you get even a little annoyed by someone use the "Just As I Do" practice by repeating to yourself:

    This person suffers physical and emotional pain, just as I do.

    This person wants to be understood and appreciated, just as I do.

10. Follow every little stressor throughout the day with pausing for a brief stress-relieving mindful moment to keep minor annoyances from escalating.

Establishing Daily Rituals as Mindful Moments

Another approach is to incorporate daily rituals as part of your mindful moment practice. We all have holiday or special occasion rituals, but done on a daily basis rituals can be another opportunity to be more mindful.

Creating a ritual establishes a routine that soon becomes familiar, and eventually turns into a habit. Rituals are activities that you do in the same way each time you do them. Ideally, your daily ritual would be done the same time every day. Your first and last waking moments are ideal times for establishing daily rituals so you begin and end your day intentionally being mindful.

A daily ritual can be incorporated into an already routine part of your day such as meals. You might institute a nightly dinner ritual where you pose a question that generates a feel-good emotion—a mindful moment version of *How was your day?* One rendition is to rotate among family members or dining mates where everyone takes his or her turn for a night posing a question that engenders a mindful response. This is an uplifting alternative to the usual complaining about everything that went wrong. Here are a few options:

What was the best thing that happened to you today?
What put a big smile on your face today?
What kindness did someone do for you today?
What kind deed did you witness today?
What did you do to make someone else's day better?

Or you might establish a ritual to transition out of your work role. For example, you can set the following ritual:

When I arrive home I will sit in my special chair and take a few minutes for myself.

This time could be spent practicing deep breathing exercises, meditating, repeating a mantra, listening to a guided meditation, or playing a favorite soundtrack. It might take some time for your household or family members to accommodate your new behavior, but you'll be surprised how soon they can adjust if you stick to it. Depending on your situation, you may be able to take a longer period or gradually extend the time period.

You can bookmark your mindful moments with a ritual to start your day and again to end your day. If you make one, or maybe even both, of these a gratitude practice it can gradually change your outlook to one where you're attuned to being grateful.

Morning and Evening Daily Ritual Mindful Moment Practices

The morning can be the most negative time of day for many people. In fact, research shows that the stress hormone cortisol typically peaks 30 minutes after waking. Having an uplifting ritual as the first thing you do can get your day off to a good start. The idea is to establish a practice to acknowledge shifting from sleep into consciousness. Launching a positive mindset from the time you open your eyes and your feet hit the floor will get your mood rising like the morning sun. By developing a morning ritual you set the tone for your day.

With the constant influx of negative news from the media, establishing an evening ritual can serve as a clearing to offset accumulated negativity. Through a nightly ritual you can recover from the demands of daily living. It's akin to resetting your inner compass so you can return tomorrow with a recharged battery. It also ensures that your last thoughts are positive ones. End your day by taking a little time to appreciate the gifts the day brought and prime your subconscious mind for pleasant dreams.

Below are examples of ways to start and end your day mindfully. Some of these practices are also included as individual mindful moments. These practices are particularly worthwhile to perform every day. And if you create morning and evening rituals, it's a way to carry out two of your mindful moments daily.

10 Morning and Evening Daily Ritual Mindful Moments

Daily Morning Rituals: .

- Welcome the day. Begin your day with something as simple as standing in front of a bedroom window for a brief moment to greet whatever kind of day nature has provided.

- Start your day with a wish for the day. At the beginning of each day, make a wish for something positive to happen that day.

- Make your first spoken words of the day positive. Even if you wake up thinking about the hassles of the day, consciously conjure up something positive or caring to say as your first utterance of the day.

- Begin your day with a statement of appreciation for something in your day. For example: *Today I am grateful for the time I'm going to spend with my friend Fran.*

- Embark on each day with a short inspirational message. Read a different life-enhancing quote, poem, or passage providing a mindful message for the day.

Daily Evening Rituals:

- Recount your day by remembering three things that you are grateful for. One rendition of this ritual could be to have two of the things you are grateful for be particular to that day, while the other one may be general, such as good health.

- Recap the day on a positive note by appreciating others' acts of kindness toward you. Scan your day for any kind deeds or gestures you received.

- Acknowledge yourself for the things you did today to help others. Take the time at the end of the day to think about the ways you contributed to the betterment of your family members, co-workers, community, or the world at large.

- Appreciate what you accomplished. Compile an "I did it list" instead of the usual "to do" list.

- Write in your journal. This is a good way to have a marker for the end of everything you have to do that day. Take a moment to think about what happened today that had significance for you. Make an entry in your journal that describes what it was about this experience that you want to capture to be able to ponder when you look through your journal at a later time.

Some Ways I've Enriched My Life with a Mindful Moment Practice

My mindful moment practice enhances my life in so many ways. Here are a few examples. Simply taking little breaks throughout the day to stand up to do something has made a huge difference in the back and neck pain I would often have from sitting and working for hours on end without a break. I'm someone who had always kept an impossibly long daily "to do" list and dutifully transferred whatever wasn't done (which typically was a lot!) to the next day's list. Now, one of my nightly rituals is to do a mental scan of my day and compile an "I did it list" in my head. It feels so much better to be spotlighting what I did get done rather than what I failed to do. I usually surprise myself with all I actually get done in a day.

Having had a hearing impairment since I was a toddler, and as is common for young children who grow up with a hearing impairment, I'm often "in my own little world," like being alone, and don't initiate conversations with strangers. But since I've been doing my mindful moment practice, I often set an intention to compliment strangers I come in contact with while waiting in line or just going about my daily business. Or, I designate a day to spend initiating conversations with new acquaintances, such as in my yoga or exercise classes, or at events. Before I embarked on my mindful moment practice, I would deliberately avoid even making eye contact with people I didn't know. I'm feeling much more connected and have some wonderful new friends.

No one looks forward to doing a bunch of errands, but I've found when I make it a practice to express gratitude, or say something positive, acknowledging, or encouraging to everyone I interact with, it takes the drudgery out of doing things I'd rather not have to do. When I'm done with my errands, rather than feeling depleted, I'm feeling pleased because when I initiate kind, friendly gestures, others reciprocate. It really is astonishing how doing everyday activities with deliberate intention can make such a difference.

Your possibilities for creating a mindful moment practice are unlimited. On some days you can do individual mindful moments every time you take a break tailored to your fluctuating needs. Other days you may want to follow a theme, or do a practice just for the day that relates to some area you want to pay more attention to or improve. Throughout the book there are over 100 different mindful moment practices you can try.

The mindful moments provided can be assembled for countless daily options and a continuous stream of endless variety. Novelty is brain food and nourishes new connections to increase your brain power.

CHAPTER 10

Optimism and Gratitude:
Essential Outlooks for Living Mindfully

An optimist expects his dreams to come true;
a pessimist expects his nightmares to.
–HERMANN HESSE

Cultivating your capacity for optimism and gratitude are skills that will serve you well. These mindsets are essential ingredients for well-being, and they can be developed, enhanced, and sustained with targeted daily practices, especially a daily mindful moment practice. Maintaining an optimistic outlook and expressing gratitude on a regular basis are both characteristics of happy people.

Why Be an Optimist?

Optimism is an attitude that you can face whatever life hands you. The old saying, "When life gives you lemons, make lemonade," portrays the essence of an optimist. There is much research supporting the numerous benefits of maintaining an optimistic outlook. For starters, optimism is a trait of happy people. Optimistic people are more socially engaged which brings a whole host of benefits. Optimists are more successful in their careers. They are more likely to live healthier lifestyles, follow low-fat diets, take vitamins, and exercise.[1] Optimists take better care of themselves and have stronger immune systems making them more resistant to infection.

RESEARCH RECAP: Overall, optimists have greater success in life. They are healthier, happier, more socially connected, and live longer. Being an optimist also protects you from heart disease and speeds up recovery from illnesses as well as surgery. (See The Research Findings)

There's a World of Difference between Optimists and Pessimists

Optimists believe that their actions matter, on the other the hand, pessimists feel helpless and believe that nothing they do will matter. While optimists try to do something, pessimists lapse into passivity. Researchers analyzing writing to assess "explanatory style" as either optimistic or pessimistic discovered that people who don't give up interpret setbacks as transitory, allowing them to bounce back quickly from them.[2] The distinguishing characteristic of people who don't give up is optimism.

Martin Seligman explains that we see the world through three lenses: permanence (always/not always), pervasiveness (everything/not everything), and personal power (unchangeable/changeable).[3]

Optimists construe setbacks as:
- Temporary (*This too shall pass.*)
- Confined (*It is just one situation.*)
- Changeable (*I can do something about this.*)

Pessimists view bad events as:
- Permanent (*Things will always be like this for me.*)
- Pervasive (*This is going to ruin my life.*)
- Unchangeable (*There is nothing I can do.*)

It's no wonder pessimists feel hopeless. When these are the explanations you tell yourself for bad events that happen to you, it leads to chronic unhappiness and more illness. Not surprising, pessimists are more susceptible to depression and are less likely to experience pleasure.[4]

Over time, pessimists learn helplessness which leaves them feeling in the dumps, often for a long, long time.[5] Pessimists struggle in all aspects of their lives. They are more likely to have limited professional success and endure challenges in their relationships. Pessimists also are more likely to get sick, get sicker earlier in life, and have more serious illnesses.[6]

People who are optimistic are able to stay resilient in the face of difficulty. When they face setbacks, optimists believe that their desired goals are still within reach. Conversely, pessimists believe their odds for success are doubtful. Holding this belief, they more easily fall victim to setbacks and discouragement, forsaking challenges that may well have been within their reach.

Optimists Cope Better with Stress

Optimists take action whereas pessimists give up. Consequently, optimists cope better with their stress, while pessimists suffer more stress. In terms of the mind-body connection, negative thoughts and beliefs affect the body by triggering the stress response.[7] On the other hand, when our beliefs are hopeful and optimistic, the brain releases chemicals that put the body in a state of physiological rest, activating the relaxation response.

Interestingly, Susan Kobasa, a psychologist who studied "stress hardiness" back in the '70s, found that those who are able to cope successfully with stressful situations hold three basic attitudes toward life that align with the attitudes of an optimist.[8] She labeled these attitudes the Three Cs: challenge, commitment, and control.

Stress-hardy people interpret crises as challenges, adventures offering opportunities to grow and learn. They have a sense of meaning in life, a commitment to a higher sense of order in the universe, allowing them to see events that happen within this larger perspective. They also believe that they have some control over their lives and feel empowered to affect change.

From Post-Traumatic Stress to Post-Traumatic Growth

People react to extreme stress and adversity on a continuum. On one end are those who fall apart into post-traumatic stress disorder (PTSD), depression, and even suicide. They go from sadness to depression to a paralyzing fear of the future. In the middle are most people, who at first react with symptoms of depression and anxiety, but within a month or so are back where they were before the stressful event.

At the other end are about one-third of people who actually show post-traumatic growth (PTG), more recently referred to as stress-related growth (SRG). They, too, first experience depression and anxiety, but within a year they are better off than they were before the trauma. After a brief period of malaise, they bounce back and have grown because of their experience.[9] Research indicates that those who are optimistic are more likely to experience SRG.[10]

Based on more than thirty years of research, Seligman maintains we have learned not only how to distinguish those who will grow after failure from those who will collapse, but also how to build the set of skills necessary to turn the most difficult experiences into catalysts for personal growth.[11] He says such resilience can be taught, and it can be taught by teaching people to think like optimists. The skills that are the building blocks of resilience and growth are the same as those discussed earlier as the five pillars of positive psychology and what it takes to flourish in life (see Chapter 6). These learnable skills are enjoying positive emotions, being engaged, sustaining relationships, having meaning in life, and feeling a sense of accomplishment. And the primary teaching tools are the validated interventions coming out of the science of positive psychology.

Optimism Can Be Learned

Seligman and colleagues have found that while optimism may change over time, the way people explain bad events tends to remain fixed throughout their lives.[12] But that doesn't mean you can't change. Richard Davidson and Sharon Begley report similar results in *The Emotional Life of Your Brain*.[13] They found that outlook about trivial events is correlated with and predicts outlook about momentous ones. They likewise maintain we can cultivate practices that will build skills that can create lasting changes in the brain.

Optimism is the antithesis of helplessness. According to Seligman, author of both *Learned Hopelessness* and *Learned Optimism* among many others, optimism can be nurtured by learning to change our patterns of negative thinking and appreciate our strengths.[14] He believes optimism is the primary route to expanding personal control.

Davidson and Begley confirm the notion that optimism is a learned skill. In their book, they identify six dimensions of emotional style, each grounded in a particular pattern of brain activity.[15] Brain imaging shows that these dimensions reflect measurable, biological activity in the brain. But that circuitry is not fixed forever. One of these dimensions, which they labeled Positive Outlook, is defined by how long we are able to sustain positive emotion. The capacity to remain upbeat to sustain positive emotions over time is the key measure of Positive Outlook, and is also a defining characteristic of optimism. The durability of positive feelings has a strong carryover effect on our overall outlook. Someone who dwells in a positive mood tends to be optimistic, while someone whose experiences of joy are only momentary flickers is chronically blue and pessimistic. But because the brain can change, our outlook can change. It can be altered not only by chance experiences but by intentional effort to cultivate this capacity at any point in life.

THE RESEARCH FINDINGS

Characteristics of Optimists and Pessimists

- Optimistic people are more successful, earn more, and save more.[16]
- Studies show that optimists catch fewer infectious diseases. Pessimists have been found to have twice as many infectious diseases and twice as many doctor visits as optimists.[17]
- Those with more positive attitudes are more resilient when exposed to common cold and influenza viruses.[18]
- Studies of optimism and heart disease show that optimism is strongly related to protection from cardiovascular disease.[19]
- Optimism protects from cardiovascular disease even when correcting for all the traditional risk factors, such as obesity, smoking, excessive alcohol use, high cholesterol, and hypertension.[20]
- Tracking 1,300 men for 10 years, Harvard psychologist Laura Kubzansky found that heart-disease rates among optimists were half the rates as those of pessimists.[21]
- Optimists fare better when suffering from heart disease and recover better from coronary bypass surgery.[22]
- Optimists have better results when suffering from conditions such as cancer and kidney failure.[23]
- Optimists live longer than pessimists.[24]
- Optimists are 77 percent less likely to die from heart disease.[25]
- One of the largest studies led by Harvard researchers analyzed data from 70,000 women in the Nurses' Health Study, who in 2004 had answered questions about how they viewed their futures. Analyzing data years later, they found that women who were optimistic had a significantly reduced risk of dying from several major causes of death over an eight-year period, compared with women who were less optimistic. The most optimistic women had a 38% lower risk of dying from heart disease; 39% lower risk of dying from stroke; 38% lower risk of dying from respiratory disease; 16% lower risk of dying from cancer; and 52% lower risk of dying from infection.[26]

> • Seligman and his colleagues using the Grant Study data found that by the age of 45, pessimists were already less healthy than optimists. This well-known study followed 268 Harvard men students carefully selected as the "top of the crop" from the time they were sophomores throughout the rest of their lives. The pessimistic men started to get sick younger and more severely than the optimistic men. And by the age of 60, pessimists were significantly sicker.[27]

The Gift of Gratitude

Blessed are those who give without remembering
and take without forgetting.
–ELIZABETH BIBESCO

Gratitude is a feeling of thankfulness and appreciation. It might be expressed toward others, nature or your God. In her final book, *Living in Gratitude*, Angeles Arrien describes gratitude as the acknowledgment of the positive things that come your way that you did not actively work toward or ask for.[28] Robert Emmons, perhaps the world's leading gratitude researcher and author of *Thanks!: How the New Science of Gratitude Can Make You Happier*, defines gratitude more specifically as "a sense of thankfulness and joy in response to receiving a gift, whether the gift be a tangible benefit from a specific other or a moment of peaceful bliss evoked by natural beauty."[29]

Gratitude and Well-Being

Expressing gratitude on a regular basis is a characteristic of happy people. Having a grateful disposition predicts increased happiness, adjustment, and psychological well-being from adolescents to older adults.[30] Ample research supports the association between intentionally noting things you are grateful for and increased well-being and life satisfaction.[31] A recent article found that of the twenty-four character strengths (see Chapter 7), which include love, kindness, and hope, gratitude is the single best predictor of emotional well-being and quality relationships.[32]

Expressing gratitude is one of the most powerful habits you can develop, and there's a large body of gratitude research supporting its benefits.[33] Expressing gratitude is at the top of nearly every self-help and happiness author's lists of mood-enhancing and well-being practices. The benefits of expressing gratitude include both improved positive emotion[34] and longer-lasting positive emotions.[35] Gratitude also predicts greater daily positive feelings in war veterans suffering from post-traumatic stress disorder.[36] David Hamilton in his book, *Why Kindness is Good For You*, reports evidence that gratitude can make you as much as 25 percent happier.[37]

One of the notable effects of gratitude is that it boosts serotonin. When you think of things you are grateful for, you focus on the positive aspects of your life which increases serotonin production. Research shows that developing the mindset of remembering to ask yourself what you're grateful for is what's important, even if you don't find much. It's the looking that matters.[38] Feeling and expressing gratitude is also a potent antidote to negative emotions. Not only does expressing gratitude decrease anxiety and depression, it also acts as a buffer against stress and negativity.[39]

Gratitude and Relationships

Gratitude is linked to healthy interpersonal relationships between friends, romantic partners, and even strangers. Reviewing studies of gratitude, researchers concluded there is strong evidence that gratitude strengthens relationships and promotes prosocial actions such as kindness and altruistic behavior.[40] Gratitude can even reduce selfishness and encourage cooperation in both friends and strangers.[41]

There is evidence that gratitude may have played a unique role in human social evolution.[42] Gratitude can inspire you to direct positive actions toward people in your social network creating a self-perpetuating chain of prosocial behavior. This has been termed "upstream reciprocity" or the "pay it forward effect."[43] Alex Korb writes in *The Upward Spiral: Using Neuroscience to Reverse the Course of Depression, One Small Change at a Time*, feeling grateful produces dopamine, and when you feel gratitude toward others, it increases activity in social dopamine circuits, making social interactions more enjoyable.[44]

Expressing gratitude creates a positive feedback loop in your relationships. The more you express gratitude to the people you care about, the more they feel grateful and want to express their gratitude. Expressing your gratitude to another person whether verbally or in writing is beneficial for you, the person who receives your appreciation, as well as the quality of the relationship between the two of you.

Gratitude alerts you to the valuable relationships in your life and motivates you to reciprocate kindness that you receive and to extend it to others. Experiencing and practicing gratitude promotes supportive exchanges between people and nurtures trusting relationships.[45]

Gratitude also significantly strengthens your professional skills. Gratitude has been linked to higher social intelligence[46] and better long-term decision making.[47] Gratitude also leads to more kindness[48] and likeability as being grateful can make you behave more altruistically and ethically.[49]

Gratitude Practices

To be grateful, you first have to notice the good things that happen to you, especially the little things, before you can feel appreciative. And you have to express thanks to those responsible. Gratitude only boosts your sense of happiness and well-being if you turn it into a conscious and regular practice. To feel gratitude, you have to do something—you can't just wait for it to visit. You have to practice gratitude by deliberately counting your blessings and expressing gratitude.

Many of the most effective practices coming out of nearly two decades of research in positive psychology are related to gratitude. Practicing gratitude is a simple, evidenced-based way to bring more happiness into your life. Through easy to implement practices, such as keeping a daily gratitude journal, writing letters of thanks, and reflecting on the good that comes across your path, you can improve your well-being, increase your optimism, and even improve your sleep quality.

Gratitude practices typically involve thinking or writing about the things you feel grateful for during a designated period of time. Gratitude practices are usually uncomplicated and quick to complete. Although they are implemented for a relatively short period, the positive outcomes can be sustained over months.

In the well-known study conducted by Martin Seligman and colleagues with hundreds of online participants, they tested the impact on well-being of a series of five positive psychology activities.[50] Participants were asked to record their responses to these exercises done every night for just one week. The results of this research identified that three of these exercises brought about the most significant changes. And two of these were gratitude practices (the third was an exercise to build character strengths). The research showed that even after six months, those completing the Three Good Things exercise below were significantly happier and less depressed than the control group.

Personal Exercise: Three Good Things
Every evening, write down three good things that happened that day. In addition, provide a causal explanation for why you think each good thing happened.

Why might this exercise be so effective? Paying attention to and being grateful for the things that went well for you and thinking about why they went well prompts you to notice the things in your life that are going right rather than wrong, where our attention usually goes. This exercise may prime you to pay closer attention to positive events going on in your life that may go unnoticed and engage in them more fully, both in the moment and later when reminiscing or sharing these experiences with others. Reflecting on why these good things happened can help attune you to the positive traits that you and others possess.

These researchers found that conducting a gratitude visit created the most positive change. Participants were instructed to complete the exercise below:

Personal Exercise: Gratitude Visit
Write a letter to someone who has been especially kind to you, but whom you have never thanked, explaining why you feel grateful for what he/she did or said. Deliver the letter to the person.

After doing this Gratitude Visit exercise, participants reported being significantly happier and less depressed. While this exercise initially created the most positive change, this change was sustained for one month but not after six months. One interpretation of this finding might be that the compelling impact of explicitly expressing gratitude weans with time. To sustain its effect, similar expressions of gratitude may need to be conducted at least on a monthly basis.

Since the original study, many other researchers have reported similar results when prompting people to write letters expressing gratitude.[51] One study included 219 men and women who wrote three letters of gratitude over a three-week period. After writing the letters of gratitude, they felt happier and more satisfied with their lives and felt less depressed compared to both a control group and how they felt before they wrote the letters.[52]

Keeping a gratitude journal has much research to indicate it is effective. Gratitude journaling leads to greater positive emotions, fewer negative emotions, less physical symptoms, better quality of sleep, and greater satisfaction with life compared to control conditions.[53] Keeping a gratitude journal for just three weeks can give you more energy and help you sleep better. Even occasional gratitude journaling can boost well-being more than a regular practice of counting your blessings. Interestingly, although women are typically more grateful than men, it is men who can benefit the most from gratitude journaling, especially men who initially have lower level feelings of gratitude before they begin to journal.

RESEARCH RECAP: Simple gratitude practices can boost happiness, enhance life satisfaction, increase positive emotions, foster kindness, heighten feelings of connectedness, improve relationships, promote better sleep, as well as decrease stress, anxiety, and depression.

Start Your Own Gratitude Practice

Gratitude needs to be practiced deliberately and consistently to take hold. If you're like me, you might often find yourself regretting that you didn't tell someone that you appreciated some small thing the person did on your behalf. In fact, there's some research showing that only 52 percent of women and 44 percent of men express gratitude to others on a regular basis.[54]

Being grateful has three components: (1) First comes the noticing, just being aware of all those little things that can so easily go unnoticed. And this is where a mindfulness meditation practice can be so beneficial. (2) Next, you need to actually experience the feeling of appreciation. (3) Finally, you have to express your gratitude in words or deeds, or both.

Some of your choices to get started with a gratitude practice include keeping a gratitude journal, having a daily gratitude ritual, acknowledging what you are grateful for, and expressing gratitude to others. The daily mindful moment practice I'm advocating can merge any of these practices as well as be an ever-changing vehicle for practicing gratitude. You might set the occasional intention to have a "Be grateful day" where all of your mindful moments for the day are about acknowledging or expressing gratitude. Or you might intersperse among your daily mindful moments expressing gratitude for what you appreciate about someone or something someone did that was helpful to you or to others.

Below is a list of ways to integrate being grateful and expressing gratitude into your daily mindful moment practice. This list combines individual mindful moments, practices you do for just a designated day, practices that follow a specified intention for a day, and rituals that you may decide to do every day.

10 Mindful Moments for Enriching Your Life with Gratitude

1. Establish the daily ritual of each night before bed trying to think of something new you are grateful for that you've never given thanks for before.

2. At each mindful moment you take for the day ask yourself the question *Did I express gratitude for the things others do to make my day a little sweeter?* Reflecting on this question will attune you to all the little things you may otherwise overlook.

3. Designate a "gratitude day" where all of your mindful moments are about expressing gratitude or thanks.

4. Mentally scan your day and identify the one accomplishment you are most proud of and spend a minute being grateful you were able to get it done. This could also become a nightly ritual.

5. In each of your mindful moment breaks, replay one of your happiest times and relish in the feeling of gratitude for the experience.

6. Think about a relationship that is not going as well as it might and set an intention to express gratitude in your interactions with that person. This puts you on the alert to start noticing all the good the person does that you miss when you're not paying attention. Expressing gratitude will promote more positive exchanges.

7. At each of your mindful moments for a day, make a list of three things you're grateful for and make at least one something that has happened since your last mindful moment check-in. At the end of the day review your list and feel gratitude for all the blessings each day brings.

8. Set an intention for a day to include some expression of gratitude, no matter how small, in either the emails or texts (or both) you initiate.

9. Pick one person to be the object of your gratitude practice for the day.

10. Ponder all the different roles you have. You may be a mother, wife, daughter, sister, aunt, friend, coworker, teacher, mentor, and volunteer. At each of your mindful moment breaks reflect on one of these roles and what it is about the role that you are most thankful for and that gives you the most joy.

CHAPTER 11

The Many Benefits of Kindness

We make a living by what we get, we make a life by what we give.
–SIR WINSTON CHURCHILL

Doing good is not only good, it feels good, and it's good for our health. As Dacher Keltner asserts in *Born to Be Good: The Science of a Meaningful Life*, when we give, share, or cooperate reward circuits light up in the brain.[1] Given that we are social beings, it makes sense that kindness toward others is intrinsically rewarding. When we help others out of genuine concern for them, our levels of endorphins surge in the brain.[2] Being kind releases serotonin and dopamine, lifting our mood to feel more positive. The warm feeling that we get from being kind also releases oxytocin which helps to strengthen bonds with others by making us feel more connected.[3] Oxytocin reduces blood pressure, slows heart rate, and softens our arteries. This important hormone speeds up wound healing and stimulates angiogenesis, the growth of new blood vessels.[4] It's no wonder that the array of activity flowing through the brain and body spawned by kind actions has been dubbed both the "helper's high" and the "giver's glow."

Kindness changes our brain and our biology. Kindness has natural healing benefits that are bestowed both on us and the people who receive our kindness.[5] Kindness impacts the heart, strengthens the immune system, and can even be an antidote to depression.[6] In his book, *Why Kindness is Good For You*, David Hamilton reports that love and kindness can make a damaged heart regenerate faster and reduce levels of inflammation.[7] Hamilton tells us that kindness occupies the same neural circuits as addictive drugs. Kindness can be as good as pain-killing drugs due to the release of endorphins that bond to cells in the part of the brain involved in transmitting pain. In other words, kindness takes the place of the chemicals that transmit pain signals and interrupts the transmission of these pain signals throughout the brain.

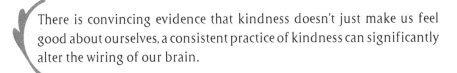

There is convincing evidence that kindness doesn't just make us feel good about ourselves, a consistent practice of kindness can significantly alter the wiring of our brain.

Kindness Is in Our Genes

Kindness is part of our DNA. Evolutionary scientists have revealed how we have evolved as kind beings.[8] Neurophysiologist Nigel Barber reported in *Kindness in a Cruel World: The Evolution of Altruism* that human brains are innately biologically wired to be altruistic.[9] Barber analyzes the motivations behind our most selfless actions to reveal their genetic, cultural, and sociological origins. He presents a compelling case that the desire to help others and the spirit of cooperation are fundamental to our human heritage.

Research suggests that the capacity to derive joy from giving might be a universal feature of human nature. Researchers have hypothesized that if altruism is a deeply rooted part of human behavior, serving an evolutionary purpose, they'd find kind or prosocial acts intrinsically rewarding from the earliest stages of life, even when these acts come at a personal cost. The notion being that performing selfless acts would make very young children happy, even before they've been socialized to fully appreciate the cultural value placed on kindness. And research bears this out.

For example, when researchers gave toddlers just under the age of two a pile of appealing treats and asked them to give one of their treats away to a puppet, the children exhibited more happiness when they gave treats away than when they received treats themselves.[10] They also showed the highest levels of happiness when they gave a treat away from their own stash rather than the experimenter's. Research also shows that adults around the world, living in poor and rich countries alike, experience emotional benefits from using their resources to help others suggesting that humans may have a deep-seated tendency to find giving rewarding.[11]

Kindness and Leadership Power

Dacher Keltner has spent a lifetime studying the power of kindness and in his latest book, *The Power Paradox: How We Gain and Lose Influence*, he reveals that kindness is also a critical factor for effective leaders.[12] To study how power actually works in the social groups we inhabit, over decades he has infiltrated college dorms, sororities, fraternities, and kid's summer camps to document who rises in power. And it's not what we've been told.

Considering the five general ways of acting in the world, or our social tendencies, known as the "big five"—enthusiasm, kindness, focus, calmness, and openness—he found those who rose as leaders had all five. Whereas the Machiavellian approach to power assumes that individuals grab it through coercive force and undermining others, his research finds that power is not *grabbed* but is actually *given* to individuals by groups.

The ability to empower others depends on their willingness to be influenced. Groups give power to those who advance the greater good and value others who do the same. It's a collaborative, cooperative, and compassionate style that draws followers. And social psychologists studying who rises to power in diverse groups, including financial and manufacturing sectors, as well as schools and the military, corroborate his findings. In these diverse samples across seventy studies, those who rose to power were those who had all of the big five.[13]

Giving of Time and Money

The meaning of life is to find your gift. The purpose of life is to give it away.
–PABLO PICASSO

There is substantial research showing that giving, both in terms of time and money, is positively related to well-being.[14] In one study, after recalling a time when they had received a kindness, people were inclined to help not only the person who had given the kindness but also those who were close to them and, to a lesser degree, strangers or persons who had been unkind to them.[15] Indeed, the ripple effect of a kindness can spread by three degrees. Even just witnessing generosity can inspire us to be more generous.

A five-year study conducted on over 800 adults 65 and older found that helping others buffered the association between stress and mortality to reduce mortality.[16] While stress did predict mortality among those who did not provide help to others, stress did not predict mortality among individuals who provided help to others in the past year. High levels of stress generally foretold earlier mortality with those who did not assist friends, neighbors, or relatives having a 30 percent higher chance of dying after a stressful life event than those who were generous.

Sadly, however, researchers report there has been a recent 10 percent decline in helping behavior in the United States, but not in Canada. One argument offered for this change in the level of help provided to strangers is the rise of neighborhood racial and ethnic diversity. In 2001 there was no variation in altruistic behavior based on neighborhood diversity. However, areas of the United States where the proportion of noncitizens increased since 2001 experienced less helping behavior, but the opposite was found in Canada. Possible explanations include changing attitudes toward noncitizens, and differences in public policy related to economic inequality, social inclusion, and the acceptance of multiculturalism.[17]

Generosity in the form of giving money also has its benefits both to well-being and health. Research demonstrates that how people spend their money matters for their happiness. Studies show that people who spend money on others report more happiness. In examining the correlation between charitable giving and happiness in 136 countries, controlling for income and other demographic variables, there was a positive relationship between giving and happiness in 120 of the countries.[18] This relationship was significant in a majority of the countries. While the strength of the relationship varied among countries, individuals in both rich and poor countries reported more happiness if they engaged in spending money on others.

To gauge the relationship between giving to others and blood pressure, researchers asked 186 older US adults who were being treated to control high blood pressure how much money they had contributed each month to friends and family, or religious, political, or charitable organizations. The more they gave to others, the lower their blood pressure was two years later. Because a correlation doesn't establish a cause-and-effect connection, the researchers did a follow-up study. In their subsequent six-week study with 72 elderly adults who were also being treated for high blood pressure, they gave the seniors some money and asked them to splurge either on themselves or on others. At the end of the study, the charitable givers exhibited lower blood pressure than the self-spenders. The difference was on par with blood pressure reductions from exercise or starting new anti-hypertension drugs.[19]

Studies also demonstrate the link between volunteering and experiencing happiness. Researchers examining the relationship between volunteering and levels of happiness in a large group of adults in the US found that the more people volunteered the happier they were.[20] One study tracked happiness throughout the day to measure its relationship to voluntary activities. The researchers found that those who devoted any time to voluntary activities during the day reported higher levels of daily happiness than those who did not engage in any voluntary activity.[21]

Performing Acts of Kindness

Performing acts of kindness is one of the staple positive psychology activities studied.[22] Doing simple acts of kindness for just brief periods can measurably increase happiness. In fact, Seligman says doing an act of kindness produces the single most reliable momentary increase in well-being of any of the multitude of personal exercises he and colleagues have tested. In these studies, participants are asked to perform random kind acts over a short period of time.

Studies on performing acts of kindness reveal some interesting results concerning the variety of kind acts performed as well as their frequency. It turns out, the variety of kind acts affects happiness more than how often they are performed. Remember, the brain loves novelty, so doing the same kind act regularly can lessen its impact once it becomes familiar. Getting creative and doing surprising, unusual, and novel acts will increase the natural high kindness brings. Other research has revealed that how often kind acts are performed makes a difference. Doing a burst of kind acts in a short period rather than spreading them out over a longer period of time has a greater impact on happiness. This finding is likely because many acts of kindness are minor, so spreading them out may make them seem inconsequential.

As an example, a friend keeps a supply of healthy granola bars in his car to give out to strangers who need food. The original intent was to give them to those who are homeless and are often standing by an exit ramp. They usually rip open the package right away, and my friend gets a little rush of those feel-good hormones. He discovered that sense of satisfaction could be amped up considerably by taking a walk through a park, where many who are homeless and hungry congregate, and giving away a bunch in a short time period. It adds to the "giver's glow" to also make eye contact and say a few encouraging words.

RESEARCH RECAP: You can increase your happiness by doing simple acts of kindness for just brief periods. Both the variety of kind acts and the frequency matter. You get more fulfilment from your kind acts by doing them in spurts and keeping them varied and novel will boost the benefits. (See The Research Findings)

Kindness and Strengthening Social Connections

As is the case with most things, doing acts of kindness may be easier to sustain with social support than going it on your own. If your kindness is just a one-shot deal, or a random act of kindness for a stranger, while it may yield a little sense of fulfillment, it's not likely to have any lasting effect unless you make it a habit. Joining a volunteer group can bolster your commitment to kindness because you are also forming social ties.

Jonathan Haidt, University of Virginia psychologist and author of *The Happiness Hypothesis: Finding Modern Truth in Ancient Wisdom*, recommends choosing deeds that strengthen existing social ties, such as bringing a meal to a sick friend.[23] He says it's not the altruism per se, it's more about building relationships. Your kind deeds will reap greater benefit when you tie them to fortifying social ties.

Research also reveals that the emotional benefits of generous spending are most likely to emerge when it fosters positive social connections. In one study, researchers showed that people feel happier after giving more to charity, but only when they give to someone they know who is connected with the cause.[24] Other studies show that the emotional rewards associated with giving to friends or acquaintances are greatest in situations that facilitate social connection.[25] Enhancing social connection is an important factor in turning good deeds into good feelings, and maximizing the feeling of connectedness between givers and receivers may increase the emotional payoff of charitable giving.

Never Underestimate the Ripple Effect of One Kind Act

Stories like the following are what sustain the passion to teach. I recently heard Jack Kornfield tell the story of a teacher noticing that her class was too rambunctious to settle down to work so she stopped and wrote the names of everyone in the class on the board. She had everyone copy the thirty-one names. Then she asked them to write down the one thing that they admired, or liked, or thought was good about that person, for every name on the list.

Over the next few weeks, she compiled an individual list for everyone in the class with the thirty-one kind comments. And on another day right before a school vacation when the students weren't ready to focus again, she handed out to each student his or her list. A number of years later she got a call from the mom of one of her class members from that year. Sadly, she informed her that her son had been killed in active duty and invited her to attend the memorial service. At the service the mom said "I want to show you something that my son always carried with him. My son only carried a few things with him and this was one of them." She handed her a piece of paper that had been folded and obviously opened and refolded countless times and was tattered and worn. When the teacher opened it, she saw that very list. Needless to say, it brought tears to her eyes.

Then something else happened. Two other classmates from that same year who were standing by chimed in with a story about their lists. The girl said "Oh yes, I always keep this in my wallet." and she took it out to show her. The boy said "I made my list part of my wedding vows."

Maybe you have an idea to bring more kindness into the world by taking some action that will impact your own little circle, your community, or beyond. You never know the ripple effect of one kind act.

Start Your Own Kindness Practice

In this digital age, if you want to find opportunities, try volunteer-match.org where you can find just about everything you might be interested in by searching by location, interest, or age group. Kindness.org, an organization that aims to leverage the power of social media to make simple acts of kindness central in our lives, is another option. You can start a kindness initiative at their website, take some action, and then post about your experience on your social networks.

If you really want to jumpstart your kindness practice you may want to do the "29-Day Giving Challenge" at 29gifts.org. Here you are challenged to give one thing away each day for the next 29 days, journal your experiences, and (optionally) share stories about your giving and how focusing on giving has had an impact on your life or someone else's.

One novel idea for a kindness initiative is to institute a "Secret Admirer Club" at your workplace. The way this Club works is the names of all the employees (or members of a unit or team if it's a larger company) are put on a piece of paper and placed in a container from which each person draws a name and becomes that person's Secret Admirer. On some mutually-decided schedule, such as once a week or once or twice a month, each person does something special or kind for the person whose name he/she has drawn. By cleverly designing a rotating schedule, someone is regularly showing a kindness while another person is expressing appreciation in return. It might be having a surprise lunch delivered, putting a small bouquet of flowers on the person's desk, or delivering a notecard acknowledging the person's special qualities and contributions. The idea is to prompt a shift in communication from the usual complaining about work and other colleagues to gratitude and appreciation. The elements of surprise, novelty, anticipation, special attention, and recognition make this kindness project especially gratifying. You could also craft this kindness practice to work at home, or with a group of friends.

Police in Juneau Alaska just spearheaded a kindness initiative campaign to turn 2017 into a community-wide year of kindness. The police kicked off the campaign with public potlucks on New Year's Eve and New Year's Day to encourage locals to commit daily acts of kindness and to reach out weekly to individuals outside their usual circles. Groups, businesses, government agencies, and others are also choosing a different week of the year for their employees to conduct "kindness surges" with correctional officers at the local prison taking the first week. Their goal is to measure the impact of kindness at the end of the year on such areas as crimes, suicides, and emergency calls. The idea was hatched in a partnership with the global kindness advocacy group, Random Acts.

An ideal way to practice kindness is to incorporate acts of kindness into a daily mindful moment practice. Your kindness practice can be one of your daily mindful moments, a theme you set for the day, a one-time novel practice you want to try, or a morning or evening ritual that you establish to do every day.

10 Mindful Moments for
Boosting Your Kindness Quotient

1. Do one kind act for each of your mindful moments for the day. Do different acts of kindness each time and challenge yourself to think of novel kindnesses.

2. Think about someone in your life who is going through a difficult time. Decide on some little act of kindness you can do for that person every day for the next week or two, or longer if necessary. Make that your first mindful moment of the day, or fit it in when you can. If you can't do it in person, call, email or text. You might text or email an uplifting quote, a picture of breathtaking scenery, a bit of humor, or simply a message that you're available for whatever the person may need or want. It doesn't matter much what you do, it's really about letting the person know you care.

3. Have a "Be a kind driver" day where you make kind gestures to other drivers. Let someone turn in ahead of you in the line of traffic, stop for someone crossing the street even if the person is not in a crosswalk, or refrain from blowing your horn if someone doesn't move quickly when stopped at a red light after the light changes to green.

4. Spend the day as a "Kindness Reporter" where your task is to watch for acts of kindness and record a brief description in a notebook. I suggest recording them in a notebook because that way you can repeat this practice periodically and your list will keep growing. At the end of the day, review your list of kind acts and savor the warm feeling of the kindness that is everywhere when you look for it. This is also a great mindful moment practice to do with children, or as a class or group activity.

5. Designate an amount of money you want to give away and divide it into 10 equal parts. At each of your mindful moments, give away the money. Or, do it all in one quick spurt by strolling through an area where those who are homeless congregate. If you don't want to give money, buy a large pack of individually wrapped snacks that usually come in packs of 24 to 36. After you've given them all away you'll be filled with a sense of satisfaction.

6. Without trying to do anything different from what you would normally do, at each of your mindful moment breaks list all the little kind acts you have done from one mindful moment check-in to

the next. The idea is to gauge your current level so you can decide if you want to increase your "kindness allotment."

7. Spend one of your mindful moments for the day reaching out beyond your usual circle. You might seek out someone at work with whom you seldom have contact and invite the person to lunch. Or, you may initiate a conversation with someone you see regularly but have never really engaged with, like the waiter or waitress at a local restaurant or coffee shop you frequent.

8. As your practice for a day, spend your mindful moments making kind gestures or doing small acts of kindness for strangers. As another rendition, do this as one of your mindful moments.

9. For a designated period of time, such as 5 or 10 days, or maybe even longer, do one kind deed.

10. Make kindness your theme for a day. To act in alignment with your kindness theme, reflect on these questions at each of your mindful moment check-ins:

   Did I act kindly to everyone I interacted with? Think back on all your interactions.

   What kindnesses did I receive? Think about the kindnesses you received and stay with that feeling of appreciation for a few seconds.

   Did I miss any opportunities when I might have shown kindness but did not? For those instances, think about what you might have done differently.

THE RESEARCH FINDINGS

Performing Acts of Kindness

- Actively helping someone for 5-15 minutes a day for just 7 days led to sustained gains in happiness.[26]
- Performing a single kind act a day over ten days produced increases in happiness.[27]
- In a study where participants were asked to perform five acts of kindness either all on one day or spread out over the course of the week for six weeks, only those performing their five acts of kindness in a single day experienced a significant boost in happiness.[28]
- Engaging in acts of kindness for four weeks, individuals with high levels of social anxiety displayed significant increases in positive emotions compared to those doing an activity designed to reduce negative emotions.[29]
- Over a ten-week period, researchers had participants either repeat the same kind acts each week or vary the acts they performed and not repeat them. Those who varied their acts of kindness reported significantly greater happiness than those doing the same kind acts. Their increased happiness was maintained even four weeks after the study. Those performing the same acts over and over actually reported diminished happiness.[30]
- Simply counting one's own acts of kindness for just one week increased happiness.[31]

CHAPTER 12

The Power of Compassion and Self-Compassion

The best path to be a good helper is to improve oneself;
but the best way to improve oneself is to help others.
−ABRAHAM MASLOW

Compassion goes beyond sympathy and empathy to include taking action. While empathy is the ability to resonate with another's emotional state, compassion merges the capacity to feel the suffering of others, the desire to relieve that suffering, and the motivation to actually do something to help.

In the absence of compassion, *empathic distress*, or the distress we have when we are feeling bad for others' pain or misfortune, can lead to experiencing negative emotions. But feeling compassion together with empathy can ignite positive emotions.[1]

Thupten Jinpa, author of *A Fearless Heart: How the Courage to Be Compassionate Can Transform Our Lives*, conceptualized compassion as having four distinct aspects.[2] These are:

164

- A cognitive aspect, an awareness of suffering
- An emotional aspect, an empathic concern where one is moved by perceived suffering
- An intentional aspect, a wish to see that suffering alleviated
- A behavioral aspect, a readiness to help to relieve the suffering.

In almost all the major religious traditions, compassion is considered one of the greatest of virtues. Compassion is a capacity intrinsic to mammals.[3] Nonetheless, compassion does require socialization and intentional practice groomed throughout a lifetime to fully flower. Jon Kabat-Zinn has recently argued that mindfulness and compassion are inextricably linked and that a mindfulness meditation practice will give rise to compassion. The viewpoint is that the heightened awareness mindfulness meditation cultivates enhances our ability to "walk in another's shoes" and this presumably leads to more altruistic actions. Shauna Shapiro, author of *The Art and Science of Mindfulness: Integrating Mindfulness Into Psychology and the Helping Professions*, posits that mindfulness meditation trains us to embrace what we are experiencing with a compassionate awareness.[4] The kind, open, and accepting attitude that we foster toward ourselves, in turn leads to extending compassion toward others. But so far, while these assertions seem feasible, they have not been empirically tested. The research that has been done looks specifically at the effects of compassion meditation, generally in the form of loving-kindness meditation.

Compassion Meditation Training

Compassion meditation training attempts to bring about a shift from self-oriented thoughts and behaviors to those oriented toward the well-being of others.[5] It aims to expand our circle of caring and concern beyond those closest to us to encompass an ever-expanding circle of others. Compassion meditation is a systematic way to practice wishing others well.

The most common and most studied type of compassion meditation is loving-kindness meditation (LKM). LKM is a type of Buddhist meditation intended to cultivate an unconditional kind attitude toward oneself and others. While the details of the practice vary across different Buddhist traditions, the core process is to keep generating one's kind intentions toward certain targets. The targets follow an order from those easy to feel compassion for to those more difficult, usually beginning with oneself, then a loved one, a neutral one, a difficult one, and finally all beings. Generally, practitioners silently repeat specific phrases, such as "may I be happy" or "may you be free from suffering." In some traditions, practitioners also visualize a mental image of the targets or light from one's heart flowing toward the targets to help generate their intentions.

There are two comprehensive compassion training programs. The Compassion Cultivation Training (CCT) program developed by Thupten Jinpa, the Dalai Lama's principal English translator, is offered through Stanford's Center for Compassion and Altruism Research and Education. It combines elements of Theravada loving-kindness and Tibetan compassion meditation. CCT is typically taught for nine sessions over nine weeks for a total 20 hours of training.

The Cognitively-Based Compassion Training (CBCT) program developed at Emory University by Geshe Lobsang Tenzin Negi is a secular compassion program that draws from the *lojong* or "mind training" tradition of Tibetan Buddhism. Three ingredients, impartiality, affection, and self-compassion, form the basis of CBCT. It involves the systematic practice of gradually training the mind through a structured and progressive series of contemplative exercises. The program is considered "cognitively-based" because it relies on analytical meditations that encourage actively working with emotions and cognitive appraisals in order to release hostility and indifference toward others and develop deep feelings of affection for, and positive connection with, others. This style of meditation fosters insight into the ways we think of and relate to others and attempts to deepen these insights through repeated reflection and practice until they transform the way we treat others. CBCT is taught in a variety of formats ranging from 10-16 hours.

In a recent comprehensive review of LKM studies, across these 25 studies the amount of training time varied widely, from as long as a ten-day retreat to more typically in the range of 6 to 20 hours of training delivered over 6 to 9 weeks. For the studies looking at the impact of a single session, the practice ranged from 7 to 25 minutes.[6]

Research on the Effect of Compassion Meditation Training on Well-Being

In a recent article, Richard Davidson reports that preliminary findings suggest that compassion training strengthens multiple networks of the brain. His research with colleagues shows that compassion meditation practice creates greater connections between brain regions to allow for better regulation of negative emotions.

Some research shows that compassion meditation training may also offer health-related benefits for those with more compassion training, such as reduced inflammation which plays an important role in heart disease. A few studies of LKM show improvements in stress indicators, but there is also research showing it can cause physiological arousal and can even activate the stress response. Compassion meditation practices may be initially challenging for some, as they can be uncomfortable. Because compassion meditation can be mentally taxing, it is not always a calming or relaxing experience.

Practicing LKM on a daily basis is associated with a variety of positive emotions, including love, joy, and gratitude. While many compassion trainings are lengthy, doing a LKM practice for just seven minutes can have an immediate impact on feelings of social connection and positive mood, but how long these changes will last is not known.

Recent systematic reviews of studies of LKM and other compassion meditation conclude that compassion meditation boosts daily positive emotions in the short-term. We don't know if more intensive meditation practice will lead to more long-term effects. There are substantial differences among individuals in the impact of different loving-kindness meditations, an indication that not everyone finds LKM a suitable practice.

RESEARCH RECAP: While loving-kindness meditation and other types of compassion meditation can lead to immediate feelings of positive emotions, they don't produce improvements in more stable measures of well-being, such as quality of life or life satisfaction. In comparisons of compassion meditation with alternative interventions, there are generally no significant differences. Compassion meditation doesn't produce positive feelings for everyone and these feelings are not enduring. (See The Research Findings)

Does Compassion Meditation Lead to Compassionate Behavior?

In all of my research, there were only two studies that hinted at compassion meditation actually leading to altruistic behavior. In the first study, twenty young adults were trained in LKM and twenty-one were trained in a cognitive reappraisal technique where they learned to reframe their thoughts to recast them in a more positive light.[7] To test if compassion training leads to more altruistic behavior, after their training participants played an online game involving two anonymous players, the "Dictator" and the "Victim." The other players were actually computer generated, but the participants were led to believe they were real people. In the game, the participants were given $5, the Dictator was given $10, and the Victim had no money. Each participant first watched as the Dictator shared an unfair amount of money (only $1 out of $10) with the Victim. They were then given the opportunity to decide how much of their own money to spend to equalize the unfair split and redistribute funds from the Dictator to the Victim. Those receiving the compassion training spent nearly twice as much as those receiving the reappraisal training, $1.14 versus $0.62, but still not very much. Giving on average about $1 of their virtual money on behalf of a Victim can hardly be considered evidence that meditation leads to compassionate behavior.

The authors' conclusion was: "We found that people trained in compassion were more likely to spend their own money altruistically to help someone who was treated unfairly than those who were trained in cognitive reappraisal." From these findings they contend that compassion meditation makes you more altruistic. But it's a huge leap from giving away virtual money to actually acting more altruistic.

Before and after their training, all participants also had their brains scanned while looking at a series of images with some depicting people in pain. Those who were the most altruistic after compassion training showed the greatest brain changes when viewing human suffering. Those receiving LKM training showed increased brain activity in areas involved in understanding the suffering of others, regulating emotions, and positive feelings in response to a reward. But the researchers saw similar brain changes in those who were the most altruistic after training in using reappraisal.

The second pair of studies looked at responding more compassionately in a relatively easy situation and one involving interpersonal conflict, finding very different results. The true test of compassion may be when it is difficult. It's much easier to show compassion to a loved one than it is to someone who you are in conflict with or who holds contrasting beliefs.

In this research, ten participants received a course on compassion meditation, another ten received mindfulness-based meditation training, and nineteen were in the control group and received no training.[8] Compassionate responding was assessed by whether participants would give up their seat for a woman on crutches who arrived to the waiting area with no empty seats. Half of those from either meditation class gave up their seat compared to 15 percent of the non-meditators. This means only half of those going through two months of either meditation training were affected enough for it to translate into compassionate behavior.

The second part of the study tested whether participation in either meditation training would increase compassionate responding toward someone following a conflict. Those who completed a meditation course were no more likely than those without meditation training to behave compassionately toward that individual. For those practicing compassion meditation, the amount of time they experienced emotional arousal in response to the angering event was actually prolonged rather than shortened.

While these studies are often referenced as an indication that both types of meditation bring about compassionate behavior, they are far from persuasive. On a scale of self-sacrifice, clearly giving away virtual money or giving up a seat, are pretty low on the totem pole. So far, there hasn't been any research that looks at more significant selfless acts of compassion. While it is often reported as one of the benefits, you can't assume that if you practice loving-kindness meditation you will become more altruistic.

RESEARCH RECAP: At this point, the research does not support that either mindfulness meditation or compassion meditation leads to helping behavior or benevolent actions toward others, especially in more difficult situations. (See The Research Findings)

Non-Meditation Compassion Practices

Most positive psychology practices have focused on performing acts of kindness that, although related, are not the same as practices specifically intended to promote compassionate acts. There is one large study with 719 participants who practiced compassionate actions for seven days.[9] The researchers found that practicing compassionate acts daily resulted in increases in happiness that lasted up to six months after the end of the study.

Participants were recruited online and were assigned to a compassionate acts intervention or a control group who wrote about an early memory. Those performing the compassionate acts were asked to act compassionately toward someone each day by actively helping or interacting with someone in a compassionate way. Participants logged onto the website daily to report their compassionate acts or early memory experiences.

At the onset of the study and at the conclusion of the seven-day study period, all participants completed self-report measures of depression, happiness, and self-esteem. At one month, and again at two, three, and six months following the exercise period, participants were asked to return to the website to complete follow-up questionnaires. The results showed that those doing compassionate acts had sustained gains in happiness and self-esteem over six months. As is often the case with longitudinal, internet-based research, a limitation of this study is the rate of attrition. Of those who provided data initially, 474 completed the one-week assessments. At one month and at six months, 356 and 179, respectively, completed the follow-up assessments. Nonetheless, these numbers are still relatively large for statistical purposes.

Consistent with positive psychology's contention that using brief, daily exercises performed over relatively short periods can produce lasting increases in positive emotions and human strengths, a one-week, online exercise involving practicing compassionate acts toward others resulted in increases in happiness and self-esteem that endured up to six months after completing the exercise.

Cultivating Compassion

Momentary compassionate acts don't lend themselves to preplanning, so it is more difficult to incorporate them into a mindful moment practice. You have to seize opportunities as they present themselves.

One option is to show compassion to someone with whom you have a constrained relationship, to a person who has not been kind to you, or to a person who has actually done something harmful to you.

Establishing a mindset or intention for a day may work better. Daily Practice #4 and Daily Practice #9 presented in Chapter 10 offer ways to foster compassion. The first involves the practice of spending the day trying to catch yourself every time you assign someone a negative label so you can become more aware of when you are being mean-spirited to prompt yourself to shift to being more kind-hearted. In the second practice, you set the theme for a day to "do no harm." This includes both your deeds and your thoughts and is directed toward others as well as yourself.

Compassion means noticing someone is suffering, being emotionally moved to alleviate that suffering, and taking action. A truer test of your own compassionate instinct is when it has potential consequences or costs to you. I had a memorable experience in one of my attempts to do a compassionate deed by coming to the aid of an elderly lady. I was going to meet three of my siblings at an outdoor concert that evening. We were planning to have a tailgate dinner before the concert. My assignment was to go to the Italian section in Providence, Rhode Island, fondly referred to as "the Hill" by locals, and get salami and cheese.

As I was walking into my favorite deli, a very old Italian lady looking quite disheveled was sitting outside mumbling to herself and fanning her dress up and down as it was well into the 90s that hot summer day. She looked so distressed I asked if she needed help. She said she wanted to go home, but she was too tired to walk. I hesitated as I was in a crunch for time and would soon be facing rush-hour traffic. I knew my siblings would be angry with me for being late, but decided I needed to take that chance and help her. I told her I would drive her home right after I bought my groceries. She immediately relaxed. I proceeded to lead her to my car and she directed me to turn right at the next corner. After making multiple turns, it became obvious she had no idea how to get home. As the thought of that saying "No good deed goes unpunished" popped into my head I was contemplating my options. Maybe she would enjoy a Billy Joel concert (just kidding—though by now I was not finding this situation very funny). I decided to keep driving around the area stopping everyone I saw to see if anyone might recognize her and might know where she lived. At last, one of the people I stopped happened to be her neighbor and pointed me in the right direction saying "Oh, she's lost again. She lives right over there." After getting her settled in her favorite chair, I continued on my journey, now an hour late, with a big smile on my face so pleased with myself for getting her home safely. I did have to contend with a lot of flak for being late. But after I told them my story they finally came around.

THE RESEARCH FINDINGS

Effects of Compassion Meditation Training on Brain Areas and Health

- Neuroscientists have identified that the brain areas associated with compassion are different from those associated with empathy. Compassion activates regions of the brain related to reward, positive emotions, and feelings of affection.[10]
- Compassion training can strengthen multiple networks of the brain affecting distinct processes.[11]
- Compassion meditation practice creates more activity in the *approach* versus the *withdrawal* area of the brain, and greater network connectivity between brain regions to allow for better regulation of the brain's alarm for threat, danger, and fear.[12]
- Compassion meditation practice is linked to brain areas associated with social affiliation and emotion regulation.[13]
- Studies of compassion training show increased activation in regions associated with executive function.[14]
- Compassion meditation training may reduce levels of inflammation.[15]
- Preliminary studies of compassion training find associations between the amount of time spent engaging in compassion training and inflammatory biomarkers, showing that more compassion training leads to decreased levels of bodily indicators related to inflammation.[16]
- Compassion meditation training can reduce immune and behavioral responses to psychosocial stress.[17]
- In a pilot study of loving-kindness meditation, chronic low back pain patients showed significant improvements in pain and psychological distress.[18]
- Some research shows compassion meditation can cause physiological arousal, such as increased heart rate, and can activate the stress response.[19]

THE RESEARCH FINDINGS

Effects of Compassion Meditation Training on Positive Emotions, Well-Being and Compassion

- Practicing compassion meditation is associated with a variety of positive emotions.[20]
- Studies of those practicing LKM on a daily basis show increases in emotions such as love, joy, and gratitude.[21]
- In-the-moment changes in feelings of social connection and positivity toward others have been found in as little as seven minutes of LKM.[22] Participants were trained in a 7-minute visualization procedure in which they were to imagine two loved ones sending loving and compassionate feelings toward themselves, and to subsequently redirect those warm feelings toward the photograph of an emotionally-neutral stranger. Participants then recited a succession of phrases wishing the stranger health, happiness, and well-being. Compared to the control group, participants who engaged in this loving-kindness visualization experienced more positive moods, though not less negative moods, and more positive responses to themselves and others.
- In a systematic review and meta-analysis considering only empirical studies on LKM with self-reported positive emotions, 25 studies were identified.[23] The reviewers concluded that LKM can produce immediate positive emotions after practicing. However, they noted that whether more intensive meditation practice or training will lead to more long-term effects remains to be validated.
- These reviewers also concluded that when LKM was compared with different interventions, the results did not often favor LKM. Of comparisons with alternative interventions, six of eight comparisons did not find any significant differences on a variety of measures of positive emotions between LKM and other trainings including mindfulness meditation,[24] progressive muscle relaxation,[25] theater therapy,[26] memory training,[27] positive emotion regulation and music.[28]

- Some of the studies included noted considerable individual differences in the impact of different loving-kindness meditations[29] as well as a high dropout rate.[30]
- One study reported that those participants with high positive emotions before LKM training experience sharper increases in positive emotions after the training.[31] Another study also found that participants experiencing high positive emotions are more likely to maintain meditation practice after the intervention.[32] Frederickson's research with colleagues shows that you first have to be moved to feel a positive emotion before the compassion meditation practice has a positive impact.[33] Her research shows that only those who feel positive emotions, and feel more connected as a result of practicing LKM, show positive outcomes.
- Another systematic review and meta-analyses considered only the evidence available from randomized controlled trials (RCTs).[34] They reviewed 22 RCTs of LKM and compassion meditation, collectively referred to as kindness-based meditation (KBM), and the effect on health and well-being against passive and active control groups in patients and the general population. They rated the methodological quality of the studies as low to moderate and had the following conclusions.

   a. KBM does facilitate positive emotions.
   b. There are no significant improvements in quality of life or satisfaction with life.
   c. KBM Is moderately effective in decreasing self-reports of depression and increasing self-reports of mindfulness, compassion, and self-compassion against passive controls, such as a waitlist or standard care.
   d. The favorable effects of KBM on self-reported compassion and self-compassion should be interpreted with caution as they may stem from positive expectancy beliefs given that kindness and compassion are explicitly addressed during KBM training. But helping behavior is an objective measure, and only one out of four measurements of helping behavior was significant.
   e. When KBM is compared with other interventions, the results do not often favor KBM. Of comparisons with

alternative interventions, the majority of comparisons did not find significant differences on a variety of measures of well-being between KBM and other trainings. The exception was against progressive relaxation where the KBM participants experienced significantly more positive emotions.

f. As indicated by high drop-out rates, these practices may be initially challenging for some people.

g. The main limitations in the studies reviewed were small sample sizes, high attrition rates, and low methodological quality. High attrition was widely reported and is a major practical issue in this area of research, as it is generally for trainings or interventions where participant demand is high. That the results are mixed and complex is not surprising given that KBM training has wide variation and may have effects at many levels, making it difficult to evaluate.

- Researchers at the Center for Healthy Minds had participants complete either LKM training or reappraisal training to test whether participants playing an online game would give some of their virtual money to offset another player's unfair distribution to a "Victim."[35] Both groups listened to guided audio instructions online for 30 minutes per day for two weeks, for a total of 7 hours of training. The reappraisal training involved recalling a stressful experience and trying to think about it in a new, less upsetting way, such as by considering it from another person's point of view. In the LKM training, participants envisioned a time when someone had suffered and then practiced wishing that suffering be relieved by repeating specific phrases. They practiced compassion for a loved one, themselves, a stranger, someone they had difficulty with, and lastly for all other beings. While those trained in compassion were more likely to spend their virtual money on behalf of the Victim than those who were trained in reappraisal, they only gave on average about $1 of the $5 of virtual money they had to give away.

- Participants with little to no prior meditation experience were randomly assigned to an eight-week course in either compassion meditation (n=10) or mindfulness-based meditation (n=10), or a no training control group (n=19).[36] At the end of the first study, participants individually arrived at a lab and upon entering a communal waiting area, participants seated themselves in the last remaining chair with actors occupying the other two chairs. Then a third female actor on crutches entered the waiting area. Those who completed either meditation course gave up their seat more frequently than did those from the control group with 50 percent (10) of those taking the meditation classes giving up their seat compared to 15 percent (3) of the non-meditators.

The second part of the study examined whether participants would respond more compassionately toward someone following an interpersonal conflict. They also recorded their physiological responses. Those who completed either meditation course were *not* more likely than controls to behave compassionately toward that individual. And those practicing compassion meditation experienced the longest cardiovascular recovery after the conflict, an indication that compassion meditation may actually prolong rather than curtail arousal in response to an angering event.

Why We Need Self-Compassion

You yourself, as much as anybody in the entire universe,
deserve your love and affection.
–BUDDHA

Being able to have compassion for yourself is as important as having compassion for others. You need to give yourself the same love and care you would give a friend or family member. Self-compassion emanates from self-love. Christine Arylo, in *Madly in Love with Me*, offers this definition of self-love: "Self-love is the unconditional, unwavering love and respect that you give to yourself so that you only choose loving situations and relationships, including the one with yourself, that are full of love and respect."[37]

Kristin Neff, pioneering researcher on self-compassion and author of *Self-Compassion: Stop Beating Yourself Up and Leave Insecurity Behind*, describes self-compassion as being warm and understanding toward ourselves when we suffer, fail or feel inadequate.[38] She defines self-compassion as having three core components which need to be combined in order to be truly self-compassionate. First, it requires self-kindness, being gentle and understanding with ourselves rather than harshly critical and judgmental. Second, it entails perceiving our experiences as part of the larger human experience. It requires recognizing our common humanity, feeling connected with others in the experience of life rather than feeling isolated by our suffering. In other words, remembering that we're all in this together and everyone has to deal with the challenges of life. Third, it necessitates mindfulness, holding painful thoughts and feelings in balanced awareness, rather than ignoring or exaggerating our pain.

Practicing self-compassion is a way to rein in your inner critic and replace it with a voice of support, understanding, and care. Treating yourself compassionately when confronting personal suffering has significant benefits. When we have self-compassion, we are better able to accept who we are regardless of what others are telling us.

Self-compassionate people recognize when they are suffering and are kind to themselves at these times so they are able to lower their levels of related stress and anxiety. Being self-compassionate not only leads to significantly less anxiety and depression, it also leads to more happiness, optimism, and positive emotions.

According to Neff, self-compassion is a powerful way to achieve emotional well-being and contentment in our lives, helping us avoid destructive patterns of fear, negativity, and isolation. The nurturing quality of self-compassion allows us to appreciate the richness of life, even in hard times. When we soothe our agitated minds with self-compassion, we're better able to notice what's right along with what's wrong.

Research on Self-Compassion

Research shows those with higher self-compassion have lower levels of stress, anxiety, and depression. Self-compassion is linked to many positive qualities, including happiness, optimism, and emotional intelligence. Neuroscientist Joseph LeDoux, author of *The Emotional Brain: The Mysterious Underpinnings of Emotional Life*, has conducted research showing that when a negative memory is recalled and then paired with a positive experience such as self-compassion, the juxtaposition can rewire the negative memory at the molecular level.[39]

While not the same, self-compassion and self-esteem do tend to go together. If you're self-compassionate, you'll tend to have higher self-esteem than if you are not.[40] Even though self-compassion and self-esteem are related, self-compassion offers some clear advantages over self-esteem when things go wrong, or when our egos are threatened. Research shows with self-compassion, feelings of self-worth are more stable than they are with self-esteem. Self-compassion is less contingent on outside factors such as social approval. We can extend self-compassion to ourselves in both good and bad times. With self-compassion, our sense of self-worth is much less easily shaken because it's not contingent on reaching certain goals or others' judgments.

People whose self-worth is vested in feeling superior and infallible tend to get angry and defensive when their status is threatened. Those who compassionately accept their imperfections don't need to protect their egos. On the other hand, self-esteem only thrives when the reviews are good and can lead to evasive and counterproductive tactics when facing unpleasant truths about oneself.

The Benefits of Practicing Self-Compassion

Self-compassion research done by Kristin Neff and Chris Germer shows that self-compassion practice can not only reduce stress and symptoms of depression and anxiety, it also increases life satisfaction. And training in self-compassion lowers stress regardless of one's level of self-compassion. This means that self-compassion practice is beneficial even for those who start out with limited capacity for self-compassion. Practicing self-compassion activates the "care circuit" which soothes negative emotions while generating a sense of calm. Brief self-compassion meditation training lowers stress responses more than mindfulness meditation training. Writing self-compassionately improves mood more than emotionally-expressive writing or distraction, two common interventions for dealing with negative emotions.

RESEARCH RECAP: Those who practice self-compassion can temper their inner critic, have more enduring feelings of self-worth, and enjoy greater happiness and optimism. By practicing self-compassion you can improve your ability to sooth your negative emotions to reduce levels of related stress and anxiety and enhance your capacity to stay emotionally balanced in difficult situations. (See The Research Findings)

Cultivating Self-Compassion

While you would expect self-compassion and compassion for others to be highly correlated, this is not true. Research bears out there is near zero correlation between self-compassion and compassion for others.[41] This means they operate almost totally independently and having the capacity for one is not related to the other. We don't need to have self-compassion in order to have compassion for others. In fact, it may be the other way around. We need to take our innate compassionate instinct for caring for the weak and vulnerable and deliberately cultivate it for ourselves by making sure we offer ourselves the self-care necessary to prevent depleting ourselves to the point of having no energy to extend compassion to others. Compassion for self, along with compassion for others, needs to be cultivated. Developing both capacities requires intentional practices to blossom to our full potential.

A self-compassion practice that has served me well is to squelch the inner voice of the *critical evaluator* and replace it with the *constructive advocate*. As I became more mindful I likewise became more attuned to the berating self-talk going on in my head which led to an important insight. When I was being critical of myself, I noticed I would address myself by my last name. So I would be saying to myself "Larrivee, you're so pathetic. Why do you keep getting yourself in the same messes?" And when I was showing myself a little self-compassion, I would use my nickname. So I might be saying to myself "It's okay Barb, you can disappoint someone to align with your own integrity." What this realization meant for me is that when I was lambasting myself, by merely switching to my nickname I could transform my voice to a kinder, gentler tone.

As suggested below, I recently made my own Sanctuary Treasure Box which brings me great comfort when I need it. I bought a beautifully-decorated box and filled it with things that spark all of my senses and soothe me. My sense of smell is the sense that's my quickest route to contentment, so I have more items in my box to activate that sense. I have rose geranium oil, lavender scented salve, a rose-scented candle in a tin, and some lemongrass incense sticks with a holder. Among many treasures, my box has a cherished ring my mom brought back for me from a trip, a few shells from a wonderful vacation in Mexico, three of my all-time favorite pictures, and a large fluffy feather. I highly recommend creating your own. Just thinking about and gathering your special items is a fulfilling experience.

You might also want to design a special sanctuary in your home you can retreat to. If you can't allocate a separate room, try to find a corner where you can put up a portable divider. You might be able to turn a walk-in closet into your own private haven with some throw pillows and an altar. Add a favorite book, a journal, soft lighting, fresh flowers, a plant, photos, or anything that is pleasing to you. Retreat to your sanctuary when you could use some self-compassion.

When you're going through something difficult, or when you're just down in the dumps, you need some self-compassion. Try using some of these self-soothing mindful moments to give yourself compassion and boost your spirits.

10 Mindful Moments When You're Feeling Blue or Need Self-Compassion

1. Label exactly what you're feeling by giving that awful, unpleasant feeling a name. Are you feeling sad, anxious, angry, unappreciated? When you consciously acknowledge the specific emotion, it reduces its impact by activating the thinking part of the brain while reducing reactivity in the part of the brain that responds to stress.

2. Do a self-squeeze. Wrap your arms around yourself, or fold your arms in a way that mirrors a hug if you need to be discreet. Just as you would hug a friend who's having a rough day, this physical gesture of self-compassion is a quick way to soothe and comfort yourself.

3. Look in a mirror and pick one thing that you like about yourself.

4. Get yourself a large soft feather and caress your face and neck. The soft touch against your skin is very self-soothing.

5. Get moving. Just two minutes of exercise is enough to change your mood, as long as you raise your heart rate. Anything from a quick brisk walk to a sprint up and down the stairs supplies a surge of dopamine and serotonin, the same targets as antidepressants.

6. Indulge yourself with some dark chocolate. The natural chemicals in cocoa can improve blood flow to the brain to increase circulation, providing a boost in mood and a spike in energy level.

7. Sniff some lemon essential oil or put it in a diffuser. Smelling lemon can quickly improve your energy level and mood. Rose and bergamot also have mood-elevating properties. Experiment to find which scents work for you.

8. Create your own Sanctuary Treasure Box you can take out whenever you want to evoke pleasant memories or need a boost. You might include a shell from a special trip, a memento from a loved one, or a cherished card from a friend. You can also put items in the box that offer encouragement or remind you of difficult times you managed to get through.

9. Read a quote, poem, or passage that has meaning for you and relates to how you're feeling. One of my favorite poems is *The Invitation* by Oriah Mountain Dreamer. It reminds me that sometimes you have to "stand in the fire."

10. Comfort your eyes with compresses. Use cold, sliced cucumber rounds, a spoon you have chilled in the freezer, a frozen gel mask, or a hot washcloth.

THE RESEARCH FINDINGS

Self-Compassion and Well-Being

- Research studies show a strong negative relationship between self-compassion and stress, anxiety, and depression.[42]
- Self-compassion is associated with many positive qualities, such as happiness, optimism, wisdom, personal initiative, and emotional intelligence, as well as curiosity and exploration.[43]
- Kristin Neff and colleague Roos Vonk investigated the benefits of self-compassion versus self-esteem in a study with more than 3,000 people from various walks of life.[44] Given that self-esteem tends to be diminished when things don't turn out well, they hypothesized that self-esteem would be associated with relatively unstable feelings of self-worth. They expected the feelings of self-worth to remain steadier over time among self-compassionate people. They had participants report on how they were feeling toward themselves at the time, doing so 12 different times over 8 months, then calculated the degree to which overall levels of self-compassion or self-esteem predicted stability in self-worth. They found:

  a. Self-compassion is clearly associated with steadier and more constant feelings of self-worth than self-esteem.

  b. Self-compassion is less likely than self-esteem to be contingent on outside factors.

  c. Self-compassion is associated with less social comparison than self-esteem.

  d. Self-compassion is also associated with less need to retaliate for perceived personal slights or to be right.

  e. Those with high self-esteem are much more narcissistic than those with low self-esteem. In contrast, self-compassion is completely unassociated with narcissism, indicating those high in self-compassion are no more likely to be narcissistic than those with low self-compassion.

THE RESEARCH FINDINGS

Benefits of Practicing Self-Compassion

- Research shows that self-compassion practice decreases symptoms of depression, anxiety, and stress while increasing life satisfaction.[45]
- Self-compassion meditation training can buffer stress regardless of initial levels of self-compassion.[46]
- Studies by the affective neuroscientist Jaak Panksepp have demonstrated that the practice of self-compassion activates the "care circuit" that generates oxytocin and other opioids that have been shown to sooth negative emotions and reduce distress as well as create feelings of calm and contentment.[47]
- Recent research demonstrates that brief self-compassion meditation training can dampen both physical and subjective responses to stress relative to attention meditation training and no-instruction control conditions.[48]
- In a study comparing the effect of self-compassionate versus emotionally-expressive writing on mood, researchers had 186 participants complete a negative mood induction, and then randomly assigned them to write about a negative event in either a self-compassionate or emotionally-expressive way. Self-compassionate writing significantly predicted improved mood more so than writing in an emotionally-expressive way. They also found that greater self-compassion significantly predicted mood improvements.[49]
- In a similar study, researchers explored whether self-compassion may be a better way to cope with negative experiences than distraction. They had 152 participants undergo a negative mood induction and then complete either a self-compassionate writing task or a distraction task. Participants who wrote self-compassionately experienced increases in positive emotions while participants who distracted themselves experienced reductions in positive emotions. Both groups had similar significant reductions in negative emotions. These findings demonstrate there are greater short-term benefits for using self-compassion rather than distraction to improve mood.[50]

CHAPTER 13

Stress: The Good, the Bad and the Ugly

Our greatest weapon against stress is the ability to choose one thought over another.
–WILLIAM CHASE

The American Psychological Association (APA) has been conducting annual polls, the *Stress in America* survey, since 2007 examining sources of stress and its impact on health and well-being. In the 2016 survey, 20 percent of Americans reported experiencing extreme stress.[1] Because many respondents to the annual August survey reported the election was a significant source of stress, this year APA commissioned an additional survey in early January 2017. Although overall stress levels have been gradually decreasing, the results showed a statistically significant increase in stress for the first time in a decade.[2] This new survey found that between August 2016 and January 2017, Americans' overall average reported stress level rose from 4.8 to 5.1 on a 10-point scale. More alarming was the fact that the percentage of Americans who reported experiencing at least one symptom of stress over the past month, such as headaches or feeling overwhelmed, anxious, sad, or depressed, rose from 71 to 80.

We have more and more reasons to feel stressed due to the political climate, natural disasters, terrorist attacks, environmental devastation, and an unending stream of dreadful news. Anxiety stemming from a continuous diet of grave news is not only upsetting, it can make us feel helpless which exacerbates stress.

Stress is an unavoidable part of life and work. While some level of stress is inherent in the workplace, many people in stressful professions, or working in highly competitive environments, have to function under chronic stress. Second only to money, work was a top cause of stress in this year's APA survey, as it has been in past years. Americans reported money and work as very or somewhat significant sources of stress in their lives, at 61 and 58 percent, respectively.[3]

We all know that unmanaged stress can run amuck. We can deal with it for a little while, but when we are exposed for long periods, the pressure builds and our system becomes flooded with stress hormones.[4] When cortisol surges through our body at high levels and stays there, we're stuck in overdrive which puts excessive wear and tear on our whole system.

The Delicate Balance of Relaxation and Stress

Our autonomic nervous system (ANS) regulates 90 percent of our body's functions.[5] *Autonomic* means involuntarily, in other words, the activity of the ANS goes on below our conscious awareness. The ANS is made up of two branches, the sympathetic nervous system (SNS) and the parasympathetic nervous system (PNS). The SNS functions like the gas pedal revving the body up to prepare us for action (the "stress response"). The PNS functions like the brakes, slowing our heart rate and other functions down to replenish our body (the "relaxation response").[6] These two systems intermingle in a complex physiologic dance between relaxation and stress. When we are exposed to enduring forms of stress, the stress response is sustained over time and this long-lasting state of stress throws the system out of equilibrium (i.e., homeostasis). Because the ANS controls so many bodily functions, it's easy to understand how prolonged imbalances can lead to serious health problems. The relaxation response engages the PNS, which is responsible for restoring the body to normal after experiencing the stress response.[7] The relaxation response is our innate asset for combating stress.

How Stress Affects Health

There is general consensus that stress is the most prevalent cause of disease and illness. Mario Martinez in *The MindBody Code* reports that 90 percent of all illness is stress-related.[8] According to the World Health Organization (WHO) that monitors global health risks, stress is literally becoming an epidemic with stress-related chronic diseases being the main source of death in developed countries.

Our response to stress is physical, mental, and emotional. Stress affects nearly all of our bodily systems with a bewildering array of health consequences. Christiane Northrup writes in her recent book, *Goddesses Never Age: The Secret Prescription for Radiance, Vitality, and Well-Being*, "When stress hormones like cortisol and adrenaline are chronically elevated in our system due to unremitting physical or emotional stress, they cause cellular inflammation, which is the primary cause of all chronic degenerative diseases including cancer."[9]

Research overwhelmingly shows that a high level of stress makes it harder to fight off disease and infections. Stress even influences how often we catch the common cold. Stress sets in motion a cascade of reactions that can affect our health even at the cellular level. Given the scope of changes that accompany a stress response, it's not surprising that estimates range from 50 to 80 percent of all visits to a doctor are for medical conditions related to stress.[10]

Signs of stress are not only physical. Psychological stress is a major contributor to exacerbating physical symptoms in many chronic conditions. High levels of stress are a factor in the development of anxiety and depression symptoms. Under stress, our minds are prone to racing thoughts. Stress also takes a toll on our cognitive capacity, especially our memory, causing mental slowness, confusion, as well as difficulty with comprehension.

RESEARCH RECAP: Under chronic stress, you get sick more often, weaken your immune system, accelerate cellular aging, and increase your chances of dying prematurely. You also increase your risk of clinical depression, harm your memory, and decrease your capacity to attend to the task at hand, solve problems, and make good decisions. (See The Research Findings)

Stress Reshapes Our Brain

Chronic stress reshapes our brain. When we have multiple things causing us stress, it leads to chronically high cortisol levels which are toxic to the brain. Too much cortisol changes two parts of the brain. One is the hippocampus, which is central to creating memories of facts, the things we know and can verbalize. Chronic stress kills neurons in the hippocampus and weakens the connections between neurons, which impairs the formation and retrieval of long-term memory.[11] The other area is our prefrontal lobe, responsible for executive functions, which literally regulates much of our behavior including recognizing the difference between good and bad and thinking about the consequences of our actions.

Chronic stress also affects the frontal cortex, which is responsible for postponement of gratification, self-discipline, long-term planning, and emotional regulation. It's the last part of the brain to fully mature and that doesn't happen until we're about twenty-five years old. Because this is the last part of the brain to fully develop, it is least constrained by genes and most sculpted by experience.[12] Chronic stress in this part of the brain causes the atrophy of neurons, disconnecting circuits that can result in poor decision making and impaired judgment.

Stress also works on the dopamine system which governs reward and pleasure. With chronic stress, the reward pathways get depleted of dopamine, and this takes away our ability to feel pleasure which can set us up for depression. Stress affects the part of the brain, the amygdala, where fear resides. Because stress feeds the amygdala, it actually gets bigger. Chronic stress creates a hyper-reactive amygdala.[13]

When we're stressed, we may find ourselves tongue-tied. This is because stress interferes with the neurological mechanisms that govern language production and perception. Under stress, the emotional circuits of the limbic brain become active, and the language circuits in the frontal lobe become less active.[14]

Short-Term Stress Can Be Productive

Although stress is most often seen in a negative light, without some stress we may not get anything done. Short-term stress can spur us to take necessary action and meet the challenges we face. A certain level of stress can improve performance, helping us to focus on the work at hand, like getting a report done by the deadline. It is well-documented that a certain level of stress can help us perform better, but once it gets too high, it gets in the way of performance. The goal is not to be stress-free, rather to keep the destructive effects of cumulative stress at bay.

Writing in *Stress without Distress*, Hans Selye in 1974 labeled the rush of adrenaline felt in the form of excitement or enthusiasm *eustress*, a kind of physiological arousal that can generate productive and vital energy.[15] Selye was also one of the first to advocate the need for stress management strategies to counteract the potentially harmful effects of stress. Occasional, moderate stress can be the impetus to act in creative and resourceful ways. As long as the stress is temporary, it is not necessarily harmful.

Robert Sapolsky, professor of neurological sciences at Stanford University and author of the well-known *Why Zebras Don't Get Ulcers*, says stress is good when it's only moderately stressful, short-lived, and happening in a context that feels safe overall.[16] Temporary, safe, and moderately stressful at most translate into *stimulation*. It's also what *play* is about. In play, we feel safe, and as a result, we are willing to give up some control and predictability, like on a roller-coaster ride. We find the surprising and stimulating aspects of stress exhilarating.

The brain is constantly responding to stress. Stress energy can motivate us to strive and get things done. It serves elite athletes, creative artists, and all kinds of high achievers well. They enjoy the burst of energy stress can provide, such as clear thinking, focus, and creative insight. According to Daniela Kaufer professor at UC Berkeley, short-lived stress can increase alertness and performance as well as boost memory. By encouraging the growth of stem cells that become brain cells, stress improves memory. Research has shown that short-term stress can lead to better mental and physical performance, especially if the individual is skilled in the task at hand, like delivering a speech or a musical performance, but only if the individual is not suffering from chronic stress.[17]

The research of Firdaus Dhabhar at Stanford University has likewise demonstrated the potentially protective effects of short-term stress, as well as the harmful effects of chronic stress.[18] He discovered that short-term stress could be harnessed to increase protection and performance.[19] His research showed stress can provide physiological benefits, including enhanced immunity.[20]

As part of the impetus for her recent book, *The Upside of Stress: Why Stress Is Good for You and How To Get Good at It*, Kelly McGonigal reports on a study that tracked 30,000 adults in the US for eight years.[21] They asked participants how much stress they had experienced in the last year as well as whether they believed that stress is harmful for your health. They found that those experiencing a lot of stress in the previous year had a 43 percent increased risk of dying. But that was only true for people who also believed that stress is harmful for your health. Surprisingly, they found those experiencing a lot of stress, but who also did not view stress as harmful, had the lowest risk of dying of anyone in the study, including people who had relatively little stress.

In support of the upside of stress, a study conducted at Harvard explored the role of mindsets—stress-is-enhancing verses stress-is-debilitating—in determining the response to stress.[22] In the study, participants were taught to rethink their responses to stress as helpful. They were told that a pounding heart was preparation for action and breathing faster gets more oxygen to the brain. For participants who learned to view their responses to stress as helpful for their performance, not only were they less anxious and more confident, their stress tests showed their blood vessels stayed relaxed and they had less cortisol in their systems.

McGonigal's message is to make stress your friend. When you change how you perceive stress, you can change your body's response to it. She tells us that the science of stress reveals that how you think about stress matters. Rising to the challenge of befriending your stress leads to a healthier response to stress. However, transforming our attitudes and beliefs is not an easy task.

Can We Learn to Manage Stress from Stressed-Out Lab Rats?

We have a lot to learn about stress from studying animal behavior.[23] But, unlike other mammals, humans can turn on the stress response with memories, emotions, and thoughts. This gives us humans a never-ending stream of opportunities to experience stress.

According to Sapolsky, experiments involving stressing out lab rats in a cage can suggest ways for humans to manage stress. Such experiments show that rats are less vulnerable to stress if they have something to distract themselves and have buddies. So having an outlet for stress-induced frustrations, like a hobby or a bunch of pals, is good. The rats were also less vulnerable to stress if they got *predictive information* and had a sense of control. However, regarding predictability and control, there are some caveats.

Sapolsky cautions that with predictive information, timing is everything in order to be protected from stress. A rat doesn't get an ulcer when the rat gets a ten-second warning before it is shocked, but if the warning light goes on one second before the shock occurs, it has no positive effect because there isn't time to adjust anything. If the warning light comes two minutes before, that will make it worse because the rat is waiting too long in anticipation—"Here it comes, here it comes, ..." When it comes to predictive information, there's only a narrow window where it helps.

In terms of a sense of control, it works when you're dealing with a mild to moderate stressor, but can backfire with major stressors. With lessor stressors, you know how much worse it could have been and can imagine that you had control over that improvement. But if it's a major stressor, you don't want to have an inflated sense of control, because then it sets you up to think that it's all your fault. In this case, what you really want is to minimize your sense of control by putting it in perspective and relinquishing a sense of responsibility. So a sense of control is only protective for mild to moderate stressors, it's worse for major ones.

Social rank can also be a source of stress, especially where rankings are unstable and people are jockeying for position. But social rank is not as important as social context. Sapolsky tells us if we have a choice between being a high-ranking baboon or a socially-affiliated one, we should definitely pick the one with friends, neighbors, and family, not the one with power, because that's the baboon who's going to have a healthier, longer life.

The implications for humans are that we are more likely to feel stressed if we:

- Have no outlets for coping with what's going on
- Lack a sense of control
- Don't pay attention to warnings or predictability
- Interpret things as getting worse
- Have nobody to soothe us

The flipside is what we can do to temper the effects of stress. Here's what we can do:

- Have outlets for dealing with our stress
- Do something in areas where we do have some control
- Be proactive when we can anticipate stress hitting us
- Construe things as temporary, not lasting forever
- Make sure we have plenty of people around to comfort us

Stress Is a Dynamic Transaction

Researchers who study stress consider stress a dynamic "transaction" between *perceived* resources and demands.[24] The key word here is perceived. The same event or situation for different individuals can be experienced as exhilarating, manageable, or overwhelming. When we encounter life demands, a transaction occurs where we weigh the perceived demands on us against our perceived capabilities for handling them. Simply stated, stress is what happens when life hands us more than we think we can handle.

When the scales tip and demands outweigh resources, stress sets in. Our resources include both internal and external resources, such as skill, patience, or energy. And the resources we have available may vary for any given point in time. This transactional view of stress underscores the active role an individual plays in responding to potential stressors.

Our *perception* of the balance between the things we have to do and our resources for getting them done is the critical variable that determines whether we will experience harmful stress levels. Our perceptions, or judgments, that lie between the comparison of existing demands and available resources are decisive factors in producing stress.

Our early life experiences will also play a role in how we judge our capacity to cope, and hence how we respond to stress. When we have a lot of stress in early life, we will be more vulnerable to the harmful effects of stress.

There's some good news for those of us getting on in years. Research clearly shows a pattern of decrease in daily stressors with age.[25] The decrease in stress ratings with age likely reflects a lifetime accumulation of experiences with which to make a comparison regarding the relative importance of individual stressors.

Daily stressors and hassles such as being stuck in traffic, losing keys, or arguing with family members may seem relatively inconsequential. But research shows that these minor stressors can have a more negative impact on well-being than bigger life events because of their regularity and cumulative effects.[26] While stress can take us by surprise, more often than not, it can be anticipated allowing us to take action in preparation.

Once stress strikes, the skills and strategies we have, or develop, for coping with stress govern how effective we will be in managing it. The more proactive we are in noticing our thoughts and judgments and using stress management strategies when stress begins, the more successful we will be in responding to the challenges stress brings.

Recognizing Your Body's Response to Stress

When demands pile up, life can seem like it's whirling out of control. When you're stressed, your body responds in an adaptive fashion, and your brain orders up a chemical surge, setting in motion the "fight-freeze-flight" survival reflex. Physiologically, a lot happens when you're experiencing the stress response.[27]

- Your heart pumps faster to get more blood to your muscles
- Your breathing becomes faster to move more oxygen to your blood
- Your muscles tense up to get ready for action
- Your blood pressure rises
- Your pupils dilate so more light can get in
- Metabolism speeds up to jolt you with a boost of energy
- Your immune system becomes suppressed
- You sweat more to cool off your body
- Blood vessels traveling to the gastrointestinal tract, hands, and feet constrict
- Stomach acid increases and digestive enzymes decrease
- Your arteries around your heart become strained
- Blood flow to the reasoning area of the brain diminishes as blood flows to the more primitive part of the brain

Your body is mobilizing to deal with a perceived threat. The nervous system basically has two modes—it fires up or it quiets down. We weren't meant to stay on red alert. Ongoing stress is unrelenting and can take over your life. It keeps sending out signals that you are exceeding the limits of your mind and body. Some of those signals include headaches, stomachaches, backaches, aching joints, or exhaustion. If you keep ignoring these early warning signs and don't take corrective action, the symptoms of the body will continue to worsen until you do pay attention, or, eventually, become immobilized by a stress-related disease.

More extreme signs of stress can take the form of being completely spent by the end of the day, lacking motivation to even get out of bed or go to work, preoccupation with negative thoughts, or persistent feelings of anger and resentment. Experiencing these feelings may signal burnout is not far away.[28] When you're feeling overwhelmed and emotionally exhausted, you have fewer inner resources to access, making it easier to fall into habits and lifestyle practices that only make stress worse.

Reactions to stress are pervasive. They permeate the way you think, feel, and act. Stress can thwart your desire for social interaction with friends and family while encouraging a sense of loneliness and an overall negative attitude. Stress can make you feel cranky, finding yourself yelling at others for no reason. When stressed, you may feel frustrated, losing your temper quickly, and often. You might feel antsy so you feel like running away, or you start to feel like you can't deal with even the smallest problem.

Building Up Your Defenses against Stress

Decades of research on regulating emotions validate the importance of tempering your initial response before it takes on a life of its own. Conditioned emotional responses unfold quickly so you need to be an "early responder" to limit the intensity and duration of a stressful experience. By paying attention to your physical sensations as soon as they kick in you can learn to intervene sooner and sooner.

The key is learning to read your body's signs by becoming more attuned to your early physical cues and using them as your signal to interrupt the stress response and precipitate its counterpart, the relaxation response. Check for bodily sensations such as a pounding heart, shortness of breath, feeling hot, tensing muscles, queasy stomach, clenched teeth, or sweaty palms. Things start to speed up, so notice if your heart's racing, you're breathing fast, you're starting to talk faster, or you're shoving food down. These are your telltale signs transmitting the message to intercept the stress response. You need to be able to turn on the relaxation response at the moment stress strikes to restore an inner state of calm.

It's not only the obvious big stresses, it's the little stresses that often go unrecognized that can take their toll. In a given day, a lot of small hassles can accumulate rapidly. A cascade of little annoyances can easily gather momentum. To build up defenses against stress you need to have a repertoire of immediate stress busters at your disposal so you can be proactive to insulate yourself from the potentially destructive effects of stress.

Below are ten evidenced-based "stress busters" gleaned from research along with why they work. These mindful moments literally take just seconds and should be part of your daily mindful moments practice because not a day goes by without stressful moments. These instant stress busters offer ways to quickly access the body's relaxation response when stress launches. When your stress is more intense, try combining two or more of these strategies. For example, while taking a few deep breaths, hold your hand on your heart and repeat some calming self-statements. Using these strategies early on can prevent a situation from escalating, help you keep your cool in the heat of the moment, and facilitate coping more effectively with a full-blown emotional flare up.

10 Mindful Moments when Stress Hits:
Instant Stress Busters

1. Take 3-4 deep breaths. This is the most immediate way to reduce stress because it acts like a control switch to shut down your body's stress response in just 6–10 seconds.

2. Place your hand on your heart and breathe deeply while remembering a time when you felt loved by someone. Just the thought is enough to release oxytocin which restores physiological equilibrium returning you to a calm state.

3. Apply pressure between your thumb and forefinger. This spot is close to bundles of nerves and pressing on them relaxes the nervous system which ramps up when you're stressed. Hold for 30 seconds.

4. Take some action, no matter how small, where you can exercise some control to reduce your stress. Taking action on your own behalf shifts you out of a sense of helplessness to regain a sense of control. This might be just walking away for a brief timeout or making a simple request for what you need.

5. Rub your hands together briskly to open up the blood vessels. Because stress pulls the blood out of your toes and fingers and sends it to your internal organs, this will jar your brain out of its stress response.

6. Repeat calming self-talk such as, *This too will pass, I am staying calm,* or *I can handle this.* This soothing talk will keep your mind from revving up interrupting your habitual negative chatter.

7. Visualize the last time you were laughing with a good friend. You'll break into a genuine smile which will lower your heart rate and lead to quicker recovery from your stressful event.

8. Use "time-distancing" by asking yourself how you might feel about what's happening a year from now. Continue to move the timeframe to a month, a week, a day, an hour. This reduces stress by helping you put it in perspective and view it with a broader lens.

9. Pop a piece of gum into your mouth. Chewing loosens jaw muscles, which hold stress, and the rhythmic act of chewing may increase blood flow to your brain.

10. Think worst-case scenario to alert you that you're overreacting, which fuels stress. Take the thought to a ludicrous point—*I'm stuck in traffic, I'm going to be way late, ... I'll probably get fired, I'll never work again.* You'll feel your anxiety dissipating as you realize you blew the situation way out of proportion.

THE RESEARCH FINDINGS

Stress and Physical Health, Mental Health and Cognitive Capacity

- Stress affects the health of our heart and leads to a higher risk of dying prematurely.[29]
- Stress lowers heart rate variability to render the heart less responsive which makes it more vulnerable.[30]
- Chronic stress makes you more prone to illness.[31]
- A high level of stress weakens your immune system, the body's natural defense system.[32]
- Stress plays a role in skin disorders, such as eczema, and respiratory problems like asthma.[33]
- Stress is linked to gastrointestinal problems. We have trillions of micro-organisms residing in the gut, and studies show that stress tips our microbial balance. This puts us at risk for dysbiosis (a shift away from normal gut microbiota diversity), which strips us of one of our prime defenses against infectious disease.[34]
- Stress may accelerate cellular aging.[35]
- Chronic stress has been shown to harm DNA by shortening telomeres, the protective caps on the ends of chromosomes.[36]
- Stress is associated with a higher risk of mortality in healthy individuals, as well as those chronically-ill.[37]
- Psychological stress can acutely provoke increases in inflammation even in otherwise healthy individuals.[38]
- High stress, especially chronic levels, is a strong contributor to the development of symptoms of anxiety and depression, as well as leads to subsequent clinical depression.[39]
- Chronic stress levels lead to other forms of psychopathology.[40]
- Continuous stress can undermine resilience, hope, and the capacity to forgive.[41]
- Stress maintained over long periods harms our memory.[42]
- When we experience stress, *mind wandering*, the tendency for our attention to drift to thoughts that are irrelevant to the task at hand, is increased.[43]
- Stress limits the ability to be creative, see situations clearly, think outside the box, solve problems skillfully, and make good decisions.[44]

CHAPTER 14

The Mind-Body Connection
Is a Two-Way Street

Sometimes your joy is the source of your smile,
but sometimes your smile can be the source of your joy.
–THICH NHAT HANH

Our mind and body are intimately connected, and that connection is a two-way street. Emotions bring on physiological reactions. The reverse is also true—changing your physiology can change how you feel. When you feel sad, you may find yourself moving at a snail's pace. And if you're feeling anxious, you may find yourself buzzing around aimlessly. When you're elated you may literally be jumping for joy.

While emotions are generally thought of as happening to us, research shows we can generate some of the same physiological changes that occur during a spontaneous emotion by adopting the congruent bodily change first. There is ample evidence to support the idea that we have biologically-wired automatic mimicking tendencies.[1]

When we view a facial expression, we produce a similar facial expression at an unconscious level. Mimicry is considered to be an automatic process that is difficult, if not impossible, to suppress.

Research shows we mimic emotional facial expressions automatically even when we are told not to move our facial muscles.[2] When Swedish researchers showed a picture of someone smiling and asked subjects to frown, their expressions went directly to imitating what they saw, and it took a conscious effort to turn their smile upside down.[3] This is even true when the emotional faces are presented subliminally.[4]

When we adopt or produce emotion-specific gestures, facial expressions, or even postures, we not only tend to experience the associated emotions, but our behavior as well as our preferences, judgments, and attitudes toward others are implicitly influenced.[5] Just as more than two decades of research has shown, when we feel happy we smile, and reciprocally, when we smile it can boost our mood, the same is true for our body language. It's important to pay attention to our posture because it not only affects our emotional state, it also changes the chemicals in our brain. Research shows that just sitting in a hunched position for two minutes starts to increase the stress hormone cortisol.[6]

Conversely, when we are feeling self-confident, we strut around like a peacock and have a zip in our step. Our posture not only affects our emotional state, it can have an impact on the outcomes we create. As we saw in Amy Cuddy's YouTube video that went viral, by adopting a power stance, we can increase our performance and sense of self-worth.[7] Cuddy, who has spent her career studying how body language affects how others see us and even how we see ourselves, has shown how "power posing" can make us feel confident even if we don't. When people adopted a Wonder Woman or Superman power pose just before a job interview, they considerably raised their chances for success. Lifting yourself up and standing with your hands on your hips, head up and chest out for just two minutes decreases cortisol and increases testosterone.

The Benefits of Touch

A friendly touch can help calm us down and buffer our stress response. A caring touch increases the release of oxytocin, the brain's direct and immediate antidote to the stress hormone cortisol.

Oxytocin is the neurotransmitter of the "calm and connect" response and accounts for our feelings of safety and trust, connection and belonging.[8] It is also called the "love hormone" and is activated during physical intimacy and maternal bonding. Oxytocin is released in response to the activation of sensory nerves in connection with positive, warm interactions between humans.[9] It is also released by interactions between humans and animals, in particular dogs.[10] Oxytocin is released in response to several kinds of massage, during sexual activity, and when we eat pleasing food.[11] The surging of oxytocin makes us feel more trusting and connected, and the cascade of electrical impulses slows our heart rate and lowers our blood pressure, making us feel less stressed and more soothed.

Light Touch Lowers Stress

Oxytocin is released when individuals of all ages touch each other, as long as the relationship is perceived as positive. Any warm, loving touch can release oxytocin—hugs, snuggles, holding hands, partner dancing, cuddles with a pet, massage, and bodywork. A recent article reviewing the research on touch concluded that the anti-stress effects of oxytocin are particularly strong when it is released in response to "low intensity" stimulation of the skin, such as touch, stroking, light pressure on the skin, or warm temperature.[12]

Safe touch is the fast-track way to calm down stress, even extreme stress.[13] Oxytocin can even be released by seeing, smelling, hearing, or by merely thinking of a beloved person.[14] We can activate the release of oxytocin by connecting with, or even just remembering connections with others. Neuroscientists have demonstrated that even remembering or imagining someone we love, or whom we feel loved by, is enough to release small but regular doses of oxytocin.[15] This can include feeling "held" by a spiritual figure or religious deity as well. Repeated exposure to the people with whom we feel close social bonds can condition the release of oxytocin so that merely being in their presence, or even just thinking about them, can trigger a dose of the good feelings that oxytocin brings.[16]

A hug, and the longer the better, calms down the brain's alarm system. According to UCLA neuroscientist Alex Korb, when people hug for twenty seconds or more, the oxytocin released serves to create a stronger bond and connection.[17] Other research shows getting five hugs a day for four weeks substantially increases happiness. Korb reports research indicating that touching can also make you more persuasive, increase team performance, and even boost math skills.

Hugging can combat feelings of loneliness that often arise as we get older. A retirement home in New York conducted a study implementing a program called "Embraceable You."[18] The idea was to encourage cross-generational contact and touch between residents and staff members in order to improve the residents' well-being. The results showed considerable benefits for residents who were touched or hugged three or more times a day. They had more energy, felt less depressed, were better able to concentrate, and got more restful sleep than their less-hugged counterparts.

Self-touching is one of the prime ways to release oxytocin. The release of oxytocin that normally occurs in response to closeness in supportive relationships can to a certain extent be mimicked by stroking and massaging our skin. Self-touch can serve as an alternative pathway for positive self-soothing and stress relief. Mark Waldman's research reveals that self-stroking of the palms and arms stimulates the self-awareness areas of the frontal lobes much more than when we are touched by others. It only takes about a minute for its effect to take hold. In fact, brain scans show that if you remain relaxed and stroke your palms and arms while having a negative experience you can stop the formation of that memory.[19]

The HeartMath System, based on how the heart communicates with the body and brain on multiple levels, offers simple tools that focus on teaching how to listen to, and follow, intuitive information from the heart.[20] One of the core tools is the Hand-on-the-Heart practice. (This practice is officially called the The Quick Coherence technique in the HeartMath System.) By doing this practice you are actually doing three things: combining touch, deep breathing, and creating a felt sense of safety. Your hand on your heart begins to activate the release of oxytocin very quickly. Deep breathing brings on board the "rest and digest" system, and feeling a sense of safety or love brought about by recalling a time that has a special emotional tag interrupts the body's stress response.

Hand-on-the-Heart Practice
Place your hand on your heart and begin to breathe deeply and slowly focusing your attention on the area around your heart. After a few breaths, bring to mind a time when you felt really good. It might be a moment of being with someone who loves you unconditionally or someone with whom you feel completely safe and accepted. Now try to re-experience the feeling by sensing in your body the positive feelings and sensations that come up with that memory. Stay with that feeling for about 30 seconds.

Smile and the Whole World Smiles with You
Feeling good makes you smile, but it also works the other way around—smiling can actually make you feel better. Not only do we smile when we feel happy, we feel happy when we smile. It turns out, we have a "facial-feedback loop." By deliberately putting a smile on your face, you turn on the same brain chemistry as if you are smiling spontaneously because you feel pleasure. The brain doesn't know the difference between a real smile driven by a positive emotion and a fake smile because it's merely interpreting the position of your facial muscles. There is a direct link between the physical action and the emotional reading.

Brain research shows that even if you are not aware that you're smiling, messages are being sent to your brain that activate the same brain chemistry associated with pleasure just as if you were deliberately smiling. Paul Ekman, notably the most preeminent researcher on emotions and their relation to facial expressions, conducted research showing that smiling registers in the area of the brain where endorphins are produced.[21] Endorphins are naturally-occurring opiates that both relieve pain and give a sense of pleasure and well-being.

While earlier research showed that not just any smile will do, the smile had to be genuine, later research found that just the act of smiling can have the same effect. Beginning in the 1990s, researchers identified that only genuine smiles that involve crucial eye muscles activate brain areas associated with enjoyment.[22] This so-called Duchenne smile is named after a 19th century French physician who was the first to identify that half-hearted smiles only involve mouth muscles while smiles involving certain muscles around the eye are "put into play by the sweet emotions of the soul."[23]

Researchers comparing brain activity in those spontaneously expressing the Duchenne smile with those expressing an inauthentic smile lacking the crucial eye muscles, showed that the authentic smile produced greater activation in the left hemisphere, the seat of positive emotions.[24] Later research revealed that asking people to simulate a Duchenne smile activated the same brain regions as a spontaneous smile.[25] In other words, the same type of brain activity occurs regardless of whether a Duchenne smile is spontaneous or voluntarily simulated. These findings indicate that by simply smiling, even if you don't feel like it, you get your brain to emit a feel-good response.

While this research showed that smiling can affect emotions, a more recent study showed that smiling can actually influence our physiological state by leading to a quicker heart rate recovery from stressful activities.[26] In the study, participants were trained to hold chopsticks in such a way that they engaged facial muscles used to create a neutral facial expression, a surface smile, or a Duchenne smile. (Using chopsticks forced participants to smile without being aware that they were doing so.) Compared to participants who held neutral facial expressions, participants who held both types of smiles had lower heart rate levels after recovery from stress-induced tasks, with genuine smiles producing more significant results. These findings indicate that smiling, with or without awareness, during a brief period of stress can have a direct impact on heart rate levels, which can help to reduce the intensity of the body's stress response.

Previous research had shown that participants who spontaneously smiled during stress returned to resting heart rate levels more rapidly than did their non-smiling counterparts.[27] The results of this new study extend the positive impact smiling can produce regardless of whether a person knowingly smiles or actually feels happy. In addition to bringing on positive emotions and speeding up recovery from stressful episodes, authentic smiles may open you up to being more receptive. Barbara Fredrickson and colleagues found that frequently displaying Duchenne smiles was associated with more flexible thinking and taking a broader perspective, making you better able to see the "big picture."[28]

Since a genuine smile is an involuntary response, it's hard to fake. Not everyone can voluntarily contract the eye muscle that raises the cheeks to produce crow's feet wrinkles at will. This is the signature movement of a heartfelt smile. According to Ekman, while most people can't come up with a genuine smile on demand, they can be trained to do so.[29] Only a sizeable minority of people can deliberately produce a Duchenne smile. Research suggests that somewhere around 40 to 50 percent of us have this capacity.[30] Duchenne smiles occur most often when we are actually experiencing a positive emotion. Berkeley researchers concluded that 95 percent of people displaying Duchenne smiles are experiencing authentic happiness.[31] This suggests that only 5 percent of people are able to fake happiness with this smile. In a study where participants were face-to face and asked to talk about a happy event in their lives, they spent only 6 percent of the time showing a non-Duchenne smile.[32]

The Many Benefits of Displaying a Genuine Smile

Researchers studying smile intensity have found that bigger smiles predict some important outcomes, such as lower divorce rates, life satisfaction, as well as longevity. They assess "smile intensity" and presumably authenticity by combining three measures of muscle action that crease the corners of the mouth, squint eyes, and raise the cheeks. Researchers found that women with bigger smiles in their college yearbook pictures had lower divorce rates and were more satisfied with their marriages 30 years later.[33] They were also more content, nurturing, and compassionate than those with lesser smiles or none at all.

Another study looking at smiles in photographs found that the larger the smile, the less likely divorce was later in life.[34] Those with the smallest smiles or no smiles, were five times more likely to be divorced. Similarly, studying photos of professional baseball players for smile intensity, researchers found that those with the biggest smiles lived an average of seven years longer than those who weren't smiling.

> RESEARCH RECAP: Get in the habit of smiling more and you'll not only boost your mood, you'll become more capable of putting things in perspective to see the big picture. Smile and you'll be able to snap out of a negative repetitive loop more quickly, be better able to handle stress, and recover sooner from a stressful event.

Smiling is Contagious

We've all experienced coming out of a bad mood with an encouraging smile from a friend. And when a child smiles at us, we find ourselves automatically smiling back. Smiling is contagious because we have a built-in empathy response that is part of the wiring of the human brain.

Much research substantiates the finding that the perceivers of smiles automatically mimic them. Those viewing a smile mimic a similar facial display at an unconscious level.[35] Perceivers will smile at almost imperceptible levels when exposed to pictures of smiling. When we view a smile, our lip muscle contracts to lift the corners of the mouth within 200 milliseconds.[36] Smiling is so contagious that even when researchers show a picture of someone smiling and ask observers to frown, their expressions go directly to a smile.[37]

In a study where participants viewed *true* or *false* smiles and were asked to rate their genuineness, participants holding a pencil in their mouths blocking their ability to mimic the smiles could not tell true from false smiles.[38] Apparently, being able to simulate the smiles they saw was a crucial cue for determining whether a smile was genuine.

The infectiousness of a smile can even make others happy. When people perceive smiles, they experience them as rewarding. Research has linked the reward areas of the brain with the perception of smiling faces.[39] The saying, "Smile and the whole world smiles with you," actually has some research clout.

Just seeing a child's smile creates a short-term high more so than getting a bunch of money or munching chocolate. To gauge the effects of various factors for creating a short-term high, researchers measured brain and heart activity to create a "mood-boosting value." Participants were shown photos of friends, family, and loved ones smiling and given money and chocolate. Those shown a child's smile had the same level of stimulation as they would have had from eating 2,000 chocolate bars or receiving $16,000 in cash. The researchers' subsequent survey found that seeing a smile was more likely to create a short-term high than sex, eating chocolate, and shopping, ranked in that order behind smiling.[40]

There is ample research indicating that genuine smiles have a greater impact than insincere smiles. Much research has been conducted over the last several decades comparing fake and genuine smiles. Yale University psychology professor Marianne LaFrance reports in *Lip Service: Smiles in Life, Death, Trust, Lies, Work, Memory, Sex, and Politics*, a genuine smile evokes an emotional current in observers and literally lights up the reward centers in the brain.[41] An authentic smile provides a distinguishable signal to observers. Most of us can readily distinguish an authentic smile from an inauthentic smile. We instinctively recognize the difference between the two types of smiles.

We assign an extensive list of positive attributes to those we see displaying genuine smiles. An authentic smile not only influences how we evaluate smiles, it also affects how we judge others' likeability, authenticity, and trustworthiness.[42] Research reveals that when we observe genuine smiles we perceive the person smiling as more attractive, extroverted, spontaneous, friendly, and authentic.[43] We also attribute positive attributes to those displaying genuine smiles, considering them to be more sincere, kind, and generous than those displaying only surface smiles.[44] We judge those displaying authentic smiles to be more intelligent, competent, as well as more employable.[45] Those displaying authentic smiles also elicit *action tendencies* in others such that they are more willing to approach, cooperate, and trust them.[46]

RESEARCH RECAP: Smiling affects how we feel, has a contagious effect on others, and influences the positive qualities others ascribe to us. When we display a genuine smile, others think well of us, finding us more likable, authentic, kind, generous, and competent. Smiling more can affect our level of life satisfaction and may even influence how long we live.

Put a Smile on Your Face

You don't have to feel like smiling, just smile anyway, even if you're feeling miserable. While a forced smile can activate brain chemistry associated with pleasure and well-being, you glean the most benefit from a heartfelt smile, one that is actually accompanied by a positive emotion.

Even a smile that starts out fake when followed up by a pleasant thought or memory, or a feeling of anticipation, can spark a genuine smile. So when you put a smile on your face, think of something that actually makes you feel happy. When you access a joyful memory, it brings on a real smile. You can turn a forced smile into a real smile by replaying a memory that makes you feel happy. The mere act of smiling can act as a catalyst to summon pleasurable memories from the recent past or long ago. When you're thinking of that special moment, you'll be smiling an authentic smile.

Try some of these mindful moments to increase your smile quotient.

10 Mindful Moments to Get More Smiles into Your Day

1. Scroll through on your smartphone some of your favorite pictures of those you care about with big smiles on their faces, and smile. First, you'll need to create a designated folder with 15 to 20 of your favorite smiling pictures. You might even include pictures of strangers that move you, like a mother smiling at her baby.

2. Plan one nice thing you will do for yourself today no matter how small. See yourself doing it, and smile.

3. Take a minute to savor a happy memory. You might recapture the happiest period in your life, revel in one of your most pleasurable moments, or bask in an early memory of being held in your mother's or father's arms.

4. Make a mental list of all the people who appreciate what you do, and smile.

5. Recall something you did recently that made someone else's day just a little, or a whole lot, better. Take time to relish in that good feeling.

6. Remind yourself of something later in the day or in the near future you are looking forward to. Be grateful that your time is coming, and smile.

7. Take a moment to remember someone else's act of kindness toward you—and smile in appreciation.

8. Close your eyes and visualize all the people who care about you lined up in front of you. Keep thinking of people to add to the line. Feel that pleasing state of receiving all their care and affection. Hold that feeling for about 10 seconds then open your eyes and you will feel a smile rolling across your face.

9. Whenever you catch yourself frowning, scowling, or rolling your eyes switch to a smile. Then follow it up with a shift in attitude by conjuring up a pleasant thought. And remember to engage those muscles around your eyes.

10. When you're really in a frump, and can't seem to muster a smile, bite on a pencil or chopstick. Then think of a loved one and recall a time you saw him or her laughing and your smile will turn genuine.

Last Words

If you take one message from this book it's to be deliberate and intentional about practicing what you want to be front and center in your life. Without conscious intention you can easily go through your day on auto pilot plodding along mindlessly.

The daily challenges of life are endless and a steady flow of mindful moments can provide the balance to keep you from becoming overwhelmed and slipping into negativity. Many mindful moments will add up to significant changes over time. Don't underestimate the colossal power of small daily acts.

If you want to be less stressed, more positive, and happier bring more mindfulness into every day with a mindful moment practice. A daily dose of mindful moments will go a long way to make your day, and can eventually change your life.

Comparison of Evidence Chart

This chart compares the evidence for mindfulness meditation with the evidence for positive emotions/positive emotion-enhancing activities and for cognitive behavioral therapy for the top 20 areas that have been studied for any of these categories. The chart indicates which of these three categories has the best evidence, and where the evidence is good, limited, and insufficient.

Comparison of Evidence for Mindfulness Meditation (MM), Positive Emotions/Positive Emotion-Enhancing Activities (PE/PEA) & Cognitive Behavioral Therapy (CBT)

	MM	PE/PEA	CBT
1. Pain	+		
2. Stress	+	*	+
3. Anxiety	+	+	*
4. Depression	+	+	*
5. Attentional Focus	*		
6. Emotional Regulation	+	+	*
7. Optimism		*	
8. Positive Emotional States		*	
9. Positive Mood		*	+
10. Happiness		*	
11. Life Satisfaction		*	
12. Compassion	+[a]		
13. Resilience	–	*	–
14. Cardiovascular Disease		*	
15. Immune Function	–	–	
16. Inflammation	–	–	
17. Longevity		*	
18. Creativity	–	+	
19. Work Performance	+	*	
20. Sleep	–		*

[a]For compassion meditation only
*Best evidence   +Good evidence   –Limited evidence
Blank=Insufficient evidence/Not Studied

Acknowledgments

There are so many people who have contributed to making this book a reality. I want to extend my gratitude to the thousands of teachers whom I have taught and who have taught me so much along the way about optimism, compassion, and generosity with all that they give every day. I am forever grateful for my husband, Chuck Bloom, who is my tower of strength and is by my side through the best and the worst. I want to thank my friends and family members for their continuous support and validation. They humored me trying out countless mindful moments, endured endless discussions about the value of a mindful moment practice, and tirelessly listened to me rant and rave about all the hype about mindfulness meditation. I am especially grateful to my sister, Constance Witham, whose background as an artist, English teacher, and librarian was invaluable for making choices about the book design, reviewing editorial changes, and scouring the internet to find the perfect quote for each chapter. I want to express my appreciation to my other siblings, Alison Witzmann, Deborah Block, and Edward DiBona, whom I can always count on to champion whatever I choose to do. I would like to extend a special thanks to my stepdaughter, Laura Bloom, who supported and inspired me every step of the way. Their love and encouragement got me through the times I was about to give up.

Many thanks to Madalyn Stone whose editing skills completely transformed the book to make it more appealing to a general audi-

213

ence. Her editing and restructuring improved the book immeasurably. I want to thank Christy Collins of Constellation Book Services, not only for her creative talent, but for her willingness to make change after change until we finally got it just right. Her interior and exterior design skills produced a book more visually appealing than I could ever have imagined. And finally, I am grateful for my own good health and perseverance and for the opportunity to share the notion of a daily dose of mindful moments with the world.

Notes

Chapter 1: My Journey to a Daily Mindful Moment Practice

1. Wieder, M. (2016). *Dream: Clarify and create what you want.* Las Vegas, NV: Century Publishing.
2. Carver, C., & Scheier, M. (1998). *On the self-regulation of behavior.* New York, NY: Cambridge University Press.
3. Chang, H. H., & Pham, M. T. (2013). Affect as a decision-making system of the present. *Journal of Consumer Research, 40*(1), 42-63.
4. Kabat-Zinn, J. (1994). *Wherever you go, there you are.* New York, NY: Hyperion.

Chapter 2: Mindfulness and Its Promise

1. Langer, E. J. (1989). *Mindfulness.* Reading, MA: Addison-Wesley.
2. Langer, E. J. (2014). *Mindfulness, 25th Anniversary Edition.* Philadelphia, PA: Da Capo Lifelong Books.
3. Kabat-Zinn (1994), op. cit. (See ch. 1, note 4).
4. Jha, A. P., Baime, M. J., & Sreenivasan, K. K. (2009). Attention and mindfulness training. In R. E. Ingram (Ed.), *The international encyclopedia of depression* (pp. 37-40). New York, NY: Springer Publishing.
5. (1) Kornfield, J. (2009). *The wise heart: A guide to the universal teachings of Buddhist psychology.* New York, NY: Bantam. (2) Salzberg, S. (1997). *Lovingkindness: The revolutionary art of happiness.* Boston, MA: Shambhala.

Chapter 3: What Do We Know about Mindfulness Meditation?

1. Kabat-Zinn (1994), op. cit. (See ch. 1, note 4).
2. Eisendrath, S. (2012, May 31). Applying Mindfulness-Based Cognitive Therapy to treatment. *University of California Television (UCTV).* Retrieved from https://youtu.be/5eQ3MWz4yrI
3. Seligman, M. (2016, May 12). Positive psychology with Martin Seligman. Retrieved from https://youtu.be/HHosssQzQGg
4. Tang, Y. Y., Rothbart, M. K., & Posner, M. I. (2012). Neural correlates of establishing, maintaining and switching brain states. *Trends in Cognitive Sciences, 16*, 330-337.

5. (1) Dickenson, J., Berkman, E. T., Arch, J., & Lieberman, M. D. (2013). Neural correlates of focused attention during a brief mindfulness induction. *Social, Cognitive & Affective Neuroscience, 8*, 40-47. (2) Jha, A. P., Krompinger, J., & Baime, M. J. (2007). Mindfulness training modifies subsystems of attention, *Cognitive, Affective, & Behavioral Neuroscience, 7*(2), 109-119. (3) Tang, Y. Y., Ma, Y., Wang, J., Fan, Y., Feng, S., Lu, Q.,...Posner, M. I. (2007). Short-term meditation training improves attention and self-regulation. *Proceedings of the National Academy of Sciences, 104*(43), 17152-17156.

6. (1) Tang, Y. Y., & Posner, M. I. (2013). Special issue on mindfulness neuroscience. *Social, Cognitive & Affective Neuroscience, 8*(1), 1-3. (2) Travis, F., & Shear, J. (2010). Focused attention, open monitoring and automatic self-transcending: Categories to organize meditations from Vedic, Buddhist and Chinese traditions. *Consciousness and Cognition, 19*, 1110-1118.

7. Tang et al. (2012), op. cit. (See ch. 3, note 4).

8. (1) Davidson, R. J., & Begley, S. (2012). *The emotional life of your brain: How its unique patterns affect the way you think, feel, and live—and how you can change them.* New York, NY: Hudson Street Press. (2) Siegel, D. J. (2010). *Mindsight: The new science of personal transformation.* New York, NY: Bantam Books.

9. (1) Farb, N. A. S., Segal, Z. V., Mayberg, H., Bean, J., McKeon, D., Fatima, Z., & Anderson, A. K. (2007). Attending to the present: Mindfulness meditation reveals distinct neural modes of self-reference. *Social, Cognitive & Affective Neuroscience, 2*, 313-322. (2) Fox, K. C., Nijeboer, S., Dixon, M. L., Floman, J. L., Ellamil, M., Rumak, S. P.,...Christoff, K. (2014). Is meditation associated with altered brain structure? A systematic review and meta-analysis of morphometric neuroimaging in meditation practitioners. *Neuroscience & Biobehavioral Reviews, 43*, 48-73.

10. (1) Lin, Y., Fisher, M. E., Roberts, S. M. M. & Moser, J. S. (2016). Deconstructing the emotion regulatory properties of mindfulness: An electrophysiological investigation. *Frontiers in Human Neuroscience, 10*, 451. (2) Boccia, M., Piccardi, L., & Guariglia, P. (2015). The meditative mind: A comprehensive meta-analysis of MRI studies. *Biomed Research International*, 1-11. (3) Brewer, J. A., & Garrison, K. A. (2014). The posterior cingulate cortex as a plausible mechanistic target of meditation: findings from neuroimaging. *Annals of the New York Academy of Sciences, 1307*, 19-27.

11. (1) Taren, A. A., Gianaros, P. J., Greco, C. M., Lindsay, E. K., Fairgrieve, A., Brown, K. W.,...Creswell, J. D. (2015). Mindfulness meditation training alters stress-related amygdala resting state functional connectivity: A randomized controlled trial. *Social, Cognitive & Affective Neuroscience, 10*(12), 1758-1768. (2) Tang, Y. Y., Hölzel, B. K., & Posner, M. I. (2015). The neuroscience of mindfulness meditation. *Nature Reviews Neuroscience, 16*, 213-225.

12. Davidson, R. (2016, May 3). Change your brain by transforming your mind. Center for Complementary and Integrative Health (NCCIH). Retrieved from https://videocast.nih.gov/Summary.asp?File=19659&bhcp=1

13. (1) Buhle, J. T., Silvers, J. A., Wager, T. D., Lopez, R., Onyemekwu, C., Kober, H.,...Ochsner, K. N. (2014). Cognitive reappraisal of emotion: A meta-analysis of human neuroimaging studies. *Cerebral Cortex, 24*(11), 2981-2990. (2) Goldin, P. R., McRae, K., Ramel, W., & Gross, J. J. (2008). The neural bases of emotion regulation: Reappraisal and suppression of negative emotion. *Biological Psychiatry, 63*, 577-588. (3) Ochsner, K., & Gross, J. (2008). Emotion regulation: Insights from social cognitive and affective neuroscience. *Current Directions in Psychological Science, 17*, 153-158.

14. Jha, A. P., Stanley, E. A., Kiyonaga, A., Wong, L., & Gelfand, L. (2010). Examining the protective effects of mindfulness training on working memory capacity and affective experience. *Emotion, 10*(1), 54-64.

15. Mrazek, M. D., Franklin, M. S., Phillips, D. T., Baird, B., & Schooler, J. W. (2013). Mindfulness training improves working memory capacity and GRE performance while reducing mind wandering. *Psychological Science, 24*, 776-781.

16. Morrison, A. B., Goolsarran, M., Rogers, S. L., & Jha, A. P. (2014). Taming a wandering attention: Short-form mindfulness training in student cohorts. *Frontiers in Human Neuroscience, 7*, 897.

17. Good, D. J., Lyddy, C. J., Glomb, T. M., Bono, J. E., Brown, K. W., Duffy, M. K.,...Lazar, S. W. (2016). Contemplating mindfulness at work: An integrative review. *Journal of Management, 42*(1), 114-142.

18. Colzato, L. S., Ozturk, A., & Hommel, B. (2012). Meditate to create: the impact of focused-attention and open-monitoring training on convergent and divergent thinking. *Frontiers in Psychology, 3*(116), 1-5.

19. Baas, M., Nevicka, B., & Ten Velden, F. S. (2014). Specific mindfulness skills differentially predict creative performance. *Personality and Social Psychology Bulletin, 40*(9), 1092-1106.

20. Black, D. S., & Slavich, G. M. (2016). Mindfulness meditation and the immune system: a systematic review of randomized controlled trials. *Annals of the New York Academy of Sciences, 1373*(1), 13-24.

21. Ellis, J. G., Perlis, M. L., Neale, L. F., Espie, C. A., & Bastien, C. H. (2012). The natural history of insomnia: focus on prevalence and incidence of acute insomnia. *Journal of Psychiatric Research, 46*(10), 1278-1285.

22. Skinner, G. (February, 2017). Secrets to a great night's sleep. *Consumer Reports, 82*(2), 6.

23. Trauer, J. M., Qian, M. Y., Doyle, J. S., Rajaratnam, S. M., & Cunnington, D. (2015). Cognitive behavioral therapy for chronic insomnia: A systematic review and meta-analysis. *Annals of Internal Medicine, 163*(3), 191-204.

24. (1) Cheng, S. K., & Dizon, J. (2012). Computerised cognitive behavioural therapy for insomnia: a systematic review and meta-analysis. *Psychotherapy and Psychosomatics, 81*(4), 206-216. (2) Seyffert, M., Lagisetty, P., Landgraf, J., Chopra, V., Pfeiffer, P. N., Conte, M. L., & Rogers, M. M. (2016). Internet-delivered cognitive behavioral therapy to treat insomnia: A systematic review and meta-analysis. *Plos ONE, 11*(2), 1-21.

25. Qaseem, A., Kansagara, D., Forciea, M. A., Cooke, M., & Denberg, T. D. (2016). Management of chronic insomnia disorder in adults: a clinical practice guideline from the American College of Physicians. *Annals of Internal Medicine, 165*(2), 125-133.

26. Davidson, R. J., & Kaszniak, A. W. (2015). Conceptual and methodological issues in research on mindfulness and meditation. *American Psychologist, 70*(7), 581-592.

27. Dahl, C. J., Lutz, A., & Davidson, R. J. (2015). Reconstructing and deconstructing the self: cognitive mechanisms in meditation practice, *Trends in Cognitive Sciences, 19*(9), 515-523.

28. Davidson (2016), op. cit. (See ch. 3, note 12).

29. Goyal, M., Singh, S., Sibinga, E. M. S., Gould, N. F., Rowland-Seymour, A., Sharma, R.,...Haythornthwaite, J. A. (2014). Meditation programs for psychological stress and well-being: A systematic review and meta-analysis. *JAMA Internal Medicine, 174*, 357-368.

30. Coronado-Montoya, S., Levis, A. W., Kwakkenbos, L., Steele, R. J., Turner, E. H., & Thombs, B. D. (2016). Reporting of positive results in randomized controlled trials of mindfulness-based mental health interventions. *Plos ONE, 11*(4), 1-18.

31. Hamilton, D. R. (2010). *How your mind can heal your body*. Carlsbad, CA: Hay House.

32. Burke, A., Chun Nok, L., Stussman, B., & Hui, Y. (2017). Prevalence and patterns of use of mantra, mindfulness and spiritual meditation among adults in the United States. *BMC Complementary & Alternative Medicine, 17*, 1-18.

33. Goyal et al. (2014), op. cit. (See ch. 3, note 29).

34. Zeng, X., Chiu, C. P. K., Wang, R., Oei, T. P. S. & Leung, F. Y. K. (2015). The effect of loving-kindness meditation on positive emotions: a meta-analytic review. *Frontiers in Psychology, 6*, 1693.

35. Beck, J. S. (2011). *Cognitive behavior therapy: Basics and beyond*, 2nd ed. New York, NY: Guilford Press.

36. Veehof, M. M., Trompetter, H. R., Bohlmeijer, E. T., & Schreurs, K. G. (2016). Acceptance- and mindfulness-based interventions for the treatment of chronic pain: A meta-analytic review. *Cognitive Behaviour Therapy, 45*(1), 5-31.

37. (1) Davidson (2016), op. cit. (See ch. 3, note 12). (2) Williams, J. M. G., Crane, C., Barnhofer, T., Brennan, K., Duggan, D. S., Fennell, M. J. V.,...Russell, I. T. (2014). Mindfulness-based cognitive therapy for preventing relapse in recurrent depression: A randomized dismantling trial. *Journal of Consulting and Clinical Psychology, 82*, 275-286.

38. (1) Van Dam, N. T., Earleywine, M., & Borders, A. (2010). Measuring mindfulness? An item response theory analysis of the Mindful Attention Awareness Scale. *Personality and Individual Differences, 49*(7), 805-810. (2) Van Dam, N. T., Earleywine, M., & Danoff-Burg, S. (2009). Differential item function across meditators and non-meditators on the Five Facet

Mindfulness Questionnaire. *Personality and Individual Differences, 47*(5), 516-521.

39. (1) Brown, K. W., & Ryan, R. M. (2003). The benefits of being present: Mindfulness and its role in psychological well-being. *Journal of Personality and Social Psychology, 84*(4), 822–848. (2) Carmody, J., & Baer, R. A. (2009). How long does a mindfulness-based stress reduction program need to be? A review of class contact hours and effect sizes for psychological distress. *Journal of Clinical Psychology, 65*(6), 627-638.

40. Feldman, G., Hayes, A., Kumar, S., Greeson, J., & Laurenceau, J. (2007). Mindfulness and emotion regulation: The development and initial validation of the Cognitive and Affective Mindfulness Scale-Revised (CAMS-R). *Journal of Psychopathology & Behavioral Assessment, 29*(3), 177-190.

41. (1) Zhuang, K., Bi, M., Li, Y., Xia, Y., Guo, X., Chen, Q.,...Qiu, J. (2017). A distinction between two instruments measuring dispositional mindfulness and the correlations between those measurements and the neuroanatomical structure. *Scientific Reports, 7*, 6252. (2) Park, T., Reilly-Spong, M., & Gross, C. R. (2013). Mindfulness: a systematic review of instruments to measure an emergent patient-reported outcome (PRO). *Quality of Life Research, 22*, 2639-2659.

42. Brown, K. W., & Ryan, R. M. (2003). The benefits of being present: Mindfulness and its role in psychological well-being. *Journal of Personality and Social Psychology, 84*(4), 822-848.

43. Baer, R. A., Smith, G. T., Lykins, E., Button, D., Krietemeyer, J., Sauer, S.,...Williams, J. (2008). Construct validity of the Five Facet Mindfulness Questionnaire in meditating and nonmeditating samples. *Assessment, 15*(3), 329–342.

44. (1) Bair, Y. A., Gold, E. B., Greendale, G. A., Sternfeld, B., Adler, S. R., Azari, R., & Harkey, M. (2002). Ethnic differences in use of complementary and alternative medicine at midlife: Longitudinal results from SWAN participants. *American Journal of Public Health, 92*(11), 1832-1840. (2) Ni, H., Simile, C., & Hardy, A. (2002). Utilization of complementary and alternative medicine by United States adults: results from the 1999 National Health Interview Survey. *Medical Care, 40*(4), 353-358.

45. Rankin, L. (2014). *Mind over medicine: Scientific proof that you can heal yourself.* Carlsbad, CA: Hay House.

46. Kirsch, I. (2010). *The emperor's new drugs: Exploding the antidepressant myth.* New York, NY: Basic Books.

47. Tuttle, A. H., Tohyama, S., Ramsay, T., Kimmelman, J., Schweinhardt, P., Bennett, G. J., & Mogil, J. S. (2015). Increasing placebo responses over time in U.S. clinical trials of neuropathic pain. *Pain, 156*(12), 2616-2626.

48. Howick, J., Friedemann, C., Tsakok, M., Watson, R., Tsakok, T., Thomas, J.,...Heneghan, C. (2013). Are treatments more effective than placebos? A systematic review and meta-analysis. *Plos ONE, 8*(5), 1-8.

49. Levine, J. D., Gordon, N. C., Smith, R., & Fields, H. L. (1981). Analgesic responses to morphine and placebo in individuals with postoperative pain. *Pain, 10*(3), 379-389.

50. Kaptchuk, T., & Miller, F. G. (2015). Placebo effects in medicine. *New England Journal of Medicine, 373*, 8-9.

51. Finniss, D., Kaptchuk, T., Miller, F., & Benedetti, F. (2010). Biological, clinical, and ethical advances of placebo effects. *Lancet, 375*, 686-695.

52. Lazar, S. W., Kerr, C. E., Wasserman, R. H., Gray, J. R., Greve, D. N., Treadway, M. T.,...Fischl, B. (2005). Meditation experience is associated with increased cortical thickness. *NeuroReport, 16*(17), 1893-1897.

53. Luders, E., & Cherbuin, N. (2016). Searching for the philosopher's stone: promising links between meditation and brain preservation. *Annals of the New York Academy of Sciences, 1373*(1), 38-44.

54. Ireland, T. (2014, June 12). What does mindfulness meditation do to your brain? *Scientific American.* Retrieved from https://blogs.scientificamerican.com/guest-blog/what-does-mindfulness-meditation-do-to-your-brain/

55. Rosenkranz, M. A., Lutz, A., Perlman, D. M., Bachhuber, D. W., Schuyler, B. S., MacCoon, D. G., & Davidson, R. J. (2016). Reduced stress and inflammatory responsiveness in experienced meditators compared to a matched healthy control group. *Psychoneuroendocrinology, 68*, 117-125.

56. Wielgosz, J., Schuyler, B. S., Lutz, A., & Davidson, R. J. (2016). Long-term mindfulness training is associated with reliable differences in resting respiration rate. *Scientific Reports, 6*, 27533.

57. Tlalka, S. (2016, February 5) How science reveals that "well-being" is a skill. *Mindful.* Retrieved from https://www.mindful.org/science-reveals-well-skill/

58. Goyal et al. (2014), op. cit. (See ch. 3, note 29).

59. Hilton, L., Hempel, S., Ewing, B., Apaydin, E., Xenakis, L., Newberry, S.,...Maglione, M. A. (2017). Mindfulness meditation for chronic pain: Systematic review and meta-analysis. *Annals of Behavioral Medicine, 51*(2), 199-213.

60. (1) Lee, C., Crawford, C., & Hickey, A. (2014). Mind-body therapies for the self-management of chronic pain symptoms. *Pain Medicine, 15*, S21-S39. (2) Bawa, F. M., Mercer, S. W., Atherton, R. J., Clague, F., Keen, A., Scott, N. W., & Bond, C. M. (2015). Does mindfulness improve outcomes in patients with chronic pain? Systematic review and meta-analysis. *British Journal of General Practice, 65*(635), e387-400.

61. Cherkin, D. C., Sherman, K. J., Balderson, B. H., Cook, A. J., Anderson, M. L., Hawkes, R. J.,...Turner, J. A. (2016). Effect of mindfulness-based stress reduction vs. cognitive behavioral therapy or usual care on back pain and functional limitations in adults with chronic low back pain: A randomized clinical trial. *JAMA, 315*(12), 1240-1249.

62. Davis, M. C., Zautra, A. J., Wolf, L. D., Tennen, H., & Yeung, E. W. (2015).

Mindfulness and cognitive-behavioral interventions for chronic pain: Differential effects on daily pain reactivity and stress reactivity. *Journal of Consulting & Clinical Psychology, 83*(1), 24-35.

63. (1) la Cour, P., & Petersen, M. (2015). Effects of mindfulness meditation on chronic pain: A randomized controlled trial. *Pain Medicine, 16*(4), 641-652. (2) Reiner, K., Tibi, L., & Lipsitz, J. D. (2013). Do mindfulness-based interventions reduce pain intensity? A critical review of the literature. *Pain Medicine, 14*, 230-242.

64. Zeidan, F., Emerson, N. M., Farris, S. R., Ray, J. N., Youngkyoo, J., McHaffie, J. G., & Coghill, R. C. (2015). Mindfulness meditation-based pain relief employs different neural mechanisms than placebo and sham mindfulness meditation-induced analgesia. *Journal of Neuroscience, 35*(46), 15307-15325.

65. Zeidan, F., Adler-Neal, A. L., Wells, R. E., Stagnaro, E., May, L. M., Eisenach, J. C.,...Coghill, R. C. (2016). Mindfulness-meditation-based pain relief is not mediated by endogenous opioids. *Journal of Neuroscience, 36*(11), 3391-3397.

66. (1) Lutz, A., McFarlin, D. R., Perlman, D. M., Salomons, T. V., & Davidson, R. J. (2013). Altered anterior insula activation during anticipation and experience of painful stimuli in expert meditators. *NeuroImage, 64*, 538-546. (2) Zeidan, F., & Vago, D. (2016). Mindfulness meditation–based pain relief: a mechanistic account. *Annals of the New York Academy of Sciences, 1373*(1), 114-127.

67. (1) Carmody, J., & Baer, R. A. (2008). Relationships between mindfulness practice and levels of mindfulness, medical and psychological symptoms and well-being in a mindfulness-based stress reduction program. *Journal of Behavioral Medicine, 31*(1), 23-33. (2) Grossman, P., Niemann, L., Schmidt, S., & Walach, H. (2004). Mindfulness-based stress reduction and health benefits. A meta-analysis. *Journal of Psychosomatic Research, 57*, 35-43. (3) Huss, D. B., & Baer, R. A. (2007). Acceptance and change: the integration of mindfulness-based cognitive therapy into ongoing dialectical behavior therapy in a case of borderline personality disorder with depression. *Clinical Case Studies, 6*, 17-33. (4) Kabat-Zinn, J. (2003). Mindfulness-based interventions in context: Past, present and future. *Clinical Psychology Science and Practice, 10*, 144-156. (5) Ramel, W., Goldin, P. R., Carmona, P. E., & McQuaid, J. R. (2004). The effects of mindfulness mediation on cognitive process and affect in patients with past depression. *Cognitive Therapy and Research, 28*, 433-455.

68. Chiesa, A., & Serretti, A. (2009). Mindfulness-based stress reduction for stress management in healthy people: A review and meta-analysis. *Journal of Alternative & Complementary Medicine, 15*(5), 593-600.

69. Bohlmeijer, E., Prenger, R., Taal, E., & Cuijpers, P. (2010). The effects of mindfulness-based stress reduction therapy on mental health of adults with a chronic medical disease: A meta-analysis. *Journal of Psychosomatic Research, 68*(6), 539-544.

70. Gotink, R. A., Chu, P., Busschbach, J. V., Benson, H., Fricchione, G. L., & Hunink, M. M. (2015). Standardised mindfulness-based interventions in healthcare: An overview of systematic reviews and meta-analyses of RCTs. *PLos ONE, 10*(4).

71. Abbott, R. A., Whear, R., Rodgers, L. R., Bethel, A., Thompson Coon, J., Kuyken, W.,...Dickens, C. (2014). Effectiveness of mindfulness-based stress reduction and mindfulness-based cognitive therapy in vascular disease: A systematic review and meta-analysis of randomized controlled trials. *Journal of Psychosomatic Research, 76*(5), 341-351.

72. (1) Beddoe, A. E., & Murphy, S. O. (2004). Does mindfulness decrease stress and foster empathy among nursing students? *Journal of Nursing Education, 19*, 26-35. (2) Cohen-Katz, J. C., Wiley, S. D., Capuano, T., Baker, M. A., & Shapiro, S. (2005). The effects of mindfulness-based stress reduction on nurse stress and burnout, part II. *Holistic Nursing Practice, 19*, 26-35. (3) Mackenzie, C. S., Poulin, P. A., & Seidman-Carlson, R. (2006). A brief-mindfulness based stress reduction intervention for nurses and nurse aides. *Nursing Research, 19*, 105-109. (4) Shapiro, S. L., Brown, K., & Biegel, G. (2007). Self-care for health care professionals: Effects of MBSR on mental well-being of counseling psychology students. *Training and Education in Professional Psychology, 1*, 105-115.

73. Dobkin, P., & Zhao, Q. (2011). Increased mindfulness – the active component of the mindfulness-based stress reduction program? *Complementary Therapies in Clinical Practice, 17*(1), 22-27.

74. Galantino, M., Baime, M., Maguire, M., Szapary, P., & Farrar, J. (2005). Association of psychological and physiological measures of stress in health-care professionals during an 8-week mindfulness meditation program: Mindfulness in practice. *Stress & Health, 21*(4), 255-261.

75. Jain, S., Shapiro, S. L., Swanick, S., Roesch, S. C., Mills, P. J., Bell, I., & Schwartz, G. E. (2007). A randomized controlled trial of mindfulness meditation versus relaxation training: Effects on distress, positive states of mind, rumination, and distraction. *Annals of Behavioral Medicine, 33*(1), 11-21.

76. Goyal et al. (2014), op. cit. (See ch. 3, note 29).

77. Sharma, M., & Rush, S. E. (2014). Mindfulness-based stress reduction as a stress management intervention for healthy individuals. *Journal of Evidence-Based Complementary & Alternative Medicine, 19*(4), 271-286.

78. Creswell, J. D., Pacilio, L. E., Lindsay, E. K., & Brown, K. W. (2014). Brief mindfulness meditation training alters psychological and neuroendocrine responses to social evaluative stress. *Psychoneuroendocrinology, 44*, 1-12.

79. Jacobs, T. L., Shaver, P. R., Epel, E. S., Zanesco, A. P., Aichele, S. R., Bridwell, D. A.,...Saron, C. D. (2013). Self-reported mindfulness and cortisol during a Shamatha meditation retreat. *Health Psychology, 32*(10), 1104-1109.

80. Oken, B. (2017). A systems approach to stress and resilience in humans: Mindfulness meditation, aging, and cognitive function. *Dissertation Abstracts International: Section B: The Sciences and Engineering, 77*(8-B(E)).

81. MacCoon, D. G., Imel, Z. E., Rosenkranz, M. A., Sheftel, J. G., Weng, H. Y., Sullivan, J. C.,...Lutz, A. (2012). The validation of an active control intervention for mindfulness-based stress reduction (MBSR). *Behaviour Research and Therapy, 50*, 3-12.

82. Creswell, D. J., Taren, A. A., Lindsaya, E. K., Grecoc, C. M., Gianaros, P. J., Fairgrieve, A.,...Ferrisa, J. L. (2016). Alterations in resting-state functional connectivity link mindfulness meditation with reduced interleukin-6: A randomized controlled trial. *Biological Psychiatry, 80*(1), 53-61.

83. Epelı, E. S., Puterman, E., Lin, J., Blackburn, E. H.,Lum, P. Y., Beckmann, N. D.,...Schadt, E. E. (2016). Meditation and vacation effects have an impact on disease-associated molecular phenotypes. *Translational Psychiatry, 6*, e880.

84. Goyal et al. (2014), op. cit. (See ch. 3, note 29).

85. Hilton, L., Hempel, S., Ewing, B., Apaydin, E., Xenakis, L., Newberry, S.,...Maglione, M. A. (2017). Mindfulness meditation for chronic pain: Systematic review and meta-analysis. *Annals of Behavioral Medicine, 51*(2), 199-213.

86. Gotink et al. (2015), op. cit. (See ch. 3, note 70).

87. Veehof et al. (2016), op. cit. (See ch. 3, note 36).

88. Ibid.

89. Huijbers, M. J., Spinhoven, P., Spijker, J., Ruhé, H. G., Dinna. J. F., van Schaik, P.,...Speckens, A. E. M. (2016). Discontinuation of antidepressant medication after mindfulness-based cognitive therapy for recurrent depression: randomised controlled non-inferiority trial. *British Journal of Psychiatry, 208*(4), 366-373.

90. Hoge, E. A., Bui, E., Goetter, E., Robinaugh, D. J., Ojserkis, R. A., Fresco, D. M., & Simon, N. M. (2015). Change in decentering mediates improvement in anxiety in mindfulness-based stress reduction for generalized anxiety disorder. *Cognitive Therapy and Research, 39*(2), 228-235.

91. Goyal et al. (2014), op. cit. (See ch. 3, note 29).

92. Gong, H., Ni, C., Liu, Y., Zhang, Y., Su, W., Lian, Y.,...Jiang, C. (2016). Mindfulness meditation for insomnia: A meta-analysis of randomized controlled trials. *Journal of Psychosomatic Research, 89*, 1-6.

93. Ibid.

94. Black, D. S., O'Reilly, G. A., Olmstead, R., Breen, E. C., Irwin, M. R. (2015). Mindfulness meditation and improvement in sleep quality and daytime impairment among older adults with sleep disturbances: a randomized clinical trial. *JAMA Internal Medicine, 175*(4), 494-501.

Chapter 4: Times They Are A-Changing

1. Newberg, A., & Waldman, M. R. (2017). *How enlightenment changes your brain: The new science of transformation.* New York, NY: Avery.

2. Kabat-Zinn (1994), op. cit. (See ch. 1, note 4).

3. Reynolds, G. (2013, May 9). The scientific 7-minute workout. *The New York Times Magazine*. Retrieved from https://well.blogs.nytimes.com/2013/05/09/the-scientific-7-minute-workout/

4. Chirles, T. J., Reiter, K., Weiss, L. R, Alfini, A. J., Nielson, K. A., & Smith, J. C. (2017). Exercise training and functional connectivity changes in mild cognitive impairment and healthy elders. *Journal of Alzheimer's Disease*, 57(3), 845-856.

5. Ten Brinke, L. F., Bolandzadeh, N., Nagamatsu, L. S., Hsu, C. L., Davis, J. C., Miran-Khan, K., & Liu-Ambrose, T. (2015). Aerobic exercise increases hippocampal volume in older women with probable mild cognitive impairment: a 6-month randomized controlled trial. *British Journal of Sports Medicine*, 49(4), 248-254.

6. Gregoire, C. (2013, June 5). How yoga changes your body, starting the day you begin. *Huffington Post*. Retrieved from http://www.huffingtonpost.com/2013/10/28/body-on-yoga_n_4109595.html?

7. Ratey, J. (2013). *Spark: The revolutionary new science of exercise and the brain.* New York, NY: Little, Brown and Company.

8. Luskin, F., & Pelletier, K. (2005). *Stress free for good: 10 scientifically proven life skills for health and happiness.* New York, NY: HarperOne.

9. Ibid.

10. Brown, R., & Gerbarg, P. (2013). *The healing power of the breath.* Boston, MA: Shambhala.

11. Waldman, M. R., & Manning, C. (2017). *NeuroWisdom: The new brain science of money, happiness, and success.* New York, NY: Diversion Publishing.

12. (1) Bernardi, L., Porta, C., & Sleight, P. (2006). Cardiovascular, cerebrovascular, and respiratory changes induced by different types of music in musicians and non-musicians: The importance of silence. *Heart*, 92(4), 445-452. (2) Kirste, I., Zeina, N., Kronenberg,G., Walker, T. L., Liu, R. C., & Kempermann, G. (2015). Is silence golden? Effects of auditory stimuli and their absence on adult hippocampal neurogenesis. *Brain Structure & Function*, 220(2), 1221-1228.

13. Salimpoor, V. N., Benovoy, M., Larcher, K., Dagher, A., & Zatorre, R. J. (2011). Anatomically distinct dopamine release during anticipation and experience of peak emotion to music. *Nature Neuroscience*, 14, 257-262.

14. Salimpoor, V. N., Benovoy, M., Longo, G., Cooperstock, J. R., & Zatorre, R. J. (2009). The rewarding aspects of music listening are related to degree of emotional arousal. *PLos ONE*, 4(10), e7487.

15. Ariga, A., & Lleras, A, (2011). Brief and rare mental "breaks" keep you focused: Deactivation and reactivation of task goals preempt vigilance decrements. *Cognition*, 118(3), 439-443.

16. Lee, K., Williams, K., Sargent, L., Williams, N., & Johnson, K. (2015). 40-second green roof views sustain attention: The role of micro-breaks in attention restoration. *Journal of Environmental Psychology*, 42, 182-189.

17. Bratman, G. N., Hamilton, J. P., & Daily, G. C. (2012). The impacts of nature experience on human cognitive function and mental health. *Annals of the New York Academy of Sciences, 1249*(1), 118-136.

18. Hartig, T., Mitchell, R., deVries, S., & Frumkin, H. (2014). Nature and health. *Annual Review of Public Health, 35*, 207-228.

19. Lee et al. (2015), op. cit. (See ch. 4, note 16).

20. Piff, P. K., Dietze, P., Feinberg, M., Stancato, D. M., & Keltner, D. (2015). Awe, the small self, and prosocial behavior. *Journal of Personality and Social Psychology, 108*(6), 883-899.

21. Thursday, R. (2016). *Yoga Journal presents your guide to reflexology*. Avon, MA: Adams Media.

22. Ibid.

23. Benson, H. (2000). *The relaxation response* (2nd ed.). New York, NY: William Morrow.

24. Benson, H., & Proctor, W. (2004). *The breakout principle: How to activate the natural trigger that maximizes creativity, athletic performance, productivity, and personal well-being*. New York, NY: Scribner.

25. Yerkes, R. M., & Dodson, J. D. (1908). The relation of strength of stimulus to rapidity of habit-formation. *Journal of Comparative Neurology and Psychology, 18*, 459-482.

26. Diamond, D. M., Campbell, A. M., Park, C. R., Halonen, J., & Zoladz. P. R. (2007). The temporal dynamics model of emotional memory processing: A synthesis on the neurobiological basis of stress-induced amnesia, flashbulb and traumatic memories, and the Yerkes-Dodson Law. *Neural Plasticity*, 1-33.

27. Benson, H., & Proctor, W. (2011). *The relaxation revolution: The science and genetics of mind body healing*. New York, NY: Scribner.

28. Waldman, M. (2014). *NeuroWisdom 101: Train your brain, transform your life*. Author.

29. Siegel, D. J. (2010). *Mindsight: The new science of personal transformation*. New York, NY: Bantam Books.

30. Waldman & Manning (2017), op. cit. (See ch. 4, note 11).

31. Ibid.

32. Marturano, J. (2015). *Finding the space to lead: A practical guide to mindful leadership*. New York, NY: Bloomsbury Press.

33. Soloway, G. (2016, January 13). The 30 Day Mindfulness Challenge. Retrieved from http://www.mindwellu.com/evidence-business

34. Mindfulness at Work. Retrieved from http://mindfulnessatwork.com/

35. Search Inside Yourself (SIY) Leadership Institute. Retrieved from https://www.siyli.org/

36. Achor, S. (2012). Positive intelligence: Three ways individuals can cultivate their own sense of well-being and set themselves up to succeed. *Harvard Business Review, 90*(1/2), 100-102.

Chapter 5: Three Key Ingredients in the Recipe for Well-Being

1. Hanson, R. (2013). *Hardwiring happiness: The new brain science of contentment, calm, and confidence.* New York, NY: Harmony.
2. Fredrickson, B. L. (2009). *Positivity: Top-notch research reveals the 3-to-1 ratio that will change your life.* New York, NY: Three Rivers Press.
3. Fredrickson, B. L., & Losada, M. F. (2005). Positive affect and the complex dynamics of human flourishing. *American Psychologist, 60*(7), 678-686.
4. Gottman, J. M. (1994). *What predicts divorce? The relationship between marital processes and marital outcomes.* Hillsdale, NJ: Lawrence Erlbaum.
5. Losada, M. (1999). The complex dynamics of high performance teams. *Mathematical and Computer Modeling, 30,* 179-192.
6. Gable, S. L., & Haidt, J. (2005). What (and why) is positive psychology? *Review of General Psychology, 9*(2), 103-110.
7. Berridge, K. C., Robinson, T. E., & Aldridge, J. W. (2009). Dissecting components of reward: 'liking', 'wanting', and learning. *Current Opinion in Pharmacology, 9*(1), 65-73.
8. Rankin (2014), op. cit. (See ch. 3, note 45).
9. Benson, H. B., Beary, J. F., & Carol, M. P. (1974). The relaxation response. *Psychiatry, 37,* 37-46.
10. Wallace, R. K., Benson, H., & Wilson, A. F. (1971). A wakeful hypometabolic physiologic state. *American Journal of Physiology, 221,* 795-799.
11. Dusek, J. A., Chang, B. H., Zaki, J, Lazar, S, & Deykin, A. (2006). Association between oxygen consumption and nitric oxide production during the relaxation response. *International Medical Journal of Experimental and Clinical Research, 12,* 1-10.
12. Rankin (2014), op. cit. (See ch. 3, note 45).
13. Benson & Proctor (2011), op. cit. (See ch. 4, note 27).
14. Ibid.
15. Rankin (2014), op. cit. (See ch. 3, note 45).
16. Snyder, K. A., Blan, M. P., & Marsolek, C. J. (2006). What form of memory underlies novelty preferences? *Psychonomic Bulletin & Review, 15*(2), 315-321.
17. Bunzeck, N. & Düzel, E. (2006). Absolute coding of stimulus novelty in the human substantia nigra/VTA. *Neuron, 51*(3), 369-379.
18. Schomakera, J., & Meeterb, M. (2015). Short- and long-lasting consequences of novelty, deviance and surprise on brain and cognition. *Neuroscience & Biobehavioral Reviews, 55,* 268-279.
19. Bunzeck & Düzel (2006), op. cit. (See ch. 5, note 17).
20. (1) Berlyne, D. E. (1970). Novelty, complexity, and hedonic value. *Perception & Psychophysics, 8,* 279-286. (2) Ebstein, R. P., Novick, O., Umansky, R., Priel, B., Osher, Y., & Blaine, D. (1996). Dopamine D4 receptor (D4DR) exon III poymorphism associated with the human personality trait of novelty seeking. *Nature Genetics, 12,* 78-80. (3) Pronin, E., & Jacobs, E. (2008). Thought speed, mood, and the experience of mental motion. *Perspectives on Psychological Science, 3,* 461-485.

Chapter 6: Sustaining Authentic Happiness and Positive Emotions

1. (1) Deci, E. L., & Ryan, R. M. (2000). Self-determination theory and the facilitation of intrinsic motivation, social development, and well-being. *American Psychologist, 55*(1), 68-78. (2) Diener, E., Kahneman, D., Tov, W., & Arora, R. (2010). Income's association with judgments of life versus feelings. In E. Diener, D. Kahneman, & J. F. Helliwell (Eds.), *International differences in well-being* (pp. 3-15). New York, NY: Oxford University Press.

2. Brooks, A. C. (2008). *Gross national happiness: Why happiness matters for America and how we can get more of it.* New York, NY: Basic Books.

3. Easterlin, R. A. (2001). Income and happiness: Towards a unified theory. *Economic Journal, 111,* 465-484.

4. Keyes, C. L. M. (2002). The mental health continuum: From languishing to flourishing in life. *Journal of Health and Social Behavior, 43,* 207-222.

5. Fredrickson, B. L. (2008). Promoting positive affect. In M. Eid, & R. J. Larsen (Eds.), *The science of subjective well-being* (pp. 449-468). New York, NY: Guilford Press.

6. Helliwell, J., Layard, R., & Sachs, J. (2017). *World Happiness Report 2017.* New York, NY: Sustainable Development Solutions Network.

7. Twenge, J. M., Sherman, R. A., & Lyubomirsky, S. (2016). More happiness for young people and less for mature adults: Time period differences in subjective well-being in the United States, 1972–2014. *Social Psychological and Personality Science, 7*(2), 131-141.

8. Stonea, A. A., Schwartza, J. E., Brodericka, J. E. & Deatonc, A. (2015). A snapshot of the age distribution of psychological well-being in the United States. *Proceedings of the National Academy of Sciences, 107*(22), 9985-9990.

9. Seligman, M. E. P., (2002). *Authentic happiness: Using the new positive psychology to realize your potential for lasting fulfillment.* New York, NY: Free Press.

10. Ibid.

11. Csikszentmihalyi, M. (1990). *Flow: The psychology of optimal experience.* New York, NY: Harper & Row.

12. (1) Lopez, S., & Snyder, C. (2003). *Positive psychology assessment: Handbook of models and measures.* Washington, DC: American Psychological Association. (2) Peterson, C., & Seligman, M. (2004). *Character strengths and virtues: A handbook and classification.* Washington, DC: American Psychological Association.

13. Seligman, M. E. P. (2011). *Flourish: A visionary new understanding of happiness and well-being.* New York, NY: Free Press.

14. Brooks (2008), op. cit. (See ch. 6, note 2).

15. Seligman (2011), op. cit. (See ch. 6, note 13).

16. Ibid.

17. Seligman, M. E. P., (2011). Building resilience. *Harvard Business Review, 89*(4), 100-106.

18. Diener, E. (1984). Subjective well-being. *Psychological Bulletin, 95,* 542-575.

19. Lyubomirsky, S. (2011). Hedonic adaptation to positive and negative experiences. In S. Folkman (Ed.), *The Oxford handbook of stress, health, and coping* (pp. 201-224). New York, NY: Oxford University Press.
20. Davidson & Begley (2012), op. cit. (See ch. 3, note 8).
21. Lyubomirsky (2011), op. cit. (See ch. 6, note 19).
22. Frederick, S., & Loewenstein, G. (1999). Hedonic adaptation. In D. Kahneman, E. Diener, & N. Schwarz (Eds.), *Well-being: The foundations of hedonic psychology* (pp. 302-329). New York, NY: Russell Sage Foundation.
23. (1) Baumeister, R. F., Bratslavsky, E., Finkenauer, C., & Vohs, K. D. (2001). Bad is stronger than good. *Review of General Psychology, 5*(4), 323-370. (2) Lawton, M. P., DeVoe, M. R., & Parmelee, P. (1995). Relationship of events and affect in the daily life of an elderly population. *Psychology and Aging, 10,* 469-477. (3) Nezlek, J. B., & Gable, S. L. (2001). Depression as a moderator of relationships between positive daily events and day to day psychological adjustment. *Personality and Social Psychology Bulletin, 27,* 1692-1704. (4) Sheldon, K. M., Ryan, R, & Reis, H. T. (1996). What makes for a good day? Competence and autonomy in the day and in the person. *Personality and Social Psychology Bulletin, 22,* 1270-1279.
24. Hanson (2013), op. cit. (See ch. 5, note 1).
25. Wilson, T. D., & Gilbert, D. T. (2008). Explaining away: A model of affective adaptation. *Perspectives on Psychological Science, 3*(5), 370-386.
26. Berridge, K., & Kringelbach, M. (2008). Affective neuroscience of pleasure: reward in humans and animals. *Psychopharmacology, 199*(3), 457-480.
27. Martinez, M. (2014). *The MindBody code: How to change the beliefs that limit your health, longevity, and success.* Boulder, CO: Sounds True.
28. Fredrickson, B. L. (2001). The role of positive psychology: The broaden-and-build theory of positive emotions. *American Psychologist, 56*(3), 218-226.
29. Fredrickson, B. L., & Branigan, C. (2005). Positive emotions broaden the scope of attention and thought-action repertoire. *Cognition & Emotion, 19*(3), 313-332.
30. Lyubomirsky, S., King, L. A., & Diener, E. (2005). The benefits of frequent positive affect: Does happiness lead to success. *Psychological Bulletin, 131*(6), 803-855.
31. (1) Diener, E., & Seligman, M. E. P. (2002). Very happy people. *Psychological Science, 13,* 81–84. (2) Lyubomirsky, S. (2007). *The how of happiness: A scientific approach to getting the life you want.* New York, NY: Penguin Press. (3) Roysamb, E., Tambs, K., Reichborn-Kjennerud, T., Neale, M. C., & Harris, J. R. (2003). Happiness and health: Environmental and genetic contributions to the relationship between subjective well-being, perceived health, and somatic illness. *Journal of Personality and Social Psychology, 85,* 1136-1146. (4) Snyder, C. R., & Lopez, S. J. (2009). *The Oxford handbook of positive psychology* (2nd ed.). New York, NY: Oxford University Press.
32. Achor, S. (2010). *The happiness advantage: The seven principles of positive psychology that fuel success and performance at work.* New York, NY: Crown.

33. Lyubomirsky et al. (2005), op. cit. (See ch. 6, note 30).
34. Bakker, A. B. (2011). An evidence-based model of work engagement. *Current Directions in Psychological Science, 20*(4), 265-269.
35. Dutton, J. E. E., Roberts, L. M., & Bednar, J. (2010). Pathways for positive identity construction at work: Four types of positive identity and the building of social resources. *Academy of Management Review, 35*(2), 265–293.
36. Isen, A. M. (2008). Some ways in which positive affect influences decision making and problem solving. In M. Lewis, J. M. Haviland-Jones, & L. F. Barrett (Eds.), *Handbook of emotions* (pp. 548–573). New York, NY: Guilford Press.
37. Subramaniam, A., Kounios, J., Parrish, T. B., & Jung-Beeman, M. (2009). A brain mechanism for facilitation of insight by positive affect. *Journal of Cognitive Neuroscience, 21*(3), 415-432.
38. Baas, M., Drew, D., Carsten, K. W, & Nijstad, B. A. (2008). A meta-analysis 25 years of mood-creativity research: Hedonic tone, activation or regulatory focus? *Psychological Bulletin, 134*(6), 779-806.
39. Lyubomirsky et al. (2005), op. cit. (See ch. 6, note 30).
40. Moskowitz, J. T. (2011). Coping interventions and the regulation of positive affect. In S. Folkman (Ed.), *The Oxford handbook of stress, health, and coping* (pp. 407-427). New York, NY: Oxford University Press.
41. Fredrickson, B. L., & Cohn, M. A. (2008). Positive emotions. In M. Lewis, J. M. Haviland-Jones, & L. F. Barrett (Eds.), *Handbook of emotions* (pp. 777-796). New York, NY: Guilford Press.
42. (1) Cohn, M. A., Fredrickson, B. L., Brown, S. L., Mikels, J. A., & Conway, A. M. (2009). Happiness unpacked: Positive emotions increase life satisfaction by building resilience. *Emotion, 9*(3), 361-368. (2) Gloria, C. T, Faulk, K. E., & Steinhart, M. A. (2013). Positive affectivity predicts successful and unsuccessful adaptation to stress. *Motivation and Emotion, 37*(1), 185-193.
43. Tugade, M. M., & Fredrickson, B. L. (2004). Resilient individuals use positive emotions to bounce back from negative emotional experiences. *Journal of Personality and Social Psychology, 86*(2), 320-333.
44. (1) Keltner, D., & Bonnano, G. A. (1997). A study of laughter and dissociation: Distinct correlates of laughter and smiling during bereavement. *Journal of Personality and Social Psychology, 73*, 687-702. (2) Ong, A. D., Bergeman, C. S., Bisconti, T. L., & Wallace, T. (2006). Psychological resilience, positive emotions and successful adaptation to stress in later life. *Journal of Personality and Social Psychology, 91*, 730-749.
45. Masten, A. S. (2015). *Ordinary magic: Resilience in development.* New York, NY: Guilford Press.
46. Tlalka, S. (2016, February 5). How science reveals that "well-being" is a skill. *Mindful.* Retrieved from https://www.mindful.org/science-reveals-well-skill/
47. Folkman, S., & Moskowitz, J. T. (2000). Positive affect and the other side of coping. *American Psychologist, 55*, 647-654.

48. Fredrickson, B. L., Tugade, M. M., Waugh, C. E., & Larkin, G. R. (2003). What good are positive emotions in crises?: A prospective study of resilience and emotions following the terrorist attacks on the United States in September 11, 2001. *Journal of Personality and Social Psychology, 84*, 365-376.

49. Gloria, C. T., & Steinhardt, M. A. (2016). Relationships among positive emotions, coping, resilience and mental health. *Stress and Health, 32*(2), 145-156.

50. Tugade, M. M., & Fredrickson, B. L. (2007). Regulation of positive emotions: Emotion regulation strategies that promote resilience. *Journal of Happiness Studies, 8*, 311–333.

51. Bargh, J. A., & Chartrand, T. L. (1999). The unbearable automaticity of being. *American Psychologist, 54*(7), 462-479.

52. (1) Chida, Y., & Steptoe, A. (2008). Positive psychological well-being and mortality: A quantitative review of prospective observational studies. *Psychosomatic Medicine, 70*(7), 741-756. (2) Cohen, S., & Pressman, S. D. (2006). Positive affect and health. *Current Directions in Psychological Science, 15*(3), 122-125. (3) Howell, R. T., Kern, M. L., & Lyubomirsky, S. (2007). Health benefits: meta-analytically determining the impact of well-being on objective health outcomes. *Health Psychology Review, 1*, 83-136.

53. Diener, E., & Chan, M. (2011). Happy people live longer: Subjective well-being contributes to health and longevity. *Applied Psychology: Health and Well-Being, 3*(1), 1-43.

54. Moskowitz, J. T., & Saslow, L. R. (2016). The importance of positive affect. In M. M. Tugade, M. N. Shiota, & L. D. Kirby (Eds.), *Handbook of positive emotions* (pp. 413-431). New York, NY: Guilford Press.

55. Vaillant, G. (2012). *Triumphs of experience: The men of the Harvard Grant Study*. Cambridge, MA: Belknap Press.

56. Danner, D. D., Snowdon, D. A., & Friesen, W. V. (2001). Positive emotions in early life and longevity: Findings from the Nun Study. *Journal of Personality and Social Psychology, 80*(5), 804-813.

57. Blazer, D. G., & Hybels, C. F. (2004). What symptoms of depression predict mortality in community-dwelling elders? *Journal of the American Geriatric Society, 52*, 2052-2056.

58. Steptoe, A., & Wardle, J. (2011). Positive affect measured using ecological momentary assessment and survival in older men and women. *Proceedings of the National Academy of Sciences, 108*(45), 18244-18248.

59. Giltay, E., Geleijnse, J., Zitman, F., Hoekstra, T., & Schouten, E. (2004). Dispositional optimism and all-cause and cardiovascular mortality in a prospective cohort of elderly Dutch men and women. *Archives of General Psychiatry, 61*, 1126-1135.

60. Krijthe, B. P., Walter, S., Newson, R. S., Hofman, A., Hunink, M. G., & Tiemeier, H. (2011). Is positive affect associated with survival? A population-based study of elderly persons. *American Journal of Epidemiology, 173*(11), 1298-1307.

61. Wiest, M., Schuz, B., Webster, N., & Wurm, S. (2011). Subjective well-being and mortality revisited: Differential effects of cognitive and emotional facets of well-being on mortality. *Health Psychology, 30*(6), 728-735.

62. Moskowitz, J. T., Epel, E. S., & Acree, M. (2008). Positive affect uniquely predicts lower risk of mortality in people with diabetes. *Health Psychology, 27*, S73-S82.

63. Ostir, G. V., Markides, K. S., Peek, M. K., & Goodwin, J. S. (2001). The association between emotional well-being and the incidence of stroke in older adults. *Psychosomatic Medicine, 63*(2), 210-215.

64. Davidson, K. W., Mostofsky, E., & Whang, W. (2010). Don't worry, be happy: Positive affect and reduced 10-year incident coronary heart disease: The Canadian Nova Scotia Health Survey. *European Heart Journal, 31*(9), 1065-1070.

65. Birket-Smith, M., Hansen, B. H., Hanash, J. A., Hansen, J. F. & Rasmussen, A. (2009). Mental disorders and general well-being in cardiology outpatients—6-year survival. *Journal of Psychosomatic Research, 67*(1), 5-10.

66. (1) Fredrickson, B. L., & Levenson, R. W. (1998). Positive emotions speed recovery from the cardiovascular sequelae of negative emotions. *Cognition and Emotion, 12*, 191-220. (2) Fredrickson, B. L., Mancuso, R. A., Branigan, C., & Tugade, M. M. (2000). The undoing effect of positive emotions. *Motivation and Emotion, 24*, 237-258.

67. Doyle, W. J., Gentile, D. A., & Cohen, S. (2006). Emotional style, nasal cytokines, and illness expression after experimental rhinovirus exposure. *Brain, Behavior and Immunity, 20*, 175-181.

68. (1) Ibid. (2) Cohen, S., Doyle, W. J., Skoner, D. P., Rabin, B. S., & Gwaltney, J. M. (1997). Social ties and susceptibility to the common cold. *Journal of the American Medical Association, 277*, 1940-1944.

69. Costanzo, E. S., Lutgendorf, S. K., Kohut, M. L., Nisly, N., Rozeboom, K., Spooner, S.,...McElhaney, J. E. (2004). Mood and cytokine response to influenza virus in older adults. *Journals of Gerontology, 59*(12), 1328-1333.

70. Fredrickson, B. L., Grewen, K. M., Coffey, K. A., Algoe, S. B., Firestine, A. M., Arevalo,...Cole, S. W. (2013). A functional genomic perspective on human well-being. *Proceedings of the National Academy of Sciences, 110*(33), 13684-13689.

71. (1) Kohut, M. L., Cooper, M. M., Nickolaus, M. S., Russell, D. R., & Cunnick, J. E. (2002). Exercise and psychosocial factors modulate immunity to influenza vaccine in elderly individuals. *Journals of Gerontology, 57*(9), 557-562. (2) Rein, G., Atkinson, M., & McCraty, R. (1995). The physiological and psychological effects of compassion and anger. *Journal of Advancement in Medicine, 8*(2), 87-105.

72. Stellar, J. E., John-Henderson, N., Anderson, C. L., Gordon, A. M., McNeil, G. D., & Keltner, D. (2015). Positive affect and markers of inflammation: Discrete positive emotions predict lower levels of inflammatory cytokines. *Emotion, 15*(2), 129-133.

73. Bhattacharyya, M. A., Whitehead, D. L., Rakhit, R., & Steptoe, A. (2008). Depressed mood, positive affect, and heart rate variability in patients with suspected coronary artery disease. *Psychosomatic Medicine, 70*(9), 1020-1027.

74. Childre, D. & Martin, H. (2000). *The Heartmath solution.* New York, NY: HarperCollins.

75. Kok, B. E., Coffey, K. A., Cohn, M. A., Catalino, L. I., Vacharkulksemsuk, T., Algoe, S. B.,...Fredrickson, B. L. (2013). How positive emotions build physical health: Perceived positive social connections account for the upward spiral between positive emotions and vagal tone. *Psychological Science, 24,* 1123-1132.

76. Diamond, L. M., Hicks, A. M., & Otter-Henderson, K. D. (2011). Individual differences in vagal regulation moderate associations between daily affect and daily couple interactions. *Personality and Social Psychology Bulletin, 37*(6), 731-744.

Chapter 7: The Emergence of Positive Psychology and Positive Psychology Activities

1. Seligman (2002), op. cit. (See ch. 6, note 9).

2. Seligman, M. E. P., & Csikszentmihalyi, M. (2000). Positive psychology. *American Psychologist, 55*(1), 5-14.

3. Peterson & Seligman (2004), op. cit. (See ch. 6, note 12).

4. Ibid.

5. Arrien, A. (2011). *Living in gratitude: A journey that will change your life.* Boulder, CO: Sounds True.

6. Peterson & Seligman (2004), op. cit. (See ch. 6, note 12).

7. Park, N., Peterson, C., & Seligman, M. E. P. (2004). Strengths of character and well-being. *Journal of Social and Clinical Psychology, 23*(5), 603-619.

8. Seligman, M. E. P., Steen, T. A., Park, N., & Peterson, C. (2005). Positive psychology progress: Empirical validation of interventions. *American Psychologist, 60*(5), 410-421.

9. Quinlan, D., Swain, N., & Vella-Brodrick, D. A. (2012). Character strengths interventions: Building on what we know for improved outcomes. *Journal of Happiness Studies, 13,* 1145-1163.

10. Seligman, M. (2016, May 12). Positive psychology with Martin Seligman. Retrieved from https://youtu.be/HHosssQzQGg

11. Hanson (2013), op. cit. (See ch. 5, note 1).

12. (1) Lyubomirsky, S. (2008). *The how of happiness: A scientific approach to getting the life you want.* New York, NY: Penguin Press. (2) Lyubomirsky, S. (2014). *The myths of happiness: What should make you happy, but doesn't, what shouldn't make you happy, but does.* New York, NY: Penguin Books.

13. Fredrickson, B. L. (2008). Promoting positive affect. In M. Eid & R. J. Larsen (Eds.), *The science of subjective well-being* (pp. 449-468). New York, NY: Guilford Press.

14. Seligman et al. (2005), op. cit. (See ch. 7, note 8).
15. (1) Bolier, L., Haverman, M., Westerhof, G. J., Riper, H., Smit, F., & Bohlmeijer, E. (2013). Positive psychology interventions: a meta-analysis of randomized controlled studies. *BMC Public Health, 13*(1), 1-20. (2) Sin, N. L., & Lyubomirsky, S. (2009). Enhancing well-being and alleviating depressive symptoms with positive psychology intervention: A practice-friendly meta-analysis. *Journal of Clinical Psychology, 65*(5), 467-487.
16. (1) Emmons, R. A., & McCullough, M. E. (2003). Counting blessings versus burdens: An experimental investigation of gratitude and subjective well-being in daily life. *Journal of Personality and Social Psychology, 84,* 377-389. (2) Froh, J. J., Sefick, W. J., & Emmons, R. A. (2008). Counting blessings in early adolescents: An experimental study of gratitude and subjective well-being. *Journal of School Psychology, 46*(2), 213-233. (3) Lyubomirsky, S., Dickerhoof, R., Boehm, J. K., & Sheldon, K. M. (2011). Becoming happier takes both a will and a proper way: An experimental longitudinal intervention to boost well-being. *Emotion, 11,* 391-402. (4) Sheldon, K. M., & Lyubomirsky, S. (2006). How to increase and sustain positive emotion: The effects of expressing gratitude and visualizing best possible selves. *Journal of Positive Psychology, 1,* 73-82.
17. (1) Boehm, J. K., Lyubomirsky, S., & Sheldon, K. M. (2011). A longitudinal experimental study comparing the effectiveness of happiness-enhancing strategies in Anglo Americans and Asian Americans. *Cognition & Emotion, 25,* 1263-1272. (2) Seligman et al. (2005), op. cit. (See ch. 7, note 8). (3) Lyubomirsky et al. (2011), op. cit. (See ch. 7, note 16).
18. Seligman et al. (2005), op. cit. (See ch. 7, note 8).
19. (1) Boehm at al. (2011), op. cit. (See ch. 7, note 17). (2) Lyubomirsky et al. (2011), op. cit. (See ch. 7, note 16).
20. (1) Emmons & McCullough (2003), op. cit. (See ch. 7, note 16). (2) Lyubomirsky, S., Sheldon, K. M., & Schkade, D. (2005). Pursuing happiness: The architecture of sustainable change. *Review of General Psychology, 9,* 111-131. (3) Seligman et al. (2005), op. cit. (See ch. 7, note 8).
21. (1) Dunn, E. W., Aknin, L. B., & Norton, M. I. (2008). Spending money on others promotes happiness. *Science, 319,* 1687-1688. (2) Lyubomirsky et al. (2005), op cit. (See ch. 6, note 30). (3) Otake, K., Shimai, S., Tanaka-Matsumi, J., Otsui, K., & Fredrickson, B. (2006). Happy people become happier through kindness: A counting kindnesses intervention. *Journal of Happiness Studies, 7*(3), 361-375.
22. (1) Fredrickson, B. L., Cohn, M. A., Coffey, K. A., Pek, J., & Finkel, S. M. (2008). Open hearts build lives: Positive emotions, induced through loving-kindness meditation build consequential personal resources. *Journal of Personality and Social Psychology, 95*(5), 1045-1962. (2) Seligman, et al. (2005), op. cit. (See ch. 7, note 8).
23. (1) Boehm at al. (2011), op. cit. (See ch. 7, note 17). (2) King, L. A. (2001). The health benefits of writing about life goals. *Personality and Social Psychology*

Bulletin, 27, 798-807. (3) Layous, K., Nelson, S. K., & Lyubomirsky, S. (2013). What is the optimal way to deliver a positive activity intervention? The case of writing about one's best possible selves. *Journal of Happiness Studies, 14*, 635–654. (4) Lyubomirsky (2011), op. cit. (See ch. 6, note 19).

24. Lyubomirsky, S., Sousa, L., & Dickerhoof, R. (2006). The costs and benefits of writing, talking, and thinking out life's triumphs and defeats. *Journal of Personality and Social Psychology, 90*(4), 692-708.

25. (1) Gander, F., Proyer, R. T., & Ruch, W. (2016). Positive psychology interventions addressing pleasure, engagement, meaning, positive relationships, and accomplishment increase well-being and ameliorate depressive symptoms: A randomized, placebo-controlled online study. *Frontiers in Psychology, 7*, 686. (2) Proyer, R. T., Gander, F., Wellenzohn, S., & Ruch, W. (2015). Strengths-based positive psychology interventions: A randomized, placebo-controlled online trial on long-term effects for a signature strengths- vs. a lesser strengths-intervention. *Frontiers in Psychology, 6*, 456. (3) Seligman et al. (2005), op. cit. (See ch. 7, note 8).

26. (1) Boehm at al. (2011), op. cit. (See ch. 7, note 17). (2) Burton, C., & King, L. (2008). Effects of (very) brief writing on health: the two-minute miracle. *British Journal of Health Psychology, 13*(1), 9-14. (3) King (2001), op. cit. (See ch. 7, note 23). (4) Layous, K., Nelson, S. K., & Lyubomirsky, S. (2012). What is the optimal way to deliver a positive activity intervention? The case of writing about one's best possible selves. *Journal of Happiness Studies, 14*(2), 635-654. (5) Lyubomirsky, S., Dickerhoof, R., Boehm, J. K., & Sheldon, K. M. (2009). Becoming happier takes both a will and a proper way: Two experimental longitudinal interventions to boost well-being. *Emotion, 11*(2), 391-402. (6) (Layous et al. (2013), op. cit. (See ch. 7, note 23).

27. Sheldon, K. M., & Lyubomirsky, S. (2006). How to increase and sustain positive emotion: The effects of expressing gratitude and visualizing best possible selves. *Journal of Positive Psychology, 1*, 73-82.

28. Seligman (2011), op. cit. (See ch. 6, note 17).

29. (1) Lyubomirsky (2008), op. cit. (See ch. 7, note 12). (2) Lyubomirsky (2014), op. cit. (See ch. 7, note 12).

30. Layous, K., & Lyubomirsky, S. (2014). The how, why, what, when, and who of happiness: Mechanisms underlying the success of positive interventions. In J. Gruber & J. Moscowitz (Eds.), *Positive emotion: Integrating the light sides and dark sides* (pp. 473-495). New York, NY: Oxford University Press.

31. Lyubomirsky (2011), op. cit. (See ch. 6, note 19).

32. Leventhal, A. M., Martin, R. I., Seals, R. W., Tapia, E., & Rehm, L. P. (2007) Investigating the dynamics of affect: Psychological mechanisms of affective adaptation to pleasurable stimuli. *Motivation and Emotion, 31*, 145-157.

33. Sheldon, K. M. & Lyubomirsky, S. (2007). Is it possible to become happier? (And if so, how?) *Social and Personality Psychology Compass, 1*, 129-145.

34. (1) Parks, A., Della Porta, M., Pierce, R. S., Zilca, R., & Lyubomirsky, S. (2012). Pursuing happiness in everyday life: The characteristics and behaviors of

online happiness seekers. *Emotion, 12*(6), 1222-1234. (2) Schueller, S. M., & Parks, A. C. (2012). Disseminating self-help: Positive psychology exercises in an online trial. *Journal of Medical Internet Research, 14*, e63. (3) Seligman et al. (2005), op. cit. (See ch. 7, note 8). (4) Sin & Lyubomirsky (2009), op. cit. (See ch. 7, note 15).

35. Schueller & Parks (2012), op. cit. (See ch. 7, note 34).

36. Parks et al. (2012), op. cit. (See ch. 7, note 34).

37. Ibid.

38. Sheldon, K. M., Boehm, J. K., & Lyubomirsky, S. (2012). Variety is the spice of happiness: The hedonic adaptation prevention (HAP) model. In I. Boniwell & S. David (Eds.), *Oxford handbook of happiness* (pp. 901–914). New York, NY: Oxford University Press.

39. Sheldon, K. M., & Lyubomirsky, S. (2012). The challenge of staying happier: Testing the hedonic adaptation prevention model. *Personality and Social Psychology Bulletin, 38*, 670–680.

40. Lyubomirsky, S., & Layous, K. (2013). How do simple positive activities increase well-being? *Current Directions in Psychological Science, 22*, 57-62.

41. (1) Lyubomirsky et al. (2011), op. cit. (See ch. 7, note 16). (2) Lyubomirsky et al. (2009), op. cit. (See ch. 7, note 26). (3) Ng, W. (2015). Boosting well-being with positive psychology interventions: Moderating role of personality and other factors. *Journal of Contemporary Psychotherapy, 45*(2), 79-87.

42. (1) Lyubomirsky et al. (2011), op. cit. (See ch. 7, note 16). (2) Seligman et al. (2005), op. cit. (See ch. 7, note 8).

43. Ibid.

44. Layous et al. (2013), op. cit. (See ch. 7, note 23).

45. Ibid.

46. (1) Schueller, S. M. (2010). Preferences for positive psychology exercises. *Journal of Positive Psychology, 5*, 192–203. (2) Schueller, S. (2011). To each his own well-being boosting intervention: Using preference to guide selection. *Journal of Positive Psychology, 6*(4), 300-313.

47. Dickerhoof, R. M. (2007). Expressing optimism and gratitude: A longitudinal investigation of cognitive strategies to increase wellbeing. *Dissertation Abstracts International, 68*, 4174 (UMI No. 3270426).

48. Lyubomirsky et al. (2005), op cit. (See ch. 7, note 20).

49. Nelson, S. K., Della Porta, M. D., Jacobs Bao, K., Lee, H. C., Choi, I., & Lyubomirsky, S. (2015). 'It's up to you': Experimentally manipulated autonomy support for prosocial behavior improves well-being in two cultures over six weeks. *Journal of Positive Psychology, 10*(5), 463-476.

50. Layous et al. (2012), op. cit. (See ch. 7, note 26).

Chapter 8: Seizing Opportunities for Mindful Moments

1. Siegel (2010), op. cit. (See ch. 3, note 8).

2. Laboratory of Neuro Imaging (LONI). Retrieved from http://loni.usc.edu/

3. Butler, P. E. (2008). *Talking to yourself: How cognitive behavior therapy can change your life*. Charleston, SC: BookSurge Publishing.

4. Helmstetter, S. (1990). *What to say when you talk to yourself*. New York, NY: Pocket Books.

5. Gollwitzer, P. M., & Sheeran, P. (2006). Implementation intentions and goal achievement: A meta-analysis of effects and processes. In M. P. Zanna (Ed.), *Advances in experimental social psychology* (vol. 38, pp. 69-119). San Diego, CA: Elsevier Academic Press.

6. Duhigg, C. (2014). *The power of habit: Why we do what we do in life and business*. New York, NY: Random House.

7. Smith, K., & Graybiel, A. (2013). A dual operator view of habitual behavior reflecting cortical and striatal dynamics. *Neuron, 79*(2), 361-374.

8. Maltz, M. (1960). *Psycho-Cybernetics*. New York, NY: Simon & Schuster.

9. Luskin & Pelletier (2005), op. cit. (See ch. 4, note 8).

10. Lally, P., van Jaarsveld, C. M., Potts, H. W., & Wardle, J. (2010). How are habits formed: Modelling habit formation in the real world. *European Journal of Social Psychology, 40*(6), 998-1009.

Chapter 10: Optimism and Gratitude: Essential Outlooks for Living Mindfully

1. Seligman (2011), op. cit. (See ch. 6, note 13).

2. Buchanan, G. M. (1995). Explanatory style and coronary heart disease. In G. M. Buchanan & M. P. Seligman (Eds.), *Explanatory style* (pp. 225-232). Hillsdale, NJ: Lawrence Erlbaum.

3. Seligman (2011), op. cit. (See ch. 6, note 17).

4. Seligman, M. E. P. (2006). *Learned optimism: How to change your mind and your life* (2nd ed.). New York, NY: Pocket Books.

5. Peterson. C., & Seligman, M. E. P. (1984). Causal explanations as a risk factor for depression: Theory and evidence. *Psychological Review, 91*(3), 347-374.

6. Peterson, C. (1988). Explanatory style as a risk factor for illness. *Cognitive Therapy and Research, 12*(2), 119-132.

7. Rankin (2014), op. cit. (See ch. 3, note 45).

8. Kobasa, S. C. (1979). Stressful life events, personality, and health: An inquiry into hardiness. *Journal of Personality and Social Psychology, 37*(1), 1-11.

9. Seligman (2011), op. cit. (See ch. 6, note 17).

10. (1) Bellizzi, K. M. (2004). Expressions of generativity and posttraumatic growth in adult cancer survivors. *International Journal of Aging and Human Development, 58*(4), 267-287. (2) Tedeschi, R. G., & Calhoun, L. G. (2004). Posttraumatic growth: Conceptual foundations and empirical evidences. *Psychological Inquiry, 15*, 1-18. (3) Updegraff, J. A., & Marshall, G. N. (2005). Predictors of perceived growth following direct exposure to community violence. *Journal of Social and Clinical Psychology, 24*(4), 538-560.

11. Seligman (2011), op. cit. (See ch. 6, note 13).

12. Seligman (2011), op. cit. (See ch. 6, note 17).

13. Davidson & Begley (2012), op. cit. (See ch. 3, note 8).

14. Seligman (2011), op. cit. (See ch. 6, note 13).

15. Davidson & Begley (2012), op. cit. (See ch. 3, note 8).

16. Seligman (2006), op. cit. (See ch. 10, note 4).

17. Peterson (1988), op. cit. (See ch. 10, note 6).

18. Cohen, S., Alper, C., Doyle, W., Treanor, J., & Turner, R. (2006). Positive emotional style predicts resistance to illness after experimental exposure to rhinovirus or influenza a virus. *Psychosomatic Medicine, 68*(6), 809-815.

19. (1) Bennett, K. & Elliott, M. (2005). Pessimistic explanatory style and cardiac health: What is the relation and the mechanism that links them? *Basic and Applied Social Psychology, 27*(3), 239-248. (2) Giltay et al (2004), op. cit. (See ch. 6, note 59). (3) Tindle, H., Chang, Y.F., Kuller, L., Manson, J. E., Robinson, J. G., Rosal, M. C.,...Matthews, K. A. (2009). Optimism, cynical hostility, & incident coronary heart disease and mortality in the Women's Health Initiative. *Circulation, 118*, 1145-1146.

20. Seligman (2011), op. cit. (See ch. 6, note 13).

21. Kubzansky, L., Sparrow, D., Vokonas, P., & Kawachi, I. (2001). Is the glass half empty or half full? A prospective study of optimism and coronary heart disease in the Normative Aging Study. *Psychosomatic Medicine, 63*, 910-916.

22. Aspinwall, L. G. & Tedeschi, R. G. (2010). The value of positive psychology for health psychology: Progress and pitfalls in examining the relation of positive phenomena to health. *Annals of Behavioral Medicine, 39*(1), 4-15.

23. Ibid.

24. Seligman (2006), op. cit. (See ch. 10, note 4).

25. Aspinwall & Tedeschi (2010), op. cit. (See ch. 10, note 22).

26. Kim, E. S., Hagan, K. A., Grodstein, F., DeMeo, D. L., De Vivo, I., & Kubzansky, L. D. (2017). Optimism and cause-specific mortality: A prospective cohort study. *American Journal of Epidemiology, 185*(1), 21-29.

27. Peterson. C., Seligman, M. E. P., & Vaillant, R. (1988). Pessimistic explanatory style is a risk factor for physical illness: A thirty-five-year longitudinal study. *Journal of Personality and Social Psychology, 55*(1), 23-27.

28. Arrien (2011), op. cit. (See ch. 7, note 5).

29. Emmons, R. A. (2007). *Thanks! How the new science of gratitude can make you happier*. New York, NY: Houghton Mifflin, 554.

30. Ahrens, A. H., & Forbes, C. N. (2016). Gratitude. In M. M. Tugade, M. N. Shiota, & L. D. Kirby (Eds.), *Handbook of positive emotions* (pp. 342-361). New York, NY: Guilford Press.

31. (1) Arrien (2011), op. cit. (See ch. 7, note 5). (2) Emmons (2007), op. cit. (See ch. 10, note 29). (3) Fredrickson, B. L. (2004). Gratitude, like other positive emotions, broadens and builds. In R. A. Emmons & M. E. McCullough (Eds.), *The psychology of gratitude* (pp. 145-166). New York, NY: Oxford University Press. (4) Lyubomirsky, Sheldon, & Schkade (2005), op. cit. (See ch. 7, note

20). (5) Wood, A. M., Joseph, S., & Maltby, J. (2008). Gratitude uniquely predicts satisfaction with life: Incremental validity above the domains and facets of the five factor model. *Personality and Individual Differences*, *45*, 49-54.

32. Kaufman, S. B. (2015, August 2). Which character strengths are most predictive of well-being? *Scientific American*. Retrieved from https://blogs. scientificamerican.com/beautiful-mindswhich-character-strengths-are-most-predictive-of-well-being/

33. (1) Emmons & McCullough (2003), op. cit. (See ch. 7, note 16). (2) Lyubomirsky (2006), op. cit. (See ch. 7, note 16). (3) Lyubomirsky (2009), op. cit. (See ch. 7, note 26).

34. (1) Emmons & McCullough (2003), op. cit. (See ch. 7, note 16). (2) Wood, A. M., Froh, J., Adam, J., & Geraghty, W.A. (2010). Gratitude and well-being: A review and theoretical integration, *Clinical Psychology Review*, *30*, 890-905.

35. Sheldon, K.M., & Lyubomirsky, S. (2006). How to increase and sustain positive emotion: The effects of expressing gratitude and visualizing best possible selves. *Journal of Positive Psychology*, 73-82.

36. Kashdan, T. B., Uswatte, G., & Julian, T. (2006). Gratitude and hedonic and eudaimonic well-being in Vietnam war veterans. *Behaviour Research and Therapy*, *44*(2), 177-199.

37. Hamilton (2010), op. cit. (See ch. 3, note 31).

38. Korb, A. (2015). *The upward spiral: Using neuroscience to reverse the course of depression, one small change at a time*. New York, NY: New Harbinger Publications.

39. (1) Emmons & McCullough (2003), op. cit. (See ch. 7, note 16). (2) Wood, A. M., Maltby, J., Gillett, R., Linley, P. A., & Joseph, S. (2008). The role of gratitude in the development of social support, stress, and depression: Two longitudinal studies. *Journal of Research in Personality*, *42*, 854-871.

40. Emmons, R. A., & Mishra, A. (2011). Why gratitude enhances well-being: What we know, what we need to know. In D. Sheldon, (Ed.), *Designing positive psychology: Taking stock and moving forward* (pp. 248-262). New York, NY: Oxford University Press.

41. Ahrens & Forbes (2016), op. cit. (See ch. 7, note 30).

42. McCullough, M., Kimeldorf, M., & Cohen, A. (2008). An adaptation for altruism? The social causes, social effects, and social evolution of gratitude. *Current Directions in Psychological Science*, *17*(4), 281-285.

43. (1) Ibid. (2) Nowak, M. A. & Roch, S. (2007). Upstream reciprocity and the evolution of gratitude. *Proceedings of the Royal Society B: Biological Sciences*, *274*, 605-610.

44. Korb (2015), op. cit. (See ch. 10, note 38).

45. McCullough, M. E., Kilpatrick, S. D., Emmons, R. A., & Larson, D. B. (2001). Is gratitude a moral affect? *Psychological Bulletin*, *127*, 249-266.

46. Wood et al. (2008), op. cit. (See ch. 10, note 39).

47. Grant, A. M., & Gino, F. (2010). A little thanks goes a long way: Explaining

why gratitude expressions motivate prosocial behavior. *Journal of Personality and Social Psychology*, 98(6), 946-955.

48. Ibid.

49. (1) McCullough et al. (2008), op. cit. (See ch. 10, note 42). (2) Bartlett, M. Y., & DeSteno, D. (2006). Gratitude and prosocial behavior: Helping when it costs you. *Psychological Science*, 17, 319-325.

50. Seligman et al. (2005), op. cit. (See ch. 7, note 8).

51. (1) Boehm et al. (2011), op. cit. (See ch. 7, note 17). (2) Froh et al. (2008), op. cit. (See ch. 7, note 16). (3) Lyubomirsky et al. (2011), op. cit. (See ch. 7, note 16).

52. Toepfer, S., Cichy, K., & Peters, P. (2012). Letters of gratitude: Further evidence for author benefits. *Journal of Happiness Studies*, 13(1), 187-201.

53. Emmons & McCullough (2003), op. cit. (See ch. 7, note 16).

54. Simon-Thomas, E. R., & Smith, J. A. (2013, January 10). How grateful are Americans? *Greater Good Magazine*. Retrieved from https://greatergood. berkeley.edu/article/item/how_grateful_are_americans.

Chapter 11: The Many Benefits of Kindness

1. Keltner, D. (2009). *Born to be good: The science of a meaningful life*. New York, NY: W. W. Norton & Company.

2. Jinpa, T. (2015). *A fearless heart: How the courage to be compassionate can transform our lives*. New York, NY: Avery.

3. Hamilton (2010), op. cit. (See ch. 3, note 31).

4. Ibid.

5. Jinpa (2015), op. cit. (See ch. 11, note 2).

6. Hamilton, D. (2017). *The five side effects of kindness: This book will make you feel better, be happier & live longer*. New York, NY: Avery.

7. Hamilton (2010), op. cit. (See ch. 3, note 31).

8. Keltner, D. (2010). *The compassionate instinct: The science of human goodness*. New York, NY: W. W. Norton & Company.

9. Barber, N. (2004). *Kindness in a cruel world: The evolution of altruism*. New York, NY: Prometheus Books.

10. Aknin, L. B., Hamlin, J. K., & Dunn, E. W. (2012). Giving leads to happiness in young children. *PLos ONE*, 7, e39211.

11. Aknin, J., Barrington-Leigh, L., Dunn, C., Helliwell, E., Burns, J., Biswas-Diener, R.,...Norton, R. (2013). Prosocial spending and well-being: Cross-cultural evidence for a psychological universal. *Journal of Personality and Social Psychology*, 104(4), 635-652.

12. Keltner, D. (2017). *The power paradox: How we gain and lose influence*. New York, NY: Penguin Books.

13. Ibid.

14. (1) Dolan, P., Peasgood, T. & White, M. (2008). Do we really know what makes us happy? A review of the economic literature on the factors associated with subjective wellbeing. *Journal of Economic Psychology*, 29, 94-

122. (2) Meier, S., & Stutzer, A. (2008). Is volunteering rewarding in itself? *Economica, 75,* 39-59.

15. Exline, J. J., Lisan, A. M., & Lisan, E. R. (2012). Reflecting on acts of kindness toward the self: Emotions, generosity, and the role of social norms. *Journal of Positive Psychology, 7*(1), 45-56.

16. Poulin, M. J., Brown, S. L., Dillard, A. J., & Smith, D. M. (2013). Giving to others and the association between stress and mortality. *American Journal of Public Health, 103*(9), 1649-1655.

17. Hampton, K. N. (2016). Why is helping behavior declining in the United States but not in Canada?: Ethnic diversity, new technologies, and other explanations. *City & Community, 15*(4), 380-399.

18. Aknin et al. (2013), op. cit. (See ch. 11, note 11).

19. Whillans, A.V., Seider, S. C., Dwyer, R., L., Chen, L., S., Novick, S., Graminga, K. J.,...Dunn, E. W. (2016). Does volunteering improve well-being?" *Comprehensive Results in Social Psychology, 1*(1-3), 35-50.

20. Binder, M., & Freytag, A. (2013). Volunteering, subjective well-being and public policy. *Journal of Economic Psychology, 34,* 97-119.

21. Gimenez-Nadal, J. I., & Molina, J. A. (2015).Voluntary activities and daily happiness in the United States. *Economic Inquiry, 53*(4), 1735-1750.

22. (1) Dunn, E. W., Aknin, L. B., & Norton, M. I. (2008). Spending money on others promotes happiness. *Science, 319,* 1687-1688. (2) Lyubomirsky et al. (2005), op. cit. (See ch. 7, note 20). (3) Otake et al. (2006), op. cit. (See ch. 7, note 21).

23. Haidt, J. (2006). *The happiness hypothesis: Finding modern truth in ancient wisdom.* New York, NY: Basic Books.

24. Norton, L. B., Aknin, E., Dunn, W., Gillian, M., & Sandstrom, M. (2013). Does social connection turn good deeds into good feelings? on the value of putting the 'social' in prosocial spending. *International Journal of Happiness and Development, 1*(2), 155-171.

25. Ibid.

26. Mongrain, M., Chin, J. M., & Shapira, L. B. (2011). Practicing compassion increases happiness and self-esteem. *Journal of Happiness Studies, 12,* 963-981.

27. Buchanan, K. E., & Bardi, A. (2010). Acts of kindness and acts of novelty affect life satisfaction. *Journal of Social Psychology, 150*(3), 235-237.

28. Sheldon et al. (2012), op. cit. (See ch. 7, note 38).

29. Alden, L. E., & Trew, J. L. (2013). If it makes you happy: Engaging in kind acts increases positive affect in socially anxious individuals. *Emotion, 13,* 64-75.

30. Lyubomirsky et al. (2005), op. cit. (See ch. 7, note 20).

31. Otake et al. (2006), op. cit. (See ch. 7, note 21).

Chapter 12: The Power of Compassion and Self-Compassion

1. Klimecki, O. M., Leiberg, S., Lamm, C., & Singer, T. (2013). Functional neural plasticity and associated changes in positive affect after compassion training. *Cerebral Cortex, 23,* 1552-1561.

2. Jinpa (2015), op. cit. (See ch. 11, note 2).

3. Ekman, P. A. (2010). Darwin's compassionate view of human nature. *Journal of the American Medical Association, 303*, 557-558.

4. Shapiro, S. L., & Carlson, L. E. (2009). *The art and science of mindfulness: Integrating mindfulness into psychology and the helping professions.* Washington, DC: American Psychological Association.

5. Ricard, M. (2015). *Altruism: The power of compassion to change yourself and the world.* New York, NY: Little, Brown & Company.

6. Zeng, X., Chiu, C. P. K., Wang, R., Oei, T. P. S. & Leung, F. Y. K. (2015). The effect of loving-kindness meditation on positive emotions: a meta-analytic review. *Frontiers in Psychology, 6*, 1693.

7. Weng, H. Y., Fox, A. S., Shackman, A. J., Stodola, D. E., Caldwell, J. Z., Olson, M. C., *et al.* (2013). Compassion training alters altruism and neural responses to suffering. *Psychological Science, 24*, 1171-1180.

8. (1) Condon, P., Desbordes, G., Miller, W. B., & DeSteno, D. (2013). Meditation increases compassionate responses to suffering. *Psychological Science, 24*(10), 2125-2127. (2) Condon, P. (2015). Cultivating compassion: The effects of compassion- and mindfulness-based meditation on pro-social mental states and behavior. *Dissertation Abstracts International: Section B: The Sciences and Engineering, 76*(1-B(E)).

9. Mongrain, M., Chin, J. M., & Shapira, L. B. (2011). Practicing compassion increases happiness and self-esteem. *Journal of Happiness Studies, 12*, 963-981.

10. Klimecki, O. M., Leiberg, S., Ricard, M., & Singer, T. (2014). Differential pattern of functional brain plasticity after compassion and empathy training. *Social, Cognitive and Affective Neuroscience, 9*(6), 873-879.

11. Davidson, R. J., & Kaszniak, A. W. (2015). Conceptual and methodological issues in research on mindfulness and meditation. *American Psychologist, 70*(7), 581-592.

12. Weng et al. (2013), op. cit. (See ch. 12, note 7).

13. (1) Klimecki et al. (2013), op. cit. (See ch. 12, note 1). (2) Hutcherson, C. A., Seppala, E. M., & Gross, J. J. (2015). The neural correlates of social connection. *Cognitive Affective Behavioral Neuroscience, 15*, 1-14.

14. (1) Weng et al. (2013), op. cit. (See ch. 12, note 7). (2) Klimecki et al. (2014), op. cit. (See ch. 12, note 10). (3) Lutz, A., Brefczynski-Lewis, J., Johnstone, T., & Davidson, R. J. (2008). Regulation of the neural circuitry of emotion by compassion meditation: Effects of meditative expertise. *PLos ONE, 3*(3), e1897.

15. Jinpa (2015), op. cit. (See ch. 11, note 2).

16. (1) Pace, T. W., Negi, L. T., Adame, D. D., Cole, S. P., Sivilli, T. I., Brown, T. D.,...Raison, C. L. (2009). Effect of compassion meditation on neuroendocrine, innate immune and behavioral responses to psychosocial stress. *Psychoneuroendocrinology, 34*, 87-98. (2) Pace, T. W., Negi, L. T., Dodson-Lavelle, B., Ozawa-de Silva, B., Reddy, S. D., Cole, S. P.,...Raison, C. L. (2013).

Engagement with cognitively-based compassion training is associated with reduced salivary C-reactive protein from before to after training in foster care program adolescents. *Psychoneuroendocrinology, 38*(2), 294-299.

17. (1) Pace, T. W. W., Negi, L. T., Sivilli, T. I., Issa, M. J., Cole, S. P., Adame, D. D., & Raison, C. L. (2010). Innate immune, neuroendocrine and behavioral responses to psychosocial stress do not predict subsequent compassion meditation practice time. *Psychoneuroendocrinology, 35*, 310-315. (2) Pace et al. (2009), op. cit. (See ch. 12, note 16).

18. Carson, J., Keefe, F., Lynch, T., Carson, K., Goli, V., Fras, A., & Thorp, S. (2005). Loving-kindness meditation for chronic low back pain: results from a pilot trial. *Journal of Holistic Nursing, 23*(3), 287-304.

19. (1) Lumma, A., Kok, B., & Singer, T. (2015). Is meditation always relaxing? investigating heart rate, heart rate variability, experienced effort and like-ability during training of three types of meditation. *International Journal of Psychophysiology, 97*(1), 38-45. (2) Condon et al. (2013), op. cit. (See ch. 12, note 8).

20. Fredrickson et al. (2008), op. cit. (See ch. 7, note 21).

21. Salzberg, S. (2002). *Lovingkindness: The revolutionary art of happiness.* Boston, MA: Shambhala.

22. Hutcherson, C. A., Seppala, E. M., & Gross, J. J. (2008). Loving-kindness meditation increases social connectedness. *Emotion, 8*, 720-724.

23. Zeng et al. (2015), op. cit. (See ch. 12, note 6).

24. Koopmann-Holm, B., Sze, J., Ochs, C., & Tsai, J. L. (2013). Buddhist-inspired meditation increases the value of calm. Performing a single kind act a day over ten days produced increases in happiness. *Emotion, 13*(3), 497-505.

25. Feldman, G., Greeson, J., & Senville, J. (2010). Differential effects of mindful breathing, progressive muscle relaxation, and loving-kindness meditation on decentering and negative reactions to repetitive thoughts. *Behaviour Research & Therapy, 48*(10), 1002-1011.

26. Koopmann-Holm et al. (2013), op. cit. (See ch. 12, note 24).

27. Leiberg, S., Klimecki, O., & Singer, T. (2011). Short-term compassion training increases prosocial behavior in a newly developed prosocial game. *PLos ONE, 6*, e17798.

28. Wheeler, E. A., & Lenick, N. W. (2014).Brief compassion meditation and re-call of positive emotion words. *Journal of Articulate Support Null Hypothesis, 11*, 12-20.

29. Kok, B. E., Coffey, K. A., Cohn, M. A., Catalino, L. I., Vacharkulksemsuk, T., Algoe, S. B., &...Fredrickson, B. L. (2013). How positive emotions build phys-ical health: Perceived positive social connections account for the upward spiral between positive emotions and vagal tone. *Psychological Science, 24*, 1123-1132.

30. Weytens, F., Luminet, O., Verhofstadt, L. L., & Mikolajczak, M. (2014). An integrative theory-driven positive emotion regulation intervention. *PLos ONE, 9*, e95677.

31. Kok et al. (2013), op. cit. (See ch. 12, note 29).

32. Cohn, M. A., & Fredrickson, B. L. (2010).In search of durable positive psychology interventions: predictors and consequences of long-term positive behavior change. *Journal of Positive Psychology*, 5, 355-366.

33. Fredrickson et al. (2008), op. cit. (See ch. 7, note 22).

34. Galante, J., Galante, I., Bekkers, M., & Gallacher, J. (2014). Effect of kindness-based meditation on health and well-being: A systematic review and meta-analysis. *Journal of Consulting and Clinical Psychology*, 82(6), 1101-1114.

35. Weng et al. (2013), op. cit. (See ch. 12, note 7).

36. Condon (2015), op. cit. (See ch. 12, note 8).

37. Arylo, C. (2012). *Madly in love with me: The daring adventure of becoming your own best friend*. Novato, CA: New World Library.

38. Neff, K. D. (2011). *Self-compassion: Stop beating yourself up and leave insecurity behind*. New York, NY: William Morrow.

39. LeDoux, J. (1998). *The emotional brain: The mysterious underpinnings of emotional life*. New York, NY: Simon & Schuster.

40. Neff, K., & Vonk, R. (2009). Self-compassion versus global self-esteem: Two different ways of relating to oneself. *Journal of Personality*, 77(1), 23-50.

41. McGonigal, K. (2016, October 22). The science and practice of compassion. Retrieved from https://youtu.be/6BN9tAVQfQg

42. (1) Kelly, A. C., Zuroff, D. C., & Shapira, L. B. (2009). Soothing oneself and resisting self-attacks: The treatment of two intrapersonal deficits in depression vulnerability. *Cognitive Therapy and Research*, 33, 301-313. (2) Leary, M. R., Tate, E. B., Adams, C. E., Allen, A. B., & Hancock, J. (2007). Self-compassion and reactions to unpleasant self-relevant events: The implications of treating oneself kindly. *Journal of Personality and Social Psychology*, 92, 887-904. (3) Pauley, G., & McPherson, S. (2010). The experience and meaning of compassion and self-compassion for individuals with depression or anxiety. *Psychology and Psychotherapy: Theory, Research and Practice*, 83, 129-143. (4) Terry, M. L., & Leary, M. R. (2011). Self-compassion, self-regulation, and health. *Self and Identity*, 10, 352-362. (5) Van Dam, N. T., Sheppard, S. C., Forsyth, J. P., & Earleywine, M. (2011). Self-compassion is a better predictor than mindfulness of symptom severity and quality of life in mixed anxiety and depression. *Journal of Anxiety Disorders*, 25, 123-130.

43. (1) Heffernan, M., Griffin, M., McNulty, S., & Fitzpatrick, J. J. (2010). Self-compassion and emotional intelligence in nurses. *International Journal of Nursing Practice*, 16, 366-373. (2) Hollis-Walker, L., & Colosimo, K. (2011). Mindfulness, self-compassion, and happiness in non-meditators: A theoretical and empirical examination. *Personality and Individual Differences*, 50, 222-227. (3) Neff, K. D., Rude, S. S., & Kirkpatrick, K. (2007). An examination of self-compassion in relation to positive psychological functioning and personality traits. *Journal of Research in Personality*, 41, 139-154. (4) Neff, K. D. (2012). The science of self-compassion. In C. Germer, & R. Siegel (Eds.), *Compassion and wisdom in psychotherapy* (pp. 79-92). New York, NY: Guilford Press.

44. Neff & Vonk (2009), op. cit. (See ch. 12, note 40).

45. Neff, K. D., & Germer, C. K. (2013). A pilot study and randomized controlled trial of the Mindful Self-Compassion program. *Journal of Clinical Psychology*, 69(1), 28-44.

46. Arch, J., Landy, L., & Brown, K. (2016). Predictors and moderators of biopsychological social stress responses following brief self-compassion meditation training. *Psychoneuroendocrinology*, 69, 35-40.

47. Desmond, T. (2015). *Self-compassion in psychotherapy: Mindfulness-based practices for healing and transformation*. New York, NY: W. W. Norton & Company.

48. Arch, J. J., Brown, K. W., Dean, D. J., Landy, L. N., Brown, K. D., & Laudenslager, M. L. (2014). Self-compassion training modulates alpha-amylase, heart rate variability, and subjective responses to social evaluative threat in women. *Psychoneuroendocrinology*, 42, 49-58.

49. Odou, N., & Brinker, J. (2014). Exploring the relationship between rumination, self-compassion, and mood. *Self & Identity*, 13(4), 449-459.

50. Odou, N., & Brinker, J. (2015). Self-compassion, a better alternative to rumination than distraction as a response to negative mood. *Journal of Positive Psychology*, 10(5), 447-457.

Chapter 13: Stress: The Good, the Bad and the Ugly

1. American Psychological Association. (2016). *Stress in America: Coping with change*. Washington, DC: American Psychological Association.

2. American Psychological Association. (2017). *Stress in America: Coping with change*. Washington, DC: American Psychological Association.

3. American Psychological Association (2016), op. cit. (See ch. 13, note 1).

4. Northrup, C. (2013). *Goddesses never age: The secret prescription for radiance, vitality, and well-being*. Carlsbad, CA: Hay House.

5. Childre, D., & Rozman, D. (2005). *Transforming stress: The Heartmath solution for relieving worry, fatigue, and tension*. New York, NY: New Harbinger Publications.

6. Childre & Martin (2000), op. cit. (See ch. 6, note 74).

7. Rankin (2014), op. cit. (See ch. 3, note 45).

8. Martinez (2014), op. cit. (See ch. 6, note 27).

9. Northrup (2013), op. cit. (See ch. 13, note 4).

10. Luskin & Pelletier (2005), op. cit. (See ch. 4, note 8).

11. Sapolsky, R. M. (1998). *Why zebras don't get ulcers: An updated guide to stress, stress-related diseases, and coping*. New York, NY: Freeman.

12. Ibid.

13. Ibid.

14. Newberg, A., & Waldman, M. R. (2010). *Words can change your brain: 12 conversation strategies to build trust, resolve conflict, and increase intimacy*. New York, NY: Avery.

15. Selye, H. (1974). *Stress without distress*. New York, NY: J. B. Lippincott.

16. Sapolsky, R. (2012, March 20). When is stress good for you? *Greater Good Science*

Center. Retrieved from https://www.youtube.com/watch?v=6x9zxSCYbVA_

17. Kaufer, D., Friedman, A., Seidman, S., & Soreq, H. (1998). Acute stress facilitates long-lasting changes in cholinergic gene expression. *Nature, 393*(6683), 373-377.

18. Dhabhar, F. S. (2014). Effects of stress on immune function: The good, the bad, and the beautiful. *Immunologic Research, 58*, 193-210.

19. Dhabhar, F. S. (2009). Enhancing versus suppressive effects of stress on immune function: Implications for immunoprotection and immunopathology. *Neuroimmunomodulation, 16*, 300-317.

20. Dhabhar, F. S., Saul, A. N., Daugherty, C., Holmes, T. H., Bouley, D. M., & Oberyszyn, T. M. (2010). Short-term stress enhances cellular immunity and increases early resistance to squamous cell carcinoma. *Brain Behavior and Immunity, 24*(1), 127-137.

21. McGonigal, K. (2015). *The upside of stress: Why stress is good for you and how to get good at it.* New York, NY: Avery.

22. Crum, A. J., Salovey. P., & Achor, S. (2013). Rethinking stress: The role of mindsets in determining the stress response. *Journal of Personality and Social Psychology, 104*(4), 716-733.

23. Sapolsky, R. M. (2017). *Behave: The biology of humans at our best and worst.* New York, NY: Penguin Press.

24. Lazarus, R. S., & Folkman, S. (1984). *Stress, appraisal, and coping.* New York, NY: Springer.

25. (1) Aldwin, C. M. (2007). *Stress, coping, and development: An integrative perspective* (2nd ed.). New York, NY: Guilford Press. (2) Aldwin, C. M., Sutton, K. J., Chiara, G., & Spiro, A., III. (1996). Age differences in stress, coping, and appraisal: Findings from the Normative Aging Study. *Journal of Gerontology: Psychological Sciences, 51B*, 179.

26. (1) Almeida, D.M. (2005). Resilience and vulnerability to daily stressors assessed via diary methods. *Current Directions in Psychological Science, 14*(2), 64-68. (2) Serido, J., Almeida, D.M., & Wethington, E. (2004). Chronic stressors and daily hassles: Unique and interactive relationships with psychological distress. *Journal of Health and Social Behavior, 45*(1), 17-33.

27. Rankin (2014), op. cit. (See ch. 3, note 45).

28. Larrivee, B. (2012). *Cultivating teacher renewal: Guarding against stress and burnout.* Lanham, MD: Rowman & Littlefield Education.

29. (1) Dimsdale, J. E. (2008). Psychological stress and cardiovascular disease. *Journal of the American College of Cardiology, 51*(13), 1237-1246. (2) Poulin, M. J., Brown, S. L., Dillard, A. J., & Smith, D. M. (2013). Giving to others and the association between stress and mortality. *American Journal of Public Health, 103*(9), 1649-1655.

30. Childre & Martin (2000), op. cit. (See ch. 6, note 74).

31. Miller, G. E., Cohen, S., Pressman, S., Barkin, A., Rabin, B. S., & Treanor, J. J. (2004). Psychological stress and antibody response to influenza vaccination:

When is the critical period for stress, and how does it get inside the body? *Psychosomatic Medicine, 66*(2), 215-223.

32. (1) Cohen, S., Janicki-Deverts, D., Doyle, W. J., Miller, G. E., Frank, E., Rabin, B. S., & Turner, R. B. (2012). Chronic stress, glucocorticoid receptor resistance, inflammation, and disease risk. *Proceedings of the National Academy of Sciences, 109*(16), 5995-5999. (2) Schneiderman, N., Ironson, G., & Siegel, S. D. (2005). Stress and health: Psychological, behavioral, and biological determinants. *Annual Review of Clinical Psychology, 1*, 607-628. (3) Segerstrom, S. C., & Miller, G. E. (2004). Psychological stress and the human immune system: A meta-analytic study of 30 years of inquiry. *Psychological Bulletin, 130*(4), 601-630.

33. Chen, E., Hanson, M. D., Paterson, L. Q., Griffin, M. J., Walker, H. A. & Miller, G. E. (2006). Socioeconomic status and inflammatory processes in childhood asthma: The role of psychological stress. *Journal of Allergy & Clinical Immunology, 117*(5), 1014-1020.

34. Perlmutter, D. (2015). *Brain maker: The power of gut microbes to heal and protect your brain–for life.* New York, NY: Little, Brown and Company.

35. Epel, E. S., Blackburn, E. H., Jue, L., Dhabhar, F. S., Adler, N. E., Morrow, J. D., & Cawthon, R. M. (2004). Accelerated telomere shortening in response to life stress. *Proceedings of the National Academy of Sciences, 101*(49), 17312-17315.

36. Blackburn, E., & Epel, E. (2017). *The telomere effect: A revolutionary approach to living younger, healthier, longer.* New York, NY: Grand Central Publishing.

37. (1) Matthews, K. A., & Gump, B. B. (2002). Chronic work stress and marital dissolution increase risk of posttrial mortality in men from the Multiple Risk Factor Intervention Trial. *Archives of Internal Medicine, 162*(3), 309-315. (2) Nielsen, N. R., Kristensen, T. S., Schnohr, P., & Gronbaek, M. (2008). Perceived stress and cause-specific morality among men and women: Results from a prospective cohort study. *American Journal of Epidemiology, 168*(5), 481-496. (3) Rosengren, A., Orth-Gomer, K., Wedel, H., & Wilhelmsen, L. (1993). Stressful life events, social support, and morality in men born in 1933. *British Medical Journal, 307*(6912), 1102-1105. (4) Turrell, G., Lynch, J. W., Leite, C., Raghunathan, T., & Kaplan, G. A. (2007). Socioeconomic disadvantage in childhood and across the life course and all-cause morality and physical function in adulthood: Evidence from the Alameda County Study. *Journal of Epidemiology & Community Health, 61*(8), 723-730.

38. Northrup (2013), op. cit. (See ch. 13, note 4).

39. (1) Brown, G. W., & Harris, T. O. (1989). Depression. In G. W. Brown & T. O. Harris (Eds.), *Life events and illness* (pp. 49-93). New York, NY: Guilford Press. (2) Hammen, C. (2005). Stress and depression. *Annual Review of Clinical Psychology, 1*, 293-319.

40. (1) Dohrenwend, B. P. (2000). The role of adversity and stress in psychopathology: Some evidence and its implications for theory and research. *Journal of Health & Social Behavior, 41*(1), 1-19. (2) Johnson, S. L., & Roberts,

J. E. (1995). Life events and bipolar disorder: Implications from biological theories. *Psychological Bulletin, 117*(3), 434-449.

41. (1) Harris, A., & Thoresen, C. (2005). Forgiveness, unforgiveness, health and disease. In Worthington, E. (Ed), *Handbook of forgiveness* (pp. 321-334). New York, NY: Routledge. (2) Lopez, S., Snyder, C. & Pedrotti, J. (2003). Hope: Many definitions, many measures. In S. Lopez & C. Snyder (Eds.), *Positive psychology assessment: Handbook of models and measures* (pp. 91-106). Washington, DC: American Psychological Association. (3) Ong, A. D., Bergeman, C. S., Bisconti, T. L., & Wallace, T. (2006). Psychological resilience, positive emotions and successful adaptation to stress in later life. *Journal of Personality and Social Psychology, 91*, 730-749.

42. (1) Kirschbaum, C., Wolf, O. T., May, M., Wippich, W., & Hellhammer, D. H. (1996). Stress- and treatment-induced elevations of cortisol levels associated with impaired declarative memory in healthy adults. *Life Sciences, 58*(17), 1475-1483. (2) Diamond, D. M., Fleshner, M., Ingersoll, N., & Rose, G. (1996). Psychological stress impairs spatial working memory: Relevance to electrophysiological studies of hippocampal function. *Behavioral Neuroscience, 110*(4), 661-672. (3) Oei, N. L., Everaerd, W. M., Elzinga, B. M., van Well, S., & Bermond, B. (2006). Psychosocial stress impairs working memory at high loads: An association with cortisol levels and memory retrieval. *Stress, 9*(3), 133-341.

43. Jha, A. P., Morrison, A. B., Parker, S. C., & Stanley, E. A. (2016). Practice is protective: Mindfulness training promotes cognitive resilience in high-stress cohorts. *Mindfulness, 7*(1), 1-13.

44. (1) Shanteau, J., & Dino, G. A. (1993). Environmental stressor effects on creativity and decision making. In O. Svenson & A. J. Maule (Eds.), *Time pressure and stress in human judgment and decision making* (pp. 293-308). New York, NY: Plenum. (2) Byron, K., Khazanchi, S., & Nazarian, D. (2010). The relationship between stressors and creativity: A meta-analysis examining competing theoretical models. *Journal of Applied Psychology, 95*, 201-212.

Chapter 14: The Mind-Body Connection is a Two-Way Street

1. Dimberg, U., Thunberg, M., & Elmehed, K. (2000). Unconscious facial reactions to emotional facial expressions. *Psychological Science, 11*, 86–89.

2. (1) Stel, M., & van Knippenberg, A. (2008). The role of facial mimicry in the recognition of affect. *Psychological Science, 19*, 984-985. (2) Oberman, L. M., Winkielman, P., & Ramachandran, V. S. (2007). Face to face: Blocking facial mimicry can selectively impair recognition of emotional expressions. *Social Neuroscience, 2*, 167-178.

3. Sonnby-Borgström, M. (2002), Automatic mimicry reactions as related to differences in emotional empathy. *Scandinavian Journal of Psychology, 43*, 433-443.

4. Baird, A. D., Scheffer, I. E., & Wilson, S. J. (2011). Mirror neuron system involvement in empathy: A critical look at the evidence. *Social Neuroscience*, 6(4), 327-335.

5. Ibid.

6. Hamilton (2010), op. cit. (See ch. 3, note 31).

7. Cuddy, A. (2012, October 1) Your body language may shape who you are. Retrieved from https://www.youtube.com/watch?v=Ks-_MhIQhMc

8. Korb (2015), op. cit. (See ch. 10, note 38).

9. Light, K. C., Grewen, K. M., & Amico, J. A. (2005). More frequent partner hugs and higher oxytocin levels are linked to lower blood pressure and heart rate in premenopausal women. *Biological Psychology*, 69, 5-21.

10. (1) Handlin, L., Hydbring-Sandberg, E., Nilsson, A., Ejdebäck, M., Jansson, A., & Uvnäs-Moberg, K. (2011). Short-term interaction between dogs and their owners—effects on oxytocin, cortisol, insulin and heart rate—an exploratory study. *Anthrozoös*, 24, 301-315. (2) Miller, S. C., Kennedy, C., Devoe, D., Hickey, M., Nelson, T., & Kogan, L. (2009). An Examination of changes in oxytocin levels in men and women before and after interaction with a bonded dog. *Anthrozoös*, 22, 31-42. (3) Odendaal, J. S., & Meintjes, R. A. (2003). Neurophysiological correlates of affiliative behaviour between humans and dogs. *Veterinarian Journal*, 165, 296-301.

11. (1) Ohlsson, B., Forsling, M. L., Rehfeld, J. F., & Sjolund, K. (2002). Cholecystokinin stimulation leads to increased oxytocin secretion in women. *European Journal of Surgery*, 168, 114-118. (2) Uvnäs-Moberg, K. (2004). Massage, relaxation and well-being: a possible role for oxytocin as an integrative principle? In T. Field (Ed.), *Touch and massage in early child development*. Calverton, NY: Johnson & Johnson Pediatric Institute.

12. Uvnäs-Moberg, K., & Petersson, M. (2010). Role of oxytocin and oxytocin related effects in manual therapies. In H. H. King, W. Jänig, & M. M. Patterson (Eds.), *The science and clinical application of manual therapy*. Amsterdam: Elsevier.

13. Graham, L. (2010). *Bouncing back: Rewiring your brain for maximum resilience and well-being*. Novato, CA: New World Library.

14. (1) Carter, C. S., & Keverne, E. B. (2002). The neurobiology of social affiliation and pair bonding. In D. Pfaff (Ed.), *Hormones, brains and behavior* (pp. 299-337). San Diego, CA: Academic Press. (2) Grewen, K. M., Girdler, S. S., Amico, J., & Light, K. C. (2005). Effects of partner support on resting oxytocin, cortisol, norepinephrine, and blood pressure before and after warm partner contact. *Psychosomatic Medicine*, 67, 531-538. (3) Holt-Lunstad, J., Birmingham, W. A., & Light, K. C. (2008). Influence of a "warm touch" support enhancement intervention among married couples on ambulatory blood pressure, oxytocin, alpha amylase, and cortisol. *Psychosomatic Medicine*, 70, 976-985.

15. Graham (2010), op. cit. (See ch. 14, note 13).

16. Goleman, D. (2007). *Social intelligence: The new science of human relationships.* New York, NY: Bantam.
17. Korb (2015), op. cit. (See ch. 10, note 38).
18. Ibid.
19. Newberg & Waldman (2017), op. cit. (See ch. 4, note 1).
20. Childre & Martin (2000), op. cit. (See ch. 6, note 74).
21. Ekman, P. (2007). *Emotions revealed: Recognizing faces and feelings to improve communication and emotional life.* New York, NY: Owl Books.
22. Ekman, P., Davidson, R. J., & Friesen, W. V. (1990). The Duchenne smile: Emotional expression and brain physiology: II. *Journal of Personality and Social Psychology, 58*(2), 342-353.
23. Duchenne, B. (1862/1990). *The mechanisms of human facial expression or an electrophysiological analysis of the expression of emotions* (A. Cuthbertson. Trans.). New York, NY: Cambridge University Press.
24. Ekman et al. (1990), op. cit. (See ch. 14, note 22).
25. Ekman, P., & Davidson, R. J. (1993). Voluntary smiling changes regional brain activity. *Psychological Science, 4,* 342-345.
26. Kraft, T. L., & Pressman, S. D. (2012). Grin and bear it: The influence of manipulated facial expression on the stress response. *Psychological Science, 23*(11), 1372-1378.
27. Fredrickson B. L., & Levenson R. W. (1998). Positive emotions speed recovery from the cardiovascular sequelae of negative emotions. *Cognition & Emotion, 12,* 191-220.
28. Johnson, K. J., Waugh, C. E., & Fredrickson, B. L. (2010). Smile to see the forest: Facially expressed positive emotions broaden cognition. *Cognition & Emotion, 24*(2), 299-321.
29. Ekman (2007), op. cit. (See ch. 14, note 21).
30. Gunnery, S. D., Hall, J. A., & Ruben, M. A. (2013). The deliberate Duchenne smile: Individual differences in expressive control. *Journal of Nonverbal Behavior, 37,* 29-41.
31. Harker, L., & Keltner, D. (2001). Expressions of positive emotion in women's college yearbook pictures and their relationship to personality and life outcomes across adulthood. *Journal of Personality and Social Psychology, 80*(1), 112-124.
32. Mehu, M., Little, A. C., & Dunbar, R. I. M. (2007). Duchenne smiles and the perception of generosity and sociability in faces. *Journal of Evolutionary Psychology, 5,* 183-196.
33. Harker & Keltner (2001), op. cit. (See ch. 14, note 33).
34. (1) Hertenstein, M. J., Hansel, C. A., Butts, A. M., & Hile, S. N. (2009). Smile intensity in photographs predicts divorce later in life. *Motivation and Emotion, 33*(2), 99-105. (2) Abel, E. L., & Kruger M. L. (2010). Smile intensity in photographs predicts longevity. *Psychological Science, 21,* 542-544.
35. Dimberg et al. (2000), op. cit. (See ch. 14, note 1).

36. Dimberg, U., Thunberg, M., & Gruneda, S. (2002). Facial reactions to emotional stimuli: Automatically controlled emotional responses. *Cognition & Emotion, 6*, 449-471.
37. Sonnby-Borgström (2002), op. cit. (See ch. 14, note 3).
38. Oberman et al. (2007), op. cit. (See ch. 14, note 2).
39. Lane, R. D. (2000). Neural correlates of conscious emotional experience. In R. D. Lane & L. Nadel (Eds.), *Cognitive neuroscience of emotion* (pp. 345–370). New York, NY: Oxford University Press.
40. Gutman, R. (2011, May 11). The hidden power of smiling. Retrieved from https://www.youtube.com/watch?v=U9cGdRNMdQQ
41. LaFrance, M. (2011). *Lip service: Smiles in life, death, trust, lies, work, memory, sex, and politics.* New York, NY: W. W. Norton & Company.
42. (1) Krumhuber, E., Likowski, K., & Weyers, P. (2014). Facial mimicry of spontaneous and deliberate Duchenne and non-Duchenne smiles. *Journal of Nonverbal Behavior, 38*(1), 1-11. (2) Maringer, M., Krumhuber, E. G., Fischer, A. H., & Niedenthal, P. M. (2011). Beyond smile dynamics: Mimicry and beliefs in judgments of smiles. *Emotion, 11*, 181-187.
43. (1) Quadflieg, S., Vermeulen, N., & Rossion, B. (2013). Differential reliance on the Duchenne marker during smile evaluations and person judgments. *Journal of Nonverbal Behavior, 37*, 69-77. (2) Surakka, V., & Hietanen, J. K. (1998). Facial and emotional reactions to Duchenne and non-Duchenne smiles. *International Journal of Psychophysiology, 29*, 23-33. (3) Mehu, M., Mortillaro, M., Banziger, T., & Scherer, K. R. (2012). Reliable facial muscle activation enhances recognizability and credibility of emotional expression. *Emotion, 12*, 701-715.
44. Johnston, L., Miles, L., & Macrae, C. N. (2010). Why are you smiling at me? Social functions of enjoyment and non-enjoyment smiles. *British Journal of Social Psychology, 49*, 107-127.
45. (1) Woodzicka, J. A. (2008). Sex differences in self-awareness of smiling during a mock job interview. *Journal of Nonverbal Behavior, 32*, 109-121. (2) Frank, M. G., Ekman, P., & Friesen, W. V. (1993). Behavioral markers and recognizability of the smile of enjoyment. *Journal of Personality and Social Psychology, 64*, 83-93.
46. (1) Krumhuber. E., Manstead, A. S. R., Cosker, D., Marshall, D., Rosin, P. L, & Kappas, A. (2007). Facial dynamics as indicators of trustworthiness and cooperative behavior. *Emotion, 7*, 730-735. (2) Miles, L. (2009). Who is approachable? *Journal of Experimental Social Psychology, 45*, 262-266.

Index

About the Author

Throughout her long career as a teacher education professor at Rhode Island College and California State University, Barbara Larrivee has published eight books, multiple chapters, and 25 articles in education, psychology, and counseling journals. Her writing spans many domains. She writes about classroom management, managing challenging student behavior, creating learning communities based on respectful and authentic communication, becoming a reflective practitioner, reducing stress, developing social and emotional skills, and cultivating mindfulness.

Being mindful is the umbrella for everything she has been writing about for decades. Being mindful means accepting your weaknesses, becoming your own best friend, being self-reflective, that is, testing your actions against your most cherished values, engaging in "respectful dialogue," and having "emotional integrity" where your feelings, your words, and your actions are in authentic alignment.

She has always been able to balance opposite ends of the continuum. Her doctoral studies combined research and statistics with humanistic education, a highly atypical combination. While studying for her master's degree in special education and remedial reading, she was also working at a detention center, doing in-house training in counseling methods for very troubled youth, and being a foster parent for a youth caught up in the juvenile justice system. Her background uniquely positions her to merge science and practice. Her writing translates research into practical tools and strategies. As a graduate of a humanistic education program, her approach to teacher education is based on the belief that good teaching begins with good human beings.

Dr. Larrivee is the creator of "authentic classroom management," an approach founded on the principle that managing student behavior begins with teachers managing their own behavior through developing reflection, self-awareness, and emotion regulation skills. It calls on teachers to develop styles of teacher talk that encourage authenticity and respectful dialogue, and use strategies that are non-punitive, solution-oriented, and focused on problem solving, not fault finding. Her text, *Authentic Classroom Management: Creating a Learning Community and Building Reflective Practice*, is widely used both nationally and internationally. She created a master's level online course on managing challenging behavior based on her book and was an early adopter of web-based technology to broadcast her lectures to remote sites.

Hearing stories of stressed-out teachers firsthand ignited her desire to help teachers cope with their stress. Teachers are largely at a loss about how to deal with the stress that comes with their job. Her last book, *Cultivating Teacher Renewal: Guarding Against Stress and Burnout*, gives teachers the stress management and coping strategies to build up defenses against stress, to become proactive in finding ways to get the vital peer support they need, to successfully navigate the spectrum of emotions teaching elicits, and to cultivate mindfulness. The book was chosen by *Choice*, the premier source for reviews of academic books, for their list of Outstanding Academic Titles of 2013. This list includes the top 10% of about 7,000 works reviewed yearly.

The two assessment instruments she developed are widely used by other researchers. *The Opinions Relative to the Integration of Students with Disabilities (ORI)* assesses teachers' attitudes toward integrating students with special needs into their classrooms. *The Survey of Reflective Practice: A Tool for Assessing Development as a Reflective Practitioner (SRP)* assesses development as a reflective practitioner, along a continuum of four levels of reflective practice.

She has consulted with metropolitan school districts, state departments, and national research centers. She has directed two research and evaluation companies, Teaching Research Associates (TRA) and New England Evaluation Designs (NEED), and has received grants from the U. S. Office of Education for her research. Dr. Larrivee has presented her work at national and international conferences and conducts workshops worldwide as well as at personal growth centers, including Esalen Institute and the Learning Annex. She is a longtime mindfulness practitioner and yogi.

Her dedication to bringing mindfulness and social-emotional learning (SEL) into schools has led to her recent establishment of the foundation, *Mindful Moments in My Classroom*, which will fund small grants to educators to implement mindful moment practices. Half of the profits from this book will go to the foundation.

CPSIA information can be obtained
at www.ICGtesting.com
Printed in the USA
LVHW04s1518010618
579263LV00002B/497/P